The Benefits of Environmental Improvement

The Benefits of Environmental Improvement

Theory and Practice

A. Myrick Freeman III

Published for Resources for the Future Inc.
by the Johns Hopkins University Press
Baltimore and London

Copyright © 1979 by Resources for the Future, Inc.
All rights reserved
Printed in the United States of America

The Johns Hopkins University Press, Baltimore, Maryland, 21218
The Johns Hopkins Press Ltd., London

Originally published in hardcover and paperback, 1979
Second printing (paperback), May 1981

Library of Congress Cataloging in Publication Data

Freeman, A   Myrick, 1936–
    The benefits of environmental improvement.

    Includes bibliographies.
    1. Environmental policy—Cost effectiveness.
I. Resources for the Future.   II. Title.
HC79.E5F7   338.4′3   78-20532
ISBN 0–8018–2163–0 (hardcover)
ISBN 0–8018–2195–9 (paperback)

Resources for the Future is a nonprofit organization for research and education in the development, conservation, and use of natural resources and the
improvement of the quality of the environment. It was established in 1952
with the cooperation of the Ford Foundation. Grants for research are accepted
from government and private sources only if they meet the conditions of a
policy established by the Board of Directors of Resources for the Future. The
policy states that RFF shall be solely responsible for the conduct of the research and free to make the research results available to the public. Part of the
work of Resources for the Future is carried out by its resident staff; part is
supported by grants to universities and other nonprofit organizations. Unless
otherwise stated, interpretations and conclusions in RFF publications are those
of the authors; the organization takes responsibility for the selection of significant subjects for study, the competence of the researchers, and their freedom of inquiry.

This book is a product of the Quality of the Environment Division, which is
directed by Walter O. Spofford, Jr. It was edited by Sally A. Skillings. The
figures for this book were drawn by Federal Graphics, and it was indexed by
Florence Robinson.

RFF editors: Joan R. Tron, Ruth B. Haas, Jo Hinkel, Sally A. Skillings

CONTENTS

Tables

Figures

FOREWORD

Since its beginning in 1952, Resources for the Future has supported, both directly and indirectly, the development of methods of economic analysis, and in particular, methods of benefit–cost analysis. The early efforts at RFF on methods of such analysis went into estimating the benefits associated with water resource development projects and outdoor recreation. In the last decade, attention at RFF has turned more toward methods for estimating the benefits and costs of environmental pollution control. This book by A. Myrick Freeman III addresses this latter concern.

Benefit–cost analysis has been used for the evaluation of water resource development in the United States for many years. The increased program of water resource development during the 1930s and the Flood Control Act of 1936, which explicitly required that projects be evaluated on the basis of benefits and costs, resulted in a substantial effort to develop tools and techniques for estimating the benefits and costs of proposed projects. This effort eventually resulted in the publication by the federal government in 1958 of the so-called Green Book. From the beginning, however, benefit–cost analysis has been plagued with both conceptual and practical problems of estimation, many of which have not been overcome to this day.

Some of the first research at RFF on broadly defined issues concerning the uses of the natural and environmental resources involved the application of welfare economics to public investment decisions in the field of water resource development. During this same period, research on methods of measuring the demand for and value of outdoor recreation also began and has continued to this day. An outgrowth of the early work at RFF on the economic evaluation of water resource projects resulted in a research program on water quality economics and management. It was through this program that RFF first attempted to deal with the problems associated with estimating the damages incurred by environmental degradation and the benefits of environmental pollution control.

Recent work at RFF on the application of benefit–cost analysis to environmental quality management problems has included the RFF book by Karl-Göran Mäler, *Environmental Economics: A Theoretical Inquiry,* in 1974, which broke new ground in several areas of basic theory including some aspects of the theory of benefit measurement, and the book by Lester B. Lave and Eugene P. Seskin, *Air Pollution and Human Health,* in 1977, which is important because of its effort to measure and quantify benefits and costs. This book by A. Myrick Freeman III represents a continuation of RFF's interest in developing methods of economic analysis. This is a book about applied methodology and is intended to advance the state of the art of environmental policy analysis. It focuses on the the theoretical and practical problems of quantifying the benefits of environmental pollution control and attempts to bridge the gap between theory and practice.

Myrick Freeman's concern with the problems of benefit measurement and estimation goes back to his earlier work on the distributional implications of environmental policy undertaken in 1969 and 1970 while a member of the RFF staff. In his paper, "The Distribution of Environmental Quality," published in Allen V. Kneese and Blair T. Bower, *Environmental Quality Analysis,* he discusses the need to develop better measures of damages and benefits associated with environmental pollution and its control. In his concluding comments in this paper, Freeman states: "The first and most obvious point is that considerable progress must be made in measuring and valuing benefits and costs before we can say much more either about their distribution or about the optimality of a given level of environmental quality." After returning to Bowdoin College in 1970 and during the next six years, he undertook a series of studies concerning the valuation of benefits of environmental pollution control. In the fall of 1976, he returned to the RFF staff to write this book.

This book represents a statement, circa 1978, of Freeman's collective experiences and concerns with the theory and practice of estimating the benefits of environmental pollution control. In publishing this book, RFF expresses its commitment to advancing methods of economic analysis, and particularly benefit–cost analysis, to aid public policymakers in making informed decisions on the uses of the nation's natural and environmental resources.

October 1978   WALTER O. SPOFFORD, JR.
                                Director, Quality of the Environment Division

PREFACE

In 1973 I was asked by Henry Peskin to prepare a paper on the techniques for estimating the benefits of water pollution control for a symposium sponsored by the Environmental Protection Agency. In the course of writing that paper I realized that many of the empirical techniques that were discussed in the economics literature have a common characteristic: they make use of linkage or connection in consumers' preferences and behavior between a public good (water quality in this case) and some private good whose price and quantity can be observed in the market place. Then two years later I was asked to review the state of the art of empirical estimation of air and water pollution control benefits as part of a study conducted by Enviro-Control, Inc. under contract to the Environmental Protection Agency. One of the things I learned from this review was that many—if not most—of the studies on which national estimates were based were flawed conceptually and theoretically. Not only were appropriate data difficult to obtain but what was being measured often did not coincide with the economist's definition of benefits; or the model on which the estimate was based diverged in important ways from accepted economic theory; or, in some cases, no theoretical justification for the estimate was offered.

I concluded from these experiences that practitioners in the field needed a book that would first of all describe the techniques for estimating various forms of benefits, show how they were related to the underlying economic welfare theory, and discuss some of the pitfalls and problems in the empirical implementation of the techniques. This is the book I have tried to write. My intended audience is professional economists and students having a good grasp of microeconomic theory. The notion of writing a laymen's guide to benefit estimation was appealing. But I felt the need first to address a number of technical issues and to provide a unified theoretical treatment. A laymen's guide might better come after the specialists have brought some order and cohesiveness to the subject.

The premises on which this book is based are orthodox in nature. They are the basis of neoclassical welfare theory. Individual preference theory is accepted as the basis for defining and measuring the gains and losses in welfare associated with alternative environmental policies. I review this theory to provide a yardstick against which the theoretical adequacy of empirical estimating techniques can be measured. Then I attempt a systematic analysis of the ways in which interactions between public goods and private goods demands can be utilized to derive conceptually sound estimates of benefits. In this effort I owe an intellectual debt to Karl-Göran Mäler who developed a number of valuable theoretical insights in his earlier book for Resources for the Future, *The Economics of Environment: A Theoretical Inquiry* (Baltimore, Johns Hopkins University Press for Resources for the Future, 1974).

Nonmarket approaches such as surveys and bidding games are also examined since they have been the basis of several estimates of benefits. But I am not optimistic about the reliability and accuracy of responses in the essentially hypothetical situations created by these approaches. Finally I examine those empirical techniques which have a sound theoretical foundation. My purpose here is to help practitioners select the appropriate empirical techniques for particular purposes, and to suggest improvements in the application of those techniques.

My principal debt in this effort is to Resources for the Future and Walter Spofford for providing me with the opportunity to work full time on this project for more than a year. I am grateful not only for the financial and intellectual support but also the flexibility which allowed me to divide my time between the stimulating atmosphere of Washington and the quieter environment of Maine.

Among my colleagues at Resources for the Future. I owe a special debt to V. Kerry Smith who in many conversations helped me to gain a better understanding of the theoretical aspects of consumer demand theory and welfare theory. He also made many helpful suggestions on several portions of the manuscript. A number of people read and commented on earlier drafts of one or more chapters. They are: Emery N. Castle, Elizabeth L. David, Richard F. Dye, Peter T. Gottschalk, David Harrison, Robert H. Haveman, William V. Hogan, John V. Krutilla, Jon P. Nelson, Henry M. Peskin, A. Mitchell Polinsky, Paul R. Portney, Eugene P. Seskin, Timothy M. Smeeding, and Jon C. Sonstelie. Peter Bohm, Edwin S. Mills, and Frederick J. Wells read the complete manuscript and provided many helpful comments. I am grateful for their help and I absolve them of all responsibility for any errors of omission or commission which remain.

Linda Perrotta typed the manuscript. Her patience, good cheer, and skill helped to make the task of writing this book a pleasure. To her a special thanks for a job well done.

A. Myrick Freeman III

The Benefits of Environmental Improvement

CHAPTER 1

Benefit Measures and Environmental Decisionmaking

Many groups have expressed their concerns that environmental policies are too strict because costs outweigh benefits—or too lax because the benefits of stricter controls exceed the costs. The debate goes on in large part because so little is known about the magnitude of the beneficial effects of pollution control policies. I do not propose to settle the debate by providing a definitive measure of benefits. Rather, in this book I attempt to clarify the concept of benefits and to outline systematically the theoretical basis and empirical approaches to benefit measurement.

The literature does contain some efforts to estimate benefits. For example, in 1974 the Environmental Protection Agency (EPA) estimated that air pollution caused damages to Americans of about $7 billion per year in 1970 (Waddell, 1974). A committee of the National Academy of Sciences (NAS) estimated that air pollution from automobiles costs about $5 billion per year (National Academy of Sciences, 1974). And more recently, the staff of the National Commission on Water Quality put the benefits to be expected from carrying out the Clean Water Amendments of 1972 at about $5.5 billion per year by 1985 (National Commission on Water Quality, 1976).

These figures come from different sources; they refer to different years; and they use different terminology (costs, damages, benefits). But they have several features in common. For one thing, although the estimates are presented cautiously and with carefully chosen qualifications and expressions of limitations on their accuracy, they are likely to take on a life of their own in public discourse where qualifications and limitations tend to be ignored. Second, these estimates have a common conceptual framework, one which is derived from the basic economic theory for measuring the monetary value to individuals of changes in the availability of goods and services. However that may be, this basic framework and the techniques for estimating values that are derived from the framework are probably not well understood by many of the people who would use the figures in one way or another.

References to estimates such as these and others raise several important questions. Foremost is the question of meaning or interpretation. What is a benefit? How are benefits related to damages or costs? What is included in the concept of benefits? What is left out? Second, how are these estimates derived? What empirical techniques are used, and how accurate are they? Third, of what use are benefit estimates in the formulation of public policy? If the damages from automotive air pollution are $5 billion per year, what should be done about it? And would it make any difference to policy if damages were estimated to be only $2.5 billion per year, or as high as $10 billion per year?[1]

Finally, how meaningful is a single national figure for the impact of all air pollution or water pollution? Can such figures be disaggregated to give more specific information about particular regions, types of effects, or categories of pollutants? National estimates of benefits share many of the same virtues and defects as gross national product. They both are single-valued numbers used to summarize and describe complex phenomena. Conceptually, they involve the adding up of a myriad of components—transactions in the case of GNP and individual values for benefit estimates. Actual estimates may be derived from samples of or extrapolation from limited information. Analysts may be more interested in examining components of the aggregate measures. But the estimating procedure may preclude disaggregation of the form and to the extent desired by the analysts.

THE CONCEPT OF BENEFITS

It is important to draw a distinction between the concept of benefits and the effects of environmental pollution. Pollutants can have effects on people directly or indirectly through a variety of channels. For example, pollutants can have effects on human health as measured by morbidity or mortality rates. Pollutants can have effects on individuals' activities such as water-based recreation. Or they can have

---

[1] These in fact are the lower and upper bound estimates for damages presented by the National Academy of Sciences. The $5 billion figure is their "most likely" or "best guess" estimate (National Academy of Sciences, 1974).

effects on the availability of goods and services through influencing agricultural productivity or the rates of deterioration of materials. Each of these types of effects has an economic aspect.

Controlling pollution means reducing the magnitude of these effects. And the values that individuals place on reducing the adverse effects of pollution constitute our measure of benefits. The basis for determining these values is taken to be individuals' preferences. This, of course presumes that individuals have information about the effects of pollutants. We define the benefit of an environmental improvement as the sum of the monetary values assigned to these effects by all individuals directly or indirectly affected by that action. These monetary values are often referred to as "willingness to pay." An alternative is to measure values in terms of the monetary compensation that would be required to induce people voluntarily to accept adverse effects. As discussed in chapter 3, practically speaking, it does not appear to make much difference which definition is accepted. Here, willingness to pay is used as a convenient shorthand way of expressing "values based on individuals' preferences."

As suggested above, the three terms "benefit," "damage," and "cost" are often used virtually interchangeably. This results in an unfortunate potential for confusion. For example, cost also refers to the value of resources absorbed in the process of controlling or reducing pollution. Thus we have the "costs of pollution control" as well as the "costs of pollution."

The distinction between benefits and damages lies in the choice of a reference point from which environmental changes are to be measured. The benefits of pollution control are measured by comparing the existing known degree of pollution with some specified hypothetical alternative where pollution has been reduced or eliminated. Benefits are the gain associated with reduced pollution. Damages represent the mirror image of benefits, that is, what is lost in moving from the hypothetical "clean" state to the existing level of pollution.

The "damage" terminology presumes that some zero-effect or zero pollution level reference point can be identified. But this may be difficult or impossible where there are naturally occurring sources or natural background levels for the pollutant in question. For conventional air and water pollutants, the existing polluted state can be taken as the reference point; and the benefit terminology is appropriate. Since the term "costs of pollution" invites confusion with the costs of controlling pollution, and since there may be ambiguity about the point of reference for measuring damages, we will use the term "benefits" in this study.[2]

ESTIMATING BENEFITS

The definition of benefits as willingness to pay implies the existence of a demand curve for the effects of improved environmental quality. As will be shown in chapter 3, benefits can be taken to be equal to the area under this demand curve. Benefit estimation, then, involves determining directly or indirectly the shape of the demand curve for environmental quality. If the services of the environment could be purchased in a perfectly functioning market, estimating the demand curve would be a fairly straightforward econometric problem. And environmental quality management would not be an important public policy matter. But environmental quality can be viewed as a kind of public good. This is because only one level of quality can be provided at a time, and individuals are not free to vary independently the level of environmental quality they consume. The public good character of environmental quality leads to market failure, and without a market, there are no price and quantity data from which the demand relationship can be estimated.

Where market processes have failed to reveal these values directly, the techniques for estimating benefits involve a kind of detective work— piecing together the clues about the values individuals place on public goods that people leave behind as they respond to other economic signals. There are three basic approaches to determining the values that individuals place on improvements in environmental quality. One is simply to ask individuals, through surveys and direct questioning. The second is to place proposals for alternative levels of improvement in environmental quality to referendum vote. Under certain circumstances the outcome of the voting process will be consistent with, and therefore reveal information about, the underlying demand for environmental im-

---

[2] There is one class of situations where the "damage" terminology would be appropriate. Consider a proposal to introduce a new chemical into commercial use, a chemical which has environmentally transmitted side effects. Then the appropriate reference point would be the present zero-effect situation. And deviations from that would be damages as defined here.

provement. The third approach involves analyzing data from market transactions in goods and services related to environmental quality. Under certain circumstances, the demand for environmental improvements can be estimated from market data about the demand for goods or services that have substitute or complementary relationships with environmental quality. All of the empirical techniques actually used in an effort to obtain quantitative estimates of benefits involve some variation on one of these basic approaches.

BENEFITS AND ENVIRONMENTAL POLICYMAKING

A basic assumption underlying this book is that estimates of the benefits of environmental improvement can be a valuable part of the information base for environmental decisionmaking. Because achieving the air and water pollution control objectives established by Congress will involve massive expenditures from both the public and private sectors, and because there is a potential for substantial gain through more effective utilization of the resources devoted to pollution control, the judicious use of the principles of benefit–cost analysis in evaluating policy alternatives can contribute to more effective resource utilization.

Of course this is true, almost by definition, if the objective of environmental management is to maximize the efficiency of the use of resources, including environmental resources. Then benefit–cost analysis becomes, in effect, a set of rules for optimum environmental management and a set of definitions and procedures for measuring benefits and costs. Once the efficiency objective has been accepted, policy becomes an almost mechanical process of working out estimates of marginal benefit and marginal cost curves and seeking their intersection point.

But current environmental policy is not based solely or even primarily on the efficiency criterion. One reason, of course, is that at the time the basic policy objectives were established, it was not within the capability of analysts to provide the kind of benefit information that was required to implement the efficiency objective. But it is also true that environmental decisionmakers may have other objectives besides economic efficiency. For example, decisionmakers may be concerned with equity considerations, intergenerational effects, or risk aversion—none of which can be incorporated in a simple equation. Thus, it is not particularly useful to advocate benefit–cost analysis as a simple decision rule. Rather it should be considered as a framework and a set of procedures to help organize available information. Viewed in this light, benefit–cost analysis does not dictate choices; nor does it replace the ultimate authority and responsibility of decisionmakers. Rather it is a tool for organizing and expressing certain kinds of information on the range of alternative courses of action. It is in the context of this framework for arraying information that the usefulness of benefit estimates must be assessed.

Although the major thrust of federal pollution control policy has already been established by the Congress, there are still many big decisions to be made. Moreover, impending problems may force the reconsideration of major elements in existing policies, and most of these issues involve either an implicit or explicit weighing of benefits versus costs. For example, EPA and Congress have repeatedly wrestled with proposals to change the emissions standards, the timetable for compliance for automobiles, or both. In addition, to defend effluent standards based upon the best practical treatment and best available treatment criteria against legal challenges, EPA will have to have information on the benefits to be expected from the standards they are setting. Although decisionmakers may have other objectives besides economic efficiency, it is clear that economic considerations, broadly defined, will play a significant role in the decision-making process.

Some people may be distrustful of the benefit–cost analyst's efforts to extend economic measurements to such things as human life, ecology, and aesthetics, and to reduce as many variables as possible to the commensurate monetary measure. Some skepticism about the economist's penchant for monetary measurement is no doubt healthy. But it should not be overdone. It is not correct to say that there are some things like human life that cannot be valued in dollar terms. The real world often creates situations where such valuation in some form is unavoidable. The question is really how the problem of valuation is to be approached and what information can be gathered to help in the problem of choice.

Consider a hypothetical and highly simplified case of an air pollutant. Assume that the following information is known with certainty. At present levels of emissions, the pollutant causes excess mortality of 1,000 deaths per year in the population at risk. Reducing emissions by 50 percent would cost $500,000 and would reduce the excess mortality to 500 deaths per year. One hundred percent control of emissions would reduce excess mortality to zero, but would cost $1,500,000.

This information can be displayed as follows:

Level of control (percentage)	Costs of control (dollars)	Excess mortality (deaths per year)
No control	0	1,000
50	500,000	500
100	1,500,000	0

The problem is clearly one of tradeoffs between human life and the value of resources used up in the process of controlling emissions. If the monetary value of life were known, the right-hand column of the table could be converted to dollar measures of benefits, and the appropriate benefit–cost rules could be applied to determine the optimum level of emissions control. But in the absence of some agreed-upon basis for making deaths and control costs commensurable in dollar terms, no simple decision rule can be applied to determine the correct choice.

Choices of this sort are made in the political realm by decisionmakers such as the administrator of the Environmental Protection Agency. Whatever the choice, there is an implicit value of human life that is consistent with that choice, and can be said to have been revealed by that choice. In this example, if the 50 percent control level is chosen, the value of life is at least $1,000 per death avoided. The 50 percent control level "buys" 500 lives saved at a cost of $500,000. The decision further reveals that the value of life is less than $2,000, since the decisionmaker declined the opportunity to "purchase" the additional 500 lives saved that the additional $1,000,000 of control costs would make possible. If the 100 percent control level had been chosen, this would have revealed a value of life of at least $2,000.[3]

In this example, choice determined the value, rather than value determining the choice. But either way, the problem of valuation cannot be avoided. It can be hidden. But I would argue that choices are likely to be better, the more open decisionmakers are about the problems in making choices and the values involved, and the more information they

---

[3] In this example with only three data points, the implicit value can only be determined within some range. If control costs and mortality as functions of the level of control were continuous relationships and known with certainty, the choice of a control level would imply a precise value of life. If it is assumed that the control level was established so as to equate marginal benefits and marginal costs, and marginal costs are known, the marginal benefit or value can be inferred.

have about the implications of their choices. Estimates of benefits in monetary terms are one such source of valuable information.

Because policy choices about environmental quality objectives are made in a political context, and are likely to involve comparisons and tradeoffs among variables for which there is no agreement about commensurate values, monetary benefit and cost data will not always be the determining factors in decisionmaking. But benefit and cost estimates are one form of important information. Their usefulness lies in the fact that they use easily understood and accepted rules to reduce complex clusters of effects and phenomena down to single-valued commensurate magnitudes, that is, dollars. The value of the benefit–cost framework lies in its ability to organize and simplify certain forms of information into commensurate measures.

EXPRESSING BENEFIT INFORMATION

A major factor influencing the usefulness of estimates of benefits in decisionmaking is the nature and quantity of specific information contained in the estimates. A statement that "air pollution costs $20 billion" contains almost no useful information for decisionmakers. Benefit estimates must meet certain minimum requirements for types of information included in order to be useful for policy purposes. Any statement about benefits must meet the following minimum standards.

1. Consistent terminology—The statement must be consistent in its use of the terms "benefit," "cost," and "damage." The term "costs" is sometimes used synonymously with damages; for example, "pollution costs X." This usage should be avoided. The term "costs" should be used only to refer to resources absorbed in the process of controlling and reducing pollution.

2. Reference points—A statement concerning benefits must clearly specify the pollution levels being compared, both the present dirty level and the hypothetical cleaner alternative. Is the polluted state defined as conditions in 1975 or in 1973 (when pollutant levels and adverse effects may have been either higher or lower)? Specifying the reference year is also important for determining the price level for expressing dollar measures of benefits (for example, in 1973 dollars), and for specifying values for other socioeconomic variables that might influence the analysis of benefits. The specification of the hypothetical al-

ternative determines the range over which benefits are to be estimated. There are four choices for the hypothetical alternative:

A. Zero ambient concentrations of pollutants. This may be unrealistic where there are natural sources of the pollutant in question, since it would be impossible to adopt a policy to reduce ambient concentrations to zero.

B. Zero man-made emissions—that is ambient levels equal to background levels from natural sources. This alternative can be used for defining the benefits of a total elimination of man-made pollutants. But it may be difficult to determine in advance what the natural background levels are.

C. Ambient levels above background levels but below all known thresholds. This alternative would be difficult to implement presently, since there is considerable controversy over the existence of threshold levels.

D. Ambient levels set at established air or water quality standards. This is the most useful alternative for evaluating present pollution control policies.

   The choice between options B and D depends upon the use to which the benefit information is to be put. In other words, the policy question being asked should help to determine the way in which information is gathered and analyzed.

3. Dimension—The statement of benefits should make clear whether the measure refers to total benefits for some nonmarginal change in pollution levels or marginal benefits for some small change in pollutant levels. The statement should also indicate whether benefits are defined on a per capita or aggregate basis.

4. Specific pollutants—Estimates should make clear which pollutant or group of pollutants is being referred to. Where the benefit estimates are provided for a group of pollutants (for example, all air pollutants), the statement should include a breakdown by individual pollutants, unless the pollutants within the group act synergistically so that a separation of effects is not analytically possible. Benefit estimates for a group of pollutants may also be useful where the group is controlled jointly.

5. Source of pollutants—For each benefit estimate, the statement should indicate whether all sources are included, or, for example, only mobile sources. Where the purpose of the benefit esti-

mate is to evaluate a pollution control policy, benefit estimates should exclude potential benefits associated with noncontrolled sources. For example, pollution control benefits associated with the control of nonpoint water pollution sources should not be included in an estimate of benefits associated with a municipal and industrial point-source control program.

The kind of information that should be contained in a statement of benefits also depends upon the nature of the policy question for which the estimate was made. For example, in the early stages of the development of a pollution control policy, the most important question might be one of priorities, that is, which classes of pollutant should be controlled most quickly. For this purpose, very rough order-of-magnitude estimates of total benefits by pollutant would be very helpful. Later, as control plans are developed, marginal benefits and benefits by source would be required.

Another question is whether benefits should be estimated on an aggregate basis for the nation as a whole or on a regional or "problem-shed" basis. Where regional environmental management policies are being pursued, national estimates are not useful. Rather, what is required is an estimate of marginal benefits for the region. However, the main thrust of federal policy since 1970 has been away from regionally differentiated air and water quality standards and toward uniform national ambient standards and national standards for emission levels and control technologies. This evolution of a nationally standardized set of policies has increased the importance of national estimates of benefits. The process of setting national primary air quality standards would be aided by national estimates of marginal benefits by pollutant. And the development of pollution control strategies, for example for the automobile, requires national estimates of benefits by source.

METHODOLOGY FOR DERIVING ESTIMATES

In addition to the criterion of adequate information in benefit estimates, the methodology employed for deriving the estimates should be subject to the following criteria.

A technique must yield measures in monetary units because the objective of the exercise is the determination of values. This means, for example, that a measurement technique that predicts the increase in recreation user-days associated with a given reduction in pollution does not pass this criterion, for although the information is useful, it does not fully meet the needs of water resource planners for benefit measures which are commensurable with their monetary estimates of pollution control costs. In similar fashion, while studies of the relationship between mortality and air pollution are essential building blocks in the estimation of benefits, they are incomplete. They contribute to the process of *measurement* of effects; but they do not determine values. In some cases—in particular that of human life—analysts may not have credible estimates of individual values. In these circumstances, the analyst may be justified in (1) making some explicit assumption about unit values, for example, value per death avoided, and (2) in determining the implications of alternative value judgments for estimates of monetary benefits.

The technique and estimating procedures must be based analytically and empirically on individual behavior and preference, given the utilitarian definition of benefits as outlined above and elaborated in chapter 3. Some measures of the value of reduced mortality have been based upon the earnings of affected individuals. Such measures do not meet this criterion, since there is no known relationship between willingness to pay on the one hand and earnings on the other. The most obvious limitation of the lost earnings measure is that it places no value on the lives or health of those who are not working because of their age, sex, or other factors. The possibility of deriving a "value-of-life" measure based on individual preference is the topic of chapter 7.

The measures of use and value must be related to changes in pollution levels or changes in ambient environmental quality. In other words, some measure of environmental quality must explicitly enter the analysis of value as a variable. For example, an analysis of the demand for water-based recreation would not be a benefit measure unless it showed how the demand is affected by changes in pollution and the quality of the water bodies being analyzed. Particularly in the realm of water quality, the difficulty of establishing the relationship between quality and use is a major barrier to better estimates of benefits. We do not yet have a clear idea of what indexes of water quality are relevant to recreational uses of the water and how people will respond to changes in quality parameters.

Benefit estimates must be based upon a correctly specified theoretical model of individual behavior and the relationships among economic units. The logic of the model must be internally consistent and also be consistent with established theory. When observed relationships are measured empirically, without benefit of an underlying theoretical model, researchers may be led to make faulty or erroneous interpretations of the data. An important example is the land value–air pollution relationship. Early researchers discovered that land value and air pollution levels were inversely related in urban areas, *ceteris paribus*. They then assumed that changes in welfare associated with reduced pollution would be adequately measured by the associated increases in land values. However, subsequent research based upon theoretical models of urban land markets, has shown that this assumption is not true in general. This theoretical work has shown researchers what kind of inferences can validly be drawn from empirically derived air pollution–property value relationships.[4]

The actual measures used in the empirical work should correspond as closely as possible to the variables of the theoretical model. For example, a priori reasoning about the relationship between air pollution exposure and mortality suggests that the time profile of cumulative exposure of an individual is the appropriate independent or causal variable. But most empirical research on the air pollution–mortality relationship has been based upon air pollution measurements taken at a point in time or over a short period (for example, annual averages) and on those which are taken at a specific geographic location within an urban area. Thus the empirical measure of air pollution is not perfectly correlated with the measure called for by the correctly specified theoretical model. Of course the correct theoretical measure may not be available to the researcher, and the researcher must proceed with what data are available. But the analyst must be sensitive to the problems that might be caused by the lack of correspondence between the theoretically correct variable and the one actually used.

Benefit studies must use the empirical techniques appropriate to the theoretical model and the data at hand. Empirical techniques must be able to cope with such matters as multicollinearity, simultaneity, and identification problems. Empirical techniques which do not adequately control for other variables must be used with great caution.[5] Researchers must be sensitive to the problems caused by misspecification of the variables used and of the functional forms estimated.

---

[4] See Freeman (1974); Lind (1973); and National Academy of Sciences (1974), chapter 4. The theoretical basis for interpreting property value data will be outlined in chapter 6.

[5] Some of these problems are of particular significance in the measurement of the effects of pollution. They will be discussed in chapter 2.

No benefit study yet done has been completely satisfactory in terms of all six of these criteria. Yet the researcher and analyst must push on and do the best they can with available data and analytical techniques using these criteria as benchmarks. Part of the art of benefit analysis involves sensitivity to the gap between the ideal and the available and knowing how much confidence to place in the estimates being generated.

It must be recognized that under some circumstances benefit estimates can be damaging rather than useful. If estimates succumb to the fault of misplaced concreteness, if they contain conceptual or analytical errors, if they do not make explicit the key assumptions and value judgments involved, and if they do not express their inherent lack of accuracy through some device such as confidence limits, the estimates may do more harm than good. They may mislead policymakers in key decisions. And as their faults and weaknesses become known, they may discredit the whole process of benefit estimation and policy analysis. But assuming that the benefit estimates are derived according to the principles outlined in this book, they can be useful to policymakers.

Finally, even if benefit information is not used explicitly in the process of making decisions, the exercise in quantification and measurement that benefit estimates require may itself be of educational value to researchers and policymakers. The exercise requires that investigators gain a better understanding of (1) the nature of different pollutants, (2) the paths that pollutants take in reaching people, and (3) the variety of ways in which pollutants affect the uses that man makes of his air and water environments. Even if the exercise does not bear fruit in the form of monetary estimates of benefits, the insights gained and the information developed may themselves be of value. The exercise may help policymakers to develop a sense of the relative importance and significance of different kinds of effects, different types of pollutants, different pathways through the environment, and so forth. And in a qualitative way, this may contribute to the development of priorities, such as those for pollution control programs and research strategies.

EX POST AND EX ANTE ANALYSIS OF BENEFITS

The decisionmaker who is trying to allocate scarce resources and is faced with a number of competing goals needs ex ante analyses of the effects of alternative pollution control policies to guide his decisions.

Ex ante analysis involves the prediction of the physical and economic consequences of pollution control policies on the basis of a model or a theory concerning the physical and economic processes involved. It involves visualizing two alternative states of the world, one with the policy in question and one without, and then comparing these alternative futures in terms of some established criterion, such as net economic efficiency. Ex post analysis involves measuring the actual consequences of the policy by comparing the observed state with a hypothetical alternative—the state of the world without the policy. Ex post analysis, in effect, treats the policy as a controlled laboratory experiment except that the control group is hypothetical rather than real.

Ex post and ex ante analyses are not competitive alternatives but should be viewed as complementary techniques for improving our knowledge. An ex post analysis of a policy can be viewed as a check on the validity of the ex ante analysis. The ex ante analysis is a prediction of what will happen; the ex post analysis is a check of what actually did happen.[6]

It is particularly important that the economic analysis of pollution control benefits include ex post analysis of existing policies because our knowledge of the physical and economic systems on which present ex ante analyses are based is extremely limited. It is necessary not only to develop more comprehensive models of the physical, biological, and economic aspects of the system but also to devote more effort to verifying these models through ex post comparisons of the predictions with observed results.

It must be emphasized that the ex post verification of the analytical models used in benefit estimation is not simply a comparison of actual results with predictions. Ex ante models are based upon some view of the future with projections of economic magnitudes such as population levels, real income, and price levels. Care must be taken in ex post analysis to sort out the effects of unforeseen developments such as war or uncontrolled inflation on the variables in question. For example, if the failure of income levels to rise on the projected path results in a shortfall of recreation benefits at a particular site, this is not a failure of the analytical model so much as a reflection on our inability to perceive the future. The real benefit of ex post analysis is in making the most of the opportunity to improve on the analytical models used.

---

[6] For further discussion of this and related points, see Haveman (1972).

PREVIEW

My main purpose in writing this book is to bridge what I perceive to be a major gap in the literature on benefit estimation. On the one hand, there has been a substantial research effort devoted to developing a rigorous and unambiguous definition and measure of changes in welfare at the theoretical level. This body of literature displays relatively little concern for translating the theoretical concepts and definitions into usable, operational empirical techniques. On the other hand, empirical estimates of benefits have often been based on ad hoc procedures which have lacked an adequate theoretical foundation. There is a major research need to develop empirical techniques which are consistent with the underlying economic theory and at the same time to develop, where possible, the theoretical underpinning for some of the empirical techniques in most common use.[7]

The major task of this book will be to review and summarize the basic theory of welfare measurement and to relate actual estimating techniques to this underlying theory. Although the concept of benefits is basically economic in nature, the benefits are produced from an underlying physical, environmental system. The next chapter is devoted to a discussion of the relationship between the physical-scientific aspect of benefit estimation and its economic aspects.

Chapters 3 through 5 constitute the theoretical core of the book. Chapter 3 lays out the basic premises and value judgments that underlie the economic concept of benefits and presents the basic theory of the measurement of economic welfare changes. Chapter 4 deals with some of the specific problems of the transition from basic theory to operational empirical techniques. It attempts to provide an answer to the question of how and under what conditions the benefits from an environmental service can be estimated from market data on the prices and quantities of other goods and services. Chapter 5 examines the possibility of obtaining conceptually valid measures of the demand for environmental quality and of welfare change by nonmarket methods— bidding games, surveys, and the analysis of voting behavior. Chapters 3 and 4 together provide a critical examination of the theoretical basis

---

[7] Mäler and Wyzga (1976) have recently provided a relatively short technical handbook on the measurement of environmental damages. It includes discussion of both the economic theory of damages or benefits and several empirical measurement techniques.

for translating the basic premises of consumer theory and the measurement of welfare change into operational empirical techniques utilizing market and nonmarket data. Subsequent chapters deal with some of the possibilities and pitfalls in applying particular techniques to specific problems. These include the analysis of property value data, estimating the willingness to pay for improved health and longevity, modeling recreation demand, and utilizing productivity and physical damage measures. A concluding chapter briefly reviews the state of the art and offers some suggestions for further research.

REFERENCES

Freeman, A. Myrick III. 1974. "On Estimating Air Pollution Control Benefits from Land Value Studies," *Journal of Environmental Economics and Management* vol. 1, no. 1 (May) pp. 74–83.

Haveman, Robert H. 1972. *The Economic Performance of Public Investments* (Baltimore, Johns Hopkins University Press for Resources for the Future).

Lind, Robert C. 1973. "Spatial Equilibrium: The Theory of Rent and the Measurement of Benefits from Public Programs," *Quarterly Journal of Economics* vol. 87, no. 2 (May) pp. 188–207.

Mäler, Karl-Göran, and Ronald E. Wyzga. 1976. *Economic Measurement of Environmental Damage* (Paris, Organisation for Economic Co-operation and Development).

National Academy of Sciences, Coordinating Committee on Air Quality Studies. 1974. *The Costs and Benefits of Automobile Emission Control,* volume 4 of *Air Quality and Automobile Emission Control* (Washington, D.C., NAS).

National Commission on Water Quality. 1976. *Staff Report* (Washington, D.C., NCWQ).

Waddell, Thomas E. 1974. *The Economic Damages of Air Pollution* (Washington, D.C., U.S. Environmental Protection Agency).

CHAPTER 2

Problems in Measuring Environmental Effects

Although measuring benefits involves the use of economic theory and technique, benefit estimates must be built on a base of other types of knowledge. For example, estimates of the health benefits from air pollution control must be based on scientific knowledge of the relationship between pollutant concentrations and human health. Estimates of recreation and fishery benefits stemming from water pollution control require knowledge of the relationship between pollutant levels and biological productivity. Lack of knowledge of these relationships may, in some instances, be a major barrier to empirical estimates of benefits.

The purpose of this chapter is to examine the relationship between economic theory and technique and the physical and scientific aspects of benefit estimation and to discuss some of the problems involved in determining the physical effects of pollution as distinct from the economic values of environmental change. If, as stated in chapter 1, there is a gap between the economic theory of value and the empirical measurement of benefits, it exists in large part because of the difficulties in determining these physical relationships.

The benefits that stem from a pollution control policy are the product of three sets of functional relationships.

1. Changes in the rates of discharge and the time and place of discharges of residuals into the environment lead to changes in various measures of ambient environmental quality.
2. Changes in ambient environmental quality lead to changes in the flows of environmental services to individuals. These changes may in turn be reflected in changes in the way individuals use the environment.
3. Changes in environmental services lead to changes in economic welfare or benefits.

The first set of relationships is almost totally noneconomic in nature since it involves a variety of physical and biological processes for transportation, dispersion, and transformation of residuals. The third set of relationships is wholly within the realm of economics since it involves the theory of economic welfare and the use of economic data. The second set of relationships represents the interface between the natural science and social science disciplines. Some aspects of these relationships are primarily behavioral or social, for example, how recreation use varies with changes in water quality. Other aspects are almost wholly physical, for example, the effects of air pollution on human health and mortality. Some types of environmental change involve blends or interactions between behavioral and physical dimensions; for example, the effects of an air pollutant on a particular type of vegetation is a biological question, but if farmers alter crop patterns as a way of adapting to changes in air pollution, then the behavioral and biological aspects of the relationship must be considered together.

Understanding this second set of functional relationships is essential if empirical estimates of benefits are to be made. Yet this seems to be the least understood of the three. This is perhaps the most serious barrier to more effective planning for environmental quality management through benefit–cost analysis.

AMBIENT QUALITY

Any complete analysis of the benefits from a given environmental policy change must begin with the effect of changes in discharge or emissions rates on some measures of environmental quality. For example, suppose the question is: what will be the effects on human health of achieving the auto emissions standards mandated by federal law? The first step in answering this question is to determine the impact of reduced emissions from automobiles on ambient concentrations of nitrogen oxides and photochemical oxidants. This is the first link in a chain of cause and effect relationships moving from the policy instrument, that is, emissions reduction, to the ultimate measure of impact, that is, benefits.

There are two kinds of problems that arise in this stage of an analysis. The first concerns the choice of parameters for describing ambient air or water quality. And the second is the determination of the transformation function relating residuals discharges and the specified quality measures.

Consider first the case of water quality. A single effluent discharge can contain many substances which affect water quality—for example oxygen-demanding organic wastes (biochemical oxygen demand), suspended solids, waste heat, or toxic chemicals. When these substances enter the waterway they affect—in sometimes simple and sometimes complex ways—such measurable components of water quality as dissolved oxygen, temperature, and concentrations of chemicals. For example, a nondegradable chemical substance will simply be diluted, and its concentration in the water body will be a calculable fraction of its concentration in the effluent stream. In contrast, organic wastes affect water quality parameters in a more complicated way. As they are degraded by bacteria, they reduce dissolved oxygen levels to an extent and at a rate which depends on water temperature, wind, river flow rates, and other physical and biological characteristics of the receiving water.

Some of the physical measures of water quality, such as turbidity and smell, affect man's uses of the water directly. In addition, these and other physical parameters affect the stream ecology in complex and not always well understood ways. The populations and species distributions of fish, algae, zooplankton, and bacteria may also be affected, and not necessarily in the same direction, by changes in the physical and chemical parameters of water quality.

Even providing a descriptive characterization of the outcome of this first stage is a formidable task. Water quality cannot be represented by a single number on some scale, but rather is an n-dimensional vector of the relevant parameters. Which subsets of these parameters are most important in influencing the uses of a water body (for example, commercial fishing, boating, swimming) is still a major question for research.

Developing predictive models for these parameters is also a major research priority. The most commonly used water quality models relate dissolved oxygen to discharges of biochemical oxygen demand. But dissolved oxygen levels are only crudely related to the suitability of a water body for fishery production or recreation use. A major theme of a recent book by Ackerman and others is the inappropriate use of a dissolved oxygen model in the water quality planning phase of the Delaware Estuary Comprehensive Study (Ackerman and coauthors, 1974).

In the case of air quality, the choice of parameters is somewhat easier, but not without pitfalls. It is only recently that attention has been turned from sulfur dioxide to its transformation products, sulfur particles. The latter parameter of air quality is now thought to be of major importance in its own right in understanding the health effects of sulfur combustion products (U.S. Environmental Protection Agency, 1975). Air quality modeling is still in a primitive state, especially where atmospheric reactions such as smog formation are involved.

TYPES OF EFFECTS

When residuals discharges change ambient environmental quality, this causes changes in the flow of environmental services and the uses man makes of the environment. There is a variety of channels through which environmental quality affects man. The following is one way of classifying the effects of environmental change according to whether the effects impinge directly upon man, or indirectly upon man through their impact on other living organisms or inanimate systems.

The Channels Through Which Environmental Changes Affect Man
Through living systems—biological mechanisms
　　Human health—morbidity, mortality
　　Economic productivity of ecological systems
　　　　Agricultural productivity
　　　　Forestry
　　　　Fisheries
　　Other ecosystem impacts
　　　　Recreational uses of ecosystems—fishing, hunting
　　　　Ecological diversity, stability
Through nonliving systems
　　Materials damages, soiling, production costs
　　Weather, climate
　　Other—odor, visibility, visual aesthetics

Human Health

Exposure to air pollution has been associated with increases in morbidity and mortality (Lave and Seskin, 1977). Outbreaks of infectious diseases have been traced to contaminants in municipal water supplies. And there is now evidence linking chemical pollutants in water supplies with elevated cancer mortality rates (Page, Harris, and Epstein, 1976).

Economic Productivity of Ecological Systems

In the arid West, runoff and return flows from irrigated fields carry with them dissolved salts leached from the soil. The consequence of irrigation in upstream areas, therefore, is degraded water quality down stream. Where there is repeated rediversion of the riverflow for irrigation purposes, the increasing salinity reduces the productivity of the irrigation water for agriculture. Reduced productivity of agricultural lands is a cost of this form of nonindustrial water pollution.

Agricultural productivity can also be affected by air pollution. Sulfur dioxide and photochemical oxidants have both been linked with various forms of leaf damage and reduced photosynthesis rates. There also may be a long-term effect on agricultural productivity due to rising soil acidity caused by acid rain.[1] The production of economically valuable forestry products (for example, lumber and pulp) may also be affected by acid rain.

Water pollution can affect commercial fisheries production in a number of ways. Pollution of rivers can reduce or eliminate spawning runs of commercially valuable species such as salmon, shad, herring, and smelt. Toxic substances can affect the biological productivity of estuarine areas, which are the foundation of the biological food chain for commercially valuable species. The toxic substances can themselves reduce or eliminate populations of commercially valuable species such as crabs and lobsters. And finally, contamination from chemicals and bacteria can render surviving commercially valuable species unfit for human consumption. Swordfish and tuna have been taken off the market because of contamination, and shellfish beds have been closed to commercial harvesting because of both bacterial and chemical contamination.

Other Ecosystem Impacts

This category includes impacts on those ecological systems which are not of direct economic significance to man. Man may have some use of the ecosystem, as in the case of recreational fishing and hunting. But pollutants can also cause changes in such ecosystem characteristics as diversity and stability which have no direct significance to man's uses of the environment. If we can identify no direct effect on man, these

---

[1] Acid rain refers to the unnaturally low pH of rain apparently caused by the entrapment of sulfate particles in the water droplets. The sulfate particles form sulfuric acid in solution.

ecological impacts cannot be captured by our definition of benefits. This is not to say that such changes are unimportant, but only that their importance must be assessed in terms of some criterion other than the economic one.

Materials Damages, Soiling, Production Costs

Some air pollutants can cause corrosion to metals and accelerate the deterioration of surface coatings. Soiling due to particulate deposition is aesthetically unappealing and can increase cleaning costs. The presence of contaminants in the water sources for municipal and industrial water supplies can raise costs of treating that water before use. The presence of corrosive substances can shorten the lives of and otherwise damage vessels and structures such as wharves and pilings. Sediment deposition in rivers and bays can lead to increased costs for channel dredging and maintenance. These are all examples of effects of pollution that do not act through biological mechanisms. Rather, their effects are on inanimate objects. And they are of significance to man.

Weather and Climate

Whether through raising the level of carbon dioxide or atmospheric particulates or through ozone depletion, there is a possibility that the discharge of pollutants can significantly affect weather and climate. The economic significance of climate change could be enormous. Climate change could affect human health directly; it could substantially alter production costs (for example, for heating); and it could have a significant impact on the economic productivity of ecological systems.[2]

Other

Both air and water pollution can cause odors which affect people's utility and welfare. When smog impairs the view of a nearby mountain range, this could result in a loss of amenity values. Since aesthetic effects are often not associated with direct use of environmental re-

---

[2] For a preliminary effort to assess the magnitude of some of these effects, see Ferrar (1976).

sources, they pose difficult measurement and valuation problems. But to the extent that they involve utility gains and willingness to pay, they are nevertheless every bit as real, in an economic sense, as the impairment of health.

THE NEED FOR MEASUREMENT OF EFFECTS

The bulk of this book is about the determination of the economic values attached to the services affected by environmental change. But the discussion cannot proceed very far without some reference to the relationship between ambient environmental quality and the uses of the environment, that is, the second set of relationships described above. For example, the value of a recreation user-day at a lake is affected by fish populations and species distribution, algae levels, the number and type of bacteria present, temperature, smell, turbidity, and concentration of toxic substances. To further complicate matters, an increase in the magnitude of one characteristic may affect one use favorably while affecting an alternative use in a negative way. For example, higher water temperatures may make for better swimming while adversely affecting trout and salmon populations. Industrial discharges of acids may adversely affect recreation and fisheries while improving the value of water for industrial uses because of retarded algae growth. The difficulties in tracing out the effects of the discharge of a pollutant on the many parameters of environmental quality and, in turn, their effects on man's use of the environment substantially limit our ability to do careful benefit–cost analyses of environmental quality and improvements. This is not fully appreciated by many advocates of greater use of benefit–cost analysis in this field. It was in 1968 that Allen Kneese wrote:

> I believe that our limited ability to evaluate the recreational losses associated with poor quality water, or conversely, the benefits of water improvement, is an extremely important barrier to rational water quality management. . . . The first [complexity] is the relationship between the level of various water quality parameters and the recreational attractiveness of the water resource. This relationship can be viewed as being composed of two linkages: a natural one and a human one. I think these are both about equally ill-understood. It is my impression . . . that the biological sciences are almost never able to tell us specifically what difference a change in measured parameters of water quality will make in those biological characteristics of the water that contribute to its recreational value. . . . Perhaps the undeveloped state

of forecasting is a result of the fact that biologists have seldom been confronted with the types of questions we would now like them to answer. . . . There is also a human linkage that is ill-understood. What quality characteristics of water do human beings find attractive for recreation? This is still largely an area of ignorance (pp. 180–181).

What Kneese said about water quality and recreation applies as well to the other effects of water pollution and to air pollution as well. And it is as true in 1978 as it was ten years ago.

MEASUREMENT BY REGRESSION ANALYSIS

The most commonly used empirical technique for estimating the magnitude of the effects of environmental quality changes on some environmental use is regression analysis. Various forms of the regression model have been used to estimate, for example, the relationship between mortality and air pollution, cancer and chemical contamination of drinking water, and recreation and water quality. However, there are a number of problems that arise in attempting to implement the regression approach to determining the relationships between environmental quality and environmental uses.

Model Specification

The first problem in specification is to know what explanatory variables should be included in the regression equation. As pointed out above, there are important cases, for example recreation, in which research has not yet provided a definitive answer to the question of what environmental variables to include. Statistical theory shows that if there is an important independent variable which is omitted in the estimation of the equation, the coefficients of the remaining variables will be biased in the statistical sense.[3]

The underlying true model may not be linear. It may be nonlinear in one or more of its variables; there can be threshold effects; and there may be synergistic or antagonistic relationships among subsets of the independent variables. Some of these problems can be examined by estimating alternative functional forms, for example, variables linear in

---

[3] An estimate of a coefficient is said to be biased if the expected value or mean of the estimate is not equal to the true value of the underlying model.

the logs, including multiplicative terms, and so forth.[4] But these procedures are time consuming. They may produce ambiguous results in that
no alternative specification is clearly superior to all others. And they
complicate the research task.

Temporal Aggregation

Typically, environmental quality measures vary over time. The dissolved oxygen level at any point in a river rises and falls with changes
in stream flow, discharge rates, water temperature, and the like. Air
pollution readings vary with the time of day, day of the week, and over
the year. One problem in empirical research on effects of pollution is
how to define a variable or set of variables which adequately reflects
the temporal variation in environmental quality while still being man-
ageable.

To put the problem in a concrete setting, consider an attempt to
estimate the relationship between an air pollutant and mortality. The
air pollution level at any particular point in an urban area is an instantaneous variable which fluctuates over time. The true exposure of an
individual located at that point is measured by a trace of the time path
of that instantaneous variable over the relevant time period. The published data on air pollution levels which are used to generate exposure
variables for empirical research involve various approaches to summarizing this instantaneous time path. Inevitably, summarizing involves
losing information. For example, a common measure is the annual
mean—either arithmetic or geometric. Moreover, at least in part because of measurement techniques, averages are struck over shorter time
periods, for example, the 24-hour average for particulates, and 8-hour
and 1-hour averages for other pollutants. The shorter averages can also
provide a basis for summary measures of exposure. For example, Lave
and Seskin used the lowest 24-hour average recorded during a year as
one measure of long-term exposure (Lave and Seskin, 1977).

No one or two of these measures can completely represent the true
exposure of any individual. Empirical research is hampered by this inability to characterize accurately the exposure of individuals over long
periods of time. There is, however, one approach to summarizing recorded air pollution data which may lead to a more accurate characteri-

[4] A good example of a thorough search for alternative functional forms is
Lave and Seskin (1977).

zation of exposure. This approach is based on the assumption that the instantaneous air pollution reading or an average struck over a short period of time (1-hour, 8-hour) can be treated as a stochastic variable drawn from a known probability distribution. That probability distribution has a mean, a variance, and perhaps other higher order moments which can be estimated from the pollution data for the one-year period.

Larsen (1971) has reported that the air pollution readings taken over a year for any given averaging period (for example, a 1-hour average) follow approximately a log normal distribution. This means that given the averaging period, the year's air pollution experience can be completely described by the geometric mean and geometric variance of the data.

In general, in those cases where it can be shown that the relevant environmental parameters are approximately following a normal or log normal distribution, the mean and variance of that distribution appear to be good candidates for summarizing the temporal variation.

Spatial Aggregation

Environmental systems cover large areas. The environmental quality measures may vary across space as well as through time. If readings taken at one or two points in the space are used to represent the space as the whole, they may introduce systematic errors in the analysis of the effects of environmental quality change. One case where this type of bias can arise is in the analysis of air pollution and mortality where standard metropolitan statistical areas (SMSAs) are the sample unit. The discussion that follows uses this example to show that systematic bias can exist.

Assume that there is some single-valued measure of the air pollution exposure of an individual. Further, assume that the "true" relationship between this pollution measure and the mortality rate (probability of death) is known. This is portrayed by the solid line in figure 1. Consider a "dirty" urban area. Air pollution measures are typically taken at one centrally located monitoring station in the smaller SMSAs. The larger SMSAs may have networks of monitoring stations. In the latter case, pollution measures are some average of readings at the several stations. Assume that for this "dirty" city the average air pollution reading at the downtown stations is $0-P_4$.

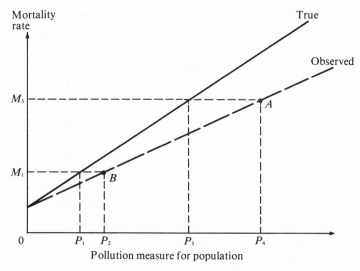

Figure 1. Mortality rates as functions of true and observed pollution exposures

Because some portion of the population lives in suburban areas quite far from the downtown monitoring stations, and some portion of the suburban population does not regularly travel to the downtown area, $0-P_4$ is an overestimate of the true average pollution exposure of this urban population. Assume that the true measure is $0-P_3$. Reference to the true pollution–mortality relationship shows that this dirty city would have a mortality rate of $0-M_3$. The observed pollution–mortality data would be plotted as point A in figure 1.

Now consider a relatively clean city. By similar reasoning, there will be a divergence between recorded and actual pollution exposures for that population. However, the divergence will be much smaller, since with a clean city, the difference between the "clean" suburbs and "almost clean" downtown area will be much smaller. If $0-P_2$ is the recorded pollution measure for the clean city, the clean city observation would be point B in figure 1. As can be seen by reference to the figure, a regression line fitted to the recorded data would lead to an underestimate of the regression coefficient relating pollution to mortality.[5]

[5] If the monitoring stations are located so as to underestimate the average pollution exposure of the urban population, regression analysis will overestimate the pollution coefficient.

However, while the estimate of the regression coefficient is biased by the error in the pollution measure, if the regression equation is used to predict changes in mortality conditional on changes in pollution, the regression equation will give "true" predictions. Consider a pollution control program which is expected to reduce recorded pollution in the dirty cities from $0-P_4$ to $0-P_2$. The regression equation predicts a reduction in mortality of $0-M_3$ to $0-M_1$. The pollution control program will actually reduce true exposure from $0-P_3$ to $0-P_1$. And the true reduction in mortality will be just that predicted by the regression equation.

Similar problems might arise for mortality or morbidity studies based on a sample of individuals if the pollution variable is measured by some proxy. For example, suppose each individual's exposure were taken to be a function of pollution levels at his residence. Then, the recorded pollution measure would understate true exposure for those individuals living in the clean part of the city and spending some part of the working day in the dirty part of the city. Similarly, for those living in the dirtiest part of the city, the recorded pollution measure is likely to overstate true exposure. By a line of reasoning similar to that developed through figure 1, it can be shown that this divergence between recorded and true exposure measures will lead to an underestimate of the slope of the regression line relating exposure to morbidity or mortality.

Multicollinearity

When two pollutants are both thought to be related to an "effect" variable such as the mortality rate, and when multiple regression techniques are used to estimate the hypothesized relationship, the process of estimation may be complicated by the problem of multicollinearity. For example, differences in mortality rates have been associated with differences in the levels of both suspended particulates and sulfates. Similarly, particulates and sulfates have both been significant variables in explaining property value differentials. Suppose the hypothesized relationship is

$$M = a_0 + a_1P + a_2S + a_3Z + e \qquad (1)$$

where M = mortality rate

   P = particulate concentration

   S = sulfate concentration

   Z = an index of other variables

   e = disturbance term

Suppose that P and S are positively correlated. Thus, multicollinearity is present. It is important to distinguish between problems in estimating the coefficients for equation (1) and problems in using equation (1) for prediction of mortality rates. It can be shown that when equation (1) is estimated with multicollinearity present, the estimates of a_1 and a_2 will be unbiased. However, they are likely to be imprecise in the sense that the estimates will have relatively large standard errors. In fact, it is possible that the equation may have an R^2 well over .95 with none of the regression coefficient estimates being significantly different from zero. It is also possible that estimated coefficients may have the wrong sign. But it is important to note that while the individual coefficient estimates may be imprecise, the equation as a whole may still provide good predictions of mortality rates when the independent variables are known.

Now suppose that equation (1) has been estimated and that the estimate of a_2 was insignificant by the ordinary statistical criterion.[6] One might be tempted to drop the sulfate variable and estimate a new equation

$$M = a_0' + a_1'P + a_3'Z + e' \tag{2}$$

However, the estimate of a_1' given by this misspecified equation will be biased. Given a positive correlation between P and the omitted sulfate variable, it can be shown that $a_1' > a_1$. This is because the estimate reflects not only the partial relationship between P and M, but also part of the relationship between the omitted variable S and M. Similarly, if P were dropped and the equation were estimated with only S, the estimated coefficient for the S variable would be biased upward.

---

[6] If neither coefficient is significant, it is possible that dropping one of the insignificant variables would improve the "t" statistic for the other variable so that it would appear to be significant in the new equation. The quest for high "t" statistics seems to be the dominant factor in the "dropping variables" strategy.

In summary, when the regression equation is to be used to predict changes in the dependent variables, the correct procedure is to estimate the equation with all variables included, and to use all of the coefficients, including those which are insignificant, to predict changes in the dependent variable conditional upon given changes in the independent variables.

In addition to the example cited here, there are a number of other situations in which multicollinearity between environmental quality variables might be present. If two different temporal measures of a single pollutant are used, they are likely to be collinear. The mean and variance measures suggested in the preceding subsection are likely to show collinearity. And different water quality parameters such as dissolved oxygen and turbidity may also be correlated.

UNCERTAINTY

Even the most careful estimate of benefits contains inaccuracies because of errors in the measurement of variables and errors in the statistical estimation of relationships. In addition, it may be necessary for the analyst to make assumptions regarding unknown parameters, relationships, and values. The uncertainty inherent in these errors must be expressed somehow in the final benefit figure. In order to accomplish this, it is necessary to adopt a framework and a language for conveying the uncertainty. The most appealing way of dealing with these problems is through the use of probabilities to quantify uncertainties. This is straightforward in theory because probability is a natural language for describing uncertain situations.[7]

Most people are accustomed to using probability informally as a language for describing uncertainty. Weather forecasts are stated in terms of probability of rain. And expectations concerning elections and sporting events are often expressed in terms of odds or probabilities. The same concepts may be used to describe uncertainties related to benefit estimates. Probability theory provides an unambiguous and logically consistent language for reasoning about uncertainty. In fact, a forceful argument can be made that any logical process for reasoning about uncertainty is equivalent to probability theory.

[7] See the recent report of the National Academy of Sciences (1975, appendix H), and National Academy of Sciences (1977, chapter 2 and appendix D) for further discussions.

The same people who use probability naturally in informal situations may be extremely reluctant to use the same ideas in important decision situations. To some extent the problem is one of measurement. Many people are accustomed to viewing probabilities as exact numbers based on objective evidence, for example as deduced from physical symmetry or observed frequencies from large-number experiments. They are uncomfortable with the idea of using subjective probabilities as a language for expressing their judgment on a matter where the available information is limited.

Consider the air pollution–human health relationship. If we had a large body of statistical data on the incidence of mortality over a range of known air pollution exposures, it would be relatively straightforward to assign a probability to a given individual's dying as the result of exposure to that air pollution. But if estimates of benefits are desired before this type of data is available, or if those data are very difficult to obtain because of cost, measurement problems, and the like, then the analyst must resort to informed judgment and logical reasoning. Judgment must be extrapolated from other information, for example, animal tests, or a review of several less than perfectly successful attempts to measure the desired relationship.

Once the basic assumption has been accepted that probability assignments are not "objective" but represent judgments—that they can summarize information or a state of mind—then the probability theory for expressing these judgments in a consistent manner is relatively straightforward. For example, what is frequently called the "best guess estimate" can be interpreted as an expected value or mean of the subjective probability distribution. The high and the low values should be expressed in terms of confidence limits. For example, "the probability is .95 that the true value lies within this range." Once the probability language has been formally adopted, the rules for carrying through uncertainties surrounding estimates or measures of underlying parameters to the final estimate are straightforward. Where the final estimate is derived from several variables in relationships each with their own estimated degrees of error or uncertainty, the uncertainty surrounding the final estimate is a compound of the component uncertainties. Probability theory thus provides a logical framework for determining the degree of uncertainty.

To those who might argue that the assignment of probability should be rejected because it is subjective, the response is that the present approach to determining best guesses and high and low bounds is also subjective. Often, the methods for deriving best guesses and high and low bounds from the underlying data are not consistent from one part of a study to the next. Probability is a language for dealing with subjective estimates in a consistent and logical manner; and it is one which can be interpreted consistently by others.

I shall return to some of these measurement problems in the concluding chapter with its discussion of the state of the art and research needs. I turn now to the essentially economic questions of defining and measuring welfare change and benefits.

REFERENCES

Ackerman, Bruce, Susan Rose-Ackerman, James Sawyer, and Dale Henderson. 1974. *The Uncertain Search for Environmental Policy* (Glencoe, Ill., Free Press).

Ferrar, Terry A., ed. 1976. *The Urban Cost of Climate Modifications* (New York, Wiley).

Kneese, Allen V. 1968. "Economics and the Quality of the Environment: Some Empirical Experiences," in Morris Garnsey and James Gibbs, eds., *Social Sciences and the Environment* (Boulder, Colo., University of Colorado Press).

Larsen, Ralph I. 1971. *A Mathematical Model for Relating Air Quality Measurements to Air Quality Standards* (Washington, D.C., U.S. Environmental Protection Agency).

Lave, Lester B., and Eugene P. Seskin. 1977. *Air Pollution and Human Health* (Baltimore, Johns Hopkins University Press for Resources for the Future).

National Academy of Sciences. 1975. *Decision Making for Regulating Chemicals in the Environment* (Washington, D.C., NAS).

———. 1977. *Decision Making in the Environmental Protection Agency* (Washington, D.C., NAS).

Page, Talbot, Robert Harris, and Samuel S. Epstein. 1976. "Drinking Water and Cancer Mortality in Louisiana," *Science* vol. 193, no. 4247 (July) pp. 55–57.

U.S. Environmental Protection Agency. 1975. *Position Paper on Regulation of Atmospheric Sulfates* (Research Triangle Park, N.C.).

CHAPTER 3

The Concept of Benefits and Welfare Change

The subject of the measurement of welfare change has been discussed by others both at the most rigorous levels of abstraction and in pragmatic, practical terms of application. My major purpose in adding to this literature is to provide a systematic and comprehensive development of the definition and measurement of welfare changes, with particular reference to the effects of environmental changes. Changes in environmental quality can affect individuals' welfares through any of the following channels: changes in the prices they pay for goods; changes in the prices they receive for their factors of production; and changes in the quantities of nonmarketed goods, for example, public goods such as air quality. Although the welfare measures discussed here have been developed primarily in the context of changes in product prices, it is shown that they can easily be generalized to encompass welfare changes occuring through the other channels.

In this chapter, I consider three sets of questions in some detail. The first is how to define an acceptable monetary measure of changes in economic welfare for an individual. The second is how changes in welfare would be measured both in theory and in practice. The third question is how any measure of welfare changes for individuals might be used to make judgments about social policies affecting many individuals. For example, is it possible to speak of a measure of aggregate welfare for the society as a whole? And what significance can be attached to changes in such a measure?

The answer to the first question requires a discussion of the compensating variation (CV) and equivalent variation (EV) measures of consumer surplus. No decisive case can be made for one measure or the other. But it is argued that in practice, this may not be an important issue since the two measures of welfare change $(EV$ and $CV)$ will usually not differ significantly. Thus the answer to the second question is that welfare changes can be measured by the area under an ordinary demand curve for an individual.

This concept of welfare change for an individual can be defined and analyzed without reference to the notions of efficiency and equity. In this sense the concept is objective; that is, one can define and measure a monetary equivalent of an individual's welfare change without being committed to any particular set of value judgments concerning aggregation across individuals or the role of such welfare measures in social choice.[1] It is in answering the third question that value judgments about the relative deservingness of individuals, the meaning of efficiency, and the objectives of public policy come into play.

In the next three sections the major concepts and measures of welfare change are developed for the case of changes in the prices of goods that individuals purchase. Subsequent sections generalize the analysis to the case of changes in factor prices and changes in quantities of nonmarketed goods. Finally, some problems in aggregation and the application of welfare measures to social choice are discussed.

WELFARE EFFECTS OF INCOME AND PRICE CHANGES

Consider an individual whose utility is a function only of private goods which can be bought and sold in markets. Assume that tastes and preferences (that is, the utility function) are given and do not change. The individual faces a set of given prices for these goods and is assumed to choose the quantities of the goods so as to maximize his utility given the constraints of prices and a fixed money income M.

We seek a money measure of the gains or losses in utility and welfare associated with changes in the individual's economic circumstances. If money income changes, the welfare effect is measured by the change in income. But the problem is more complicated if one or more of the prices are changed. What is required is a method for calculating a measure of the welfare effects of price changes—a measure that is commensurate with the money measure of the welfare effects of income changes.

---

[1] Of course in a more fundamental sense, focusing attention on changes in income and consumption to the exclusion of other aspects of well-being, such as social relationships or sense of self-worth, involves a kind of value judgment. But it is implicit in the division of labor between economists and others.

Here, we develop the exposition for the special case where there are only two goods and one price change. This is so that the exposition can be developed graphically. However, the analysis can be developed mathematically and generalized to the case of many goods and more than one price change. References will be provided where appropriate.

I shall define five alternative measures of welfare change for the case where the price of one good is decreased. The first is the change in ordinary consumer's surplus, a concept whose origin can be traced back through Marshall to Dupuit.[2] Ordinary consumer's surplus is measured by the area under a Marshallian ordinary demand curve but above the horizontal price line. As I will show, the consumer surplus measure cannot be defined in terms of the underlying indifference curves of figure 2. And in general, it will be different from the other four measures defined below.

The other four measures are theoretical refinements of the ordinary consumer's surplus. Each can be defined in terms of the underlying individual preference mapping. Figure 2 shows two indifference curves for an individual. Assume that air pollution control reduces the cost of producing x_1 so that its price drops from p_1' to p_1''. In response to the price reduction, the individual shifts from the consumption bundle marked A at utility level U_1 to consumption bundle B at utility level U_2. What is the welfare benefit of the price reduction to this individual? The welfare measure is defined in terms of good x_2, which we take to be a numeraire good. The units of x_2 are chosen so that the price of x_2 is equal to one. Thus, x_2 can be taken to represent income.[3]

The four remaining measures of welfare change are:

1. Compensating Variation (CV)—This measure asks what compensating payment or offsetting change in income is necessary to make the individual indifferent between the original situation (A in figure 2) and the new price set. Given the new price set with consumption point B, the individual could have his income reduced by the amount of CV and still be as well off at point C as he was at point A with the

---

[2] See Mishan (1960) or Currie, Murphy, and Schmitz (1971) for discussions of the history and evolution of the concept of consumer's surplus.

[3] In the many-good case, x_2 is a composite good or an index of the consumption levels of all other goods except x_1. This aggregation of all other goods into a composite good for graphical representation is valid so long as the prices of all of the goods are assumed to move in the same proportion, that is, that there are no changes in the relative prices of components of the composite good bundle. This assumption can be maintained since we are analyzing only the consequences of the change in the price of x_1.

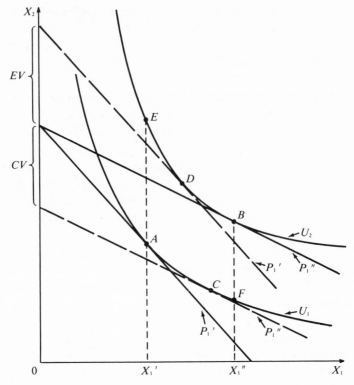

Figure 2. Four measures of the welfare gain from a price decrease

original price set and money income. The measure CV is often interpreted as the maximum amount that the individual would be willing to
pay for the opportunity to consume at the new price set. However for
a price increase, CV measures what must be paid to the individual to
make him indifferent to the price change. For price decreases the CV
can not be greater than the individual's income. But for a price increase, the CV could exceed income.

2. Equivalent Variation (EV)—This measure asks what change
in income (given the original prices) would lead to the same utility
change as the change in the price of x_1. As shown in figure 2, given the
original prices, the individual could reach utility level U_2 at point D
with an income increase equal to EV. EV is the income change equivalent to the welfare gain due to the price change. The EV measure has
also been described as the minimum lump sum payment the individual

would have to receive to induce him voluntarily to forego the opportunity to purchase at the new price set. But for a price increase, *EV* is the maximum amount the individual would be willing to pay to avoid the change in prices.

Note that both the *EV* and *CV* measures allow the individual to adjust the quantities consumed of both goods in response to both changes in relative prices and income levels. The remaining two measures are defined so as to place restrictions on the individual's adjustment of his consumption bundles.

3. Compensating Surplus (*CS*)—This measure asks what compensating payment or offsetting income change will make the individual indifferent between the original situation and the opportunity to purchase the new quantity x_1'' of the good whose price has changed. The *CS* measure is the vertical distance between the indifference curves at the new quantity x_1'', or *B–F* in figure 2. This measure is closely related to the *CV* measure, the only difference being the restriction on adjusting the purchases of x_1 in response to the compensating or offsetting income change.

4. Equivalent Surplus (*ES*)—This measure asks what change in income is required, given the old prices *and* consumption level of x_1, in order to make the individual as well off as he would be with the new price set and consumption point *B*. In figure 2 the *ES* measure is the vertical distance between the two indifference curves holding the consumption of good x_1 at the original level, that is, the vertical distance from *A* to *E*. The *ES* measure is closely related to the *EV* measure, the only difference being in the restriction on the adjustment of the consumption of x_1 in the former case. The *ES* measure is larger than the *EV* measure for price decreases because it must include an income equivalent to the individual's welfare loss stemming from the inability to adjust the consumption of x_1 so as to equate the marginal rate of substitution with the price ratio.

Each of these concepts measures something different and has a different meaning. Each has its advantages and disadvantages as a form of welfare measure. The remainder of the chapter will be devoted primarily to the compensating variation and equivalent variation measures and their relationship to the ordinary consumer surplus. The compensating surplus and equivalent surplus measures are too restrictive in their assumptions to be useful. Even in those cases, such as public goods, where the individual faces fixed quantities which may change rather than fixed prices, there is no need for the *CS* and *ES* concepts as separate measures. I will show below that in this case, the *CS* and *CV* measures are identical and the *ES* and *EV* measures are identical.

A subsequent section will be devoted to a comparison and evaluation of the *CV* and *EV* measures. But first there is a new concept to be introduced, one which will be useful in discussing both the conceptual and theoretical bases of the *CV* and *EV* concepts, and the estimation of these measures from market data. This new tool is the expenditure function.

THE EXPENDITURE FUNCTION

The expenditure function represents an another way of looking at the problem of utility maximization for an individual.[4] The conventional maximization problem can be expressed as

maximize $U = U(X)$

subject to $\sum_i p_i x_i = M$

where X is the vector of quantities $(X = x_1, \ldots, x_i, \ldots, x_n)$ and M is money income.

The solution to this problem leads to a set of ordinary or Marshallian demand functions

$$x_i = x_i(P, M)$$

and some maximum utility level U_m. The dual of this problem is

minimize $\sum_i p_i x_i$

subject to $U(X) = U^0 = U_m$

The solution to this problem is the expenditure function. The expenditure function gives the minimum dollar expenditure necessary to achieve a specified utility level, given market prices. In functional notation

$$E = E(P, U^0)$$

---

[4] For a general discussion of the expenditure function, see Diamond and McFadden (1974). See also Moss (1976) for a correction of one of the derivations. Mäler (1974) develops the concept of the expenditure function and relates it specifically to the welfare effects of changes in environmental quality.

where E is dollar expenditure, P is the vector of prices ($P = p, \ldots,$ $p_i, \ldots, p_n$), and U^0 is the specified utility level.

Just as the solution to the utility maximization problem yields a set of ordinary demand curves conditional on prices and money income, the solution of the expenditure minimization problem yields a set of demand functions conditional on prices and utility. These demand functions are of the form

$$x_i^* \, (P, \, U^0)$$

These are Hicks-compensated demand functions which show the quantities consumed at various prices assuming that income is adjusted (compensated), so that utility is held constant at U^0. The difference between the Hicks-compensated and the ordinary demand functions is one of the main considerations in the comparison of EV, CV, and consumer surplus measures of welfare change.

Panel a in figure 3 shows one individual's preference mapping in the simple two-good case. Suppose that the price of good x_1 falls from p_1' to p_1''. The individual responds by moving from the original equilibrium at point A to point B on the new budget line. In panel b of figure 3, these equilibrium positions are plotted in the price and quantity plane. Points A and B are on the ordinary demand curve holding the price of good x_2 and money income constant.

Suppose instead that as the price of good x_1 is decreased, income is taken away from the individual so that he remains at the initial utility level and indifference curve U_1. Given the price change and the compensating income change, the individual would be in equilibrium at point C in panel a of figure 3. The amount of income that must be withdrawn from the individual to hold him on this indifference curve can be calculated from the expenditure function. Point C is also plotted in panel b of figure 3. Points A and C are on the Hicks-compensated demand curve, a demand curve which reflects only the substitution effect of the change in relative prices. The income effect of the price change has been eliminated by the device of compensating withdrawals of money income. Since by assumption, x_1 is a normal good, that is, it has an income elasticity greater than zero, the Hicks-compensated demand curve is less elastic than the ordinary demand curve.

Panel a of figure 3 shows the compensating variation measure of the welfare change associated with the price decrease. The CV can also be defined in terms of the expenditure function. The CV is the differ-

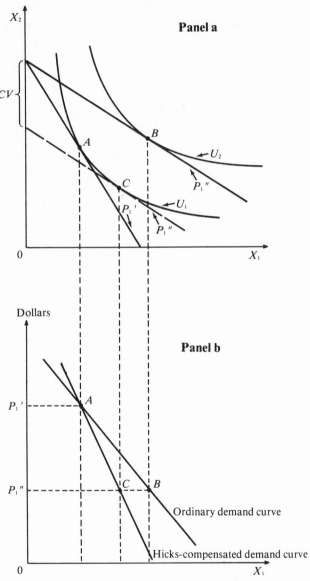

Figure 3. The compensating variation and the Hicks-compensated demand curve

ence between the expenditure function (income) required to sustain utility level U_1 at the two price sets.

$$CV = E(p_1', p_2, U_1) - E(p_1'', p_2, U_1)$$

In the two-good case with one price change, it can be shown that the CV is equal to the area to the left of the Hicks-compensated demand curve between the two prices, that is, the area $P_1'ACP_1''$. The partial derivative of the expenditure function with respect to p_1 gives the change in expenditure (income) necessary to keep the individual on U_1 for small changes in p_1. As shown above, this derivative gives the Hicks-compensated demand curve, that is, it gives the optimal quantity for x_1, holding utility constant. For finite changes, the integral of this derivative is the area to the left of the Hicks-compensated demand curve, that is, the CV.[5] In the many-good cases when several prices change, the CV of the price changes taken together is the integral of the set of compensated demand functions evaluated by taking each price change successively. The order in which the price changes are evaluated is irrelevant.[6]

The equivalent variation can also be derived through the expenditure function. Panel a of figure 4 shows the same preference mapping and price change for an individual. With a price decrease, the EV is defined as the additional expenditure (income) necessary to reach utility level U_2, given the initial set of prices. In the figure, the EV is the additional expenditure necessary to sustain point C' over point A. Thus,

$$EV = E(p_1', p_2, U_2) - E(p_1', p_2, U_1)$$

But since the money expenditure levels are the same at point A and point B [$E(p_1', p_2, U_1) = E(p_1'', p_2, U_2)$], this can be written as

$$EV = E(p_1', p_2, U_2) - E(p_1'', p_2, U_2)$$

In other words, the EV can be defined in terms of the expenditure function associated with utility level U_2. The price derivative of this expenditure function (this time holding utility constant at U_2) generates another Hicks-compensated demand curve through point B in panel b of figure 4. The area to the left of this Hicks-compensated demand curve between the two prices is the equivalent variation welfare measure.

[5] For a mathematical treatment, see Diamond and McFadden (1974, pp. 14–15), Willig (1976, pp. 591–592), or Mäler (1974, pp. 125–128).
[6] See Diamond and McFadden (1974), or Mohring (1971).

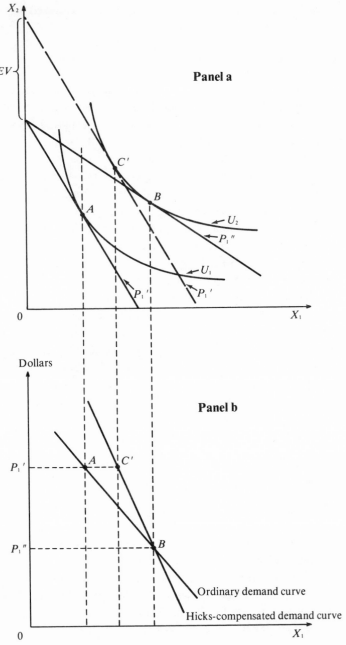

Figure 4. The equivalent variation and the Hicks-compensated demand curve

This discussion has all been in terms of the welfare gain due to a price decrease. The derivation of the welfare cost of a price increase can be worked out in a symmetrical fashion. In general, for any price change, the CV welfare measure is the area to the left of the Hicks-compensated demand curve which passes through the initial position. The EV measure of the welfare change is the area to the left of the Hicks-compensated demand curve which passes through the final position.

The two measures EV and CV will be the same if the income elasticity of demand for good x_1 is zero. In this case the ordinary and Hicks-compensated demand curves are identical. With a positive income elasticity, the EV exceeds the CV for price decreases, but the CV exceeds the EV when price increases are considered. The difference between points C and B in figure 3 and between points A and C' in figure 4 is one of income level. If the income elasticity of demand for x_1 were zero, the income differences would have no effect on the purchase of x_1. The CV and EV would be exactly equal; and they could both be measured by the area under the ordinary demand curve. The higher the income elasticity of demand for x_1, the larger is the difference between the EV and CV. And the larger is the difference between either measure and the ordinary consumer surplus.

THREE WELFARE MEASURES: A COMPARISON

In this section we offer a comparison and evaluation of three measures of welfare change: the compensating variation, the equivalent variation, and the ordinary consumer surplus as an empirical approximation. This evaluation is in terms of four criteria: practicability, the implied property rights, the uniqueness of the measures, and their consistency.

A practical consideration is whether the welfare measure can be calculated from readily obtainable market data. Ideally the answer is yes in the case of the ordinary consumer's surplus. If an econometric estimation of the demand curve for the good in question can be obtained, calculating the area under it over the range of the price change is straightforward. But things are not so easy with the EV and CV. These are both measured by areas under Hicks-compensated demand curves which are compensated to different levels of utility. Hicks-compensated demand curves are not directly observable from market data.

It is in principle possible to calculate Hicks-compensated demand functions from market data in the following manner. The first step is to estimate the complete set of demand functions as a system of equations. This system of demand functions must satisfy the integrability conditions. This assures that the demand equations are of a functional form derivable from an underlying utility function. If the integrability conditions are satisfied, the expenditure function can be derived from the system of demand equations.[7] Given the expenditure function, computing the Hicks-compensated demand functions and *EV* or *CV* measures is relatively straightforward. The practical difficulty in all this lies in the econometric problems of estimating complete systems of demand functions in sufficient detail to permit the derivation of the appropriate compensated demand functions for specific commodities. On the criterion of practicability, the ordinary consumer surplus measure gets the nod.

All three measures meet the criterion of being in dollar units for facilitating comparison with, for example, real resource costs of projects. However, these dollar measures for the *CV* and *EV* represent quite different aspects of the welfare effects of price changes. The *EV* more closely conforms to the concept of welfare change. By definition, it is a money equivalent of a price change, that is, the income change having the same effect on utility as the price change being evaluated. The *CV* does not measure a utility change, but rather the offsetting income change necessary to "prevent" a utility change. As Silberberg put it, "the [*EV*] imputes a dollar evaluation to a change in utility levels for a particular path of price changes, while the [*CV*] derives dollar values necessary to hold utility constant when prices change" (1972, p. 948).

The *CV* is sometimes described as the maximum willingness to pay for the right to purchase the good at the new price level, that is, that lump sum payment which the individual would be willing to make

---

[7] See Mäler (1974, pp. 121–125). If the price and quantity data are not fully consistent with the first order marginal conditions for utility maximization, then it will not be possible to solve for the utility function. This would be the case where there is a public good in fixed supply at a zero price. See Mäler (pp. 183–189) and chapter 4 of the present book for further discussion of this case.

which would just exhaust the potential for welfare gain from the new price. This description is accurate only for a price decrease. For a price increase, the *CV* defines a *payment to* the individual sufficient to prevent a utility decrease. Whatever the direction of the price change, the *CV* takes the initial or *status quo ante* utility as the reference point. These descriptions carry with them implicitly the presumption that the individual has no right or claim to make purchases at the new set of prices. In contrast, the *EV* is that lump sum payment (tax) which would have to be given to (taken from) the individual to make him willing to forego a price decrease (increase). This explanation contains the presumption that the individual has a right to the new price set and must be compensated if the new price set is not to be attained. Some economists using this interpretation of these two measures have argued that the choice between them is basically an ethical one, that is, one that depends on a value judgment as to which underlying distribution of property rights is more equitable.[8] But there are other objectives and factors on which to base an evaluation and comparison.

Sometimes the policy or project being evaluated will cause changes in the price of more than one good. For example, reducing the price of an air pollution-affected agricultural product may cause a reduction in the price of substitute products as well.[9] The third criterion for evaluating the alternative welfare measures is whether the measure is independent of the order in which price changes are evaluated. The welfare change measure for the set of price changes taken together must be aggregated from the measures of the welfare effects of each price change separately. The question is whether the welfare measure is independent of the choice of the order for evaluating individual price changes. For reasons that lie in the mathematics of the measurement technique, the answers are different for the two measures being considered. In general, the *EV* is not independent of the order in which multiple price changes are evaluated.[10] The *CV* is independent of the order of evaluation. The *EV* will be independent of the order of the evaluation only in the special case of a homothetic utility function, that is, where the income elasticities of the goods are unitary. Unless this

---

[8] See Krutilla (1967), and Mishan (1976).

[9] The decrease in the price of the affected good will cause a leftward shift in the ordinary demand curve for the substitute. If it is not a constant-cost industry, then its price will fall also.

[10] See Mohring (1971) or Silberberg (1972) for a complete discussion of this point.

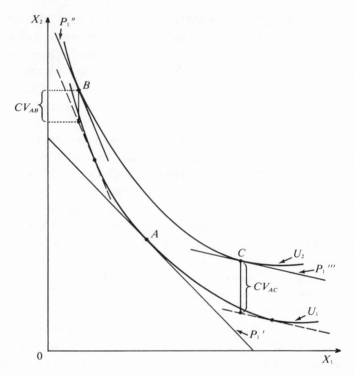

Figure 5. The compensating variation incorrectly ranks two alternative policies

condition is met, there is no unique EV in the case of multiple price changes.

The fourth criterion to be considered is the consistency of the ranking of alternatives with the underlying preference function of the individual. If the policy moves an individual to a higher indifference curve, a welfare measure should indicate a positive welfare change. Furthermore, for two alternative price changes, the welfare measures should be the same if they both place the individual on the same higher indifference curve. But if the two policy alternatives place the individual on different indifference curves, the welfare measure should correctly indicate the preference ranking of the two alternatives. It turns out that in the two-good case, the EV measure always provides a consistent ranking; but the CV does not.

Figure 5 shows an individual in equilibrium at point A, given prices and money income. One policy proposal would increase the price of x_1 and increase money income simultaneously. The individual would achieve a new equilibrium at point *B*. The *CV* measure of the welfare change CV_{AB} is shown. The second policy alternative would decrease money income while decreasing the price of x_1. This would lead to a new consumer's equilibrium at point *C*. Point *C* has been drawn to be on the same indifference curve as point *B*. Therefore, the measure of welfare change should be the same for the two policy alternatives. But as can seen by inspection, the *CV* for the second policy CV_{AC} is larger. The *CV* measure would indicate a preference for the second policy while the individual is in fact indifferent between the two.[11] The *EV* gives the same welfare measure for the two policy alternatives. This is because the *EV* measure bases its comparison on a point on the indifference curve passing through the new equilibrium, but with the old prices. If two policies are on the same new indifference curve, the *EV* measure picks the same point for measuring the welfare effects for both policies.

To summarize the comparison up to this point, the *CV* and *EV* measure different concepts. Neither is readily observable from market data. The *EV* does not provide a unique measure of welfare change when a project involves changes in more than one price (except for the special case of unitary income elasticities). When there is more than one project alternative to be evaluated and ranked, the *CV* may not provide a ranking of alternative policies that is consistent with individual preferences. Finally, the ordinary consumer surplus (*S*) is not consistent with any theoretical definition of welfare change. But it generally lies between the *CV* and *EV* measures for any particular proposal. And the ordinary consumer surplus is equal to the *CV* and the *EV* in the special case of zero income effects. This leads to the question of how important the differences are between ordinary consumers surplus and the *CV* and *EV* measures in practice.

Willig (1976) has offered rigorous derivations of expressions relating *CV, S,* and *EV*. These expressions provide a way of calculating the magnitude of the differences among the three measures for given prices, quantities, and income. The differences among the three measures depend on the income elasticity of demand for the good in question and consumer surplus as a percentage of income or expenditure. The differences among the measures appear to be small and almost trivial for most realistic cases. The differences are probably smaller than

---

[11] See Hause (1975).

the errors in the estimation of the parameters of demand functions by econometric methods.[12]

Willig takes into account the possibility that for finite changes in price and quantity, the income elasticity of demand may vary over the range of the price change. He derives rules of thumb for estimating the maximum error in using S as an approximation for EV or CV. The rules of thumb are applicable if the following conditions are met

$$\left| \frac{S}{M} \frac{\underline{E}_m}{2} \right| \leq .05$$

$$\left| \frac{S}{M} \frac{\bar{E}_m}{2} \right| \leq .05 \tag{1}$$

and

$$\left| \frac{S}{M} \right| \leq .9 \tag{2}$$

Given these conditions, the rule of thumb for CV is

$$\frac{|S|}{M} \frac{\underline{E}_m}{2} \leq \frac{CV - S}{|S|} \leq \frac{|S|}{M} \frac{\bar{E}_m}{2} \tag{3}$$

The rule of thumb for the EV is

$$\frac{|S|}{M} \frac{\underline{E}_m}{2} \leq \frac{S - EV}{|S|} \leq \frac{|S|}{M} \frac{\bar{E}_m}{2} \tag{4}$$

where S = ordinary consumer surplus (defined as positive for a price increase)
CV = compensating variation
EV = equivalent variation
M = the individual's base income
$\underline{E}_m$ = smallest value of income elasticity of demand for the good in the region under consideration
$\bar{E}_m$ = largest value of income elasticity of demand for the good in the region under consideration

[12] As was discussed in chapter 2, estimation errors and the approximation errors discussed here should be carried through in the analysis to the final benefit estimates and presented in terms of probability or confidence intervals.

The first thing to note is the conditions under which these rules of thumb are valid. Consider equation (2) first. Consumer surplus (S) as a percentage of income depends on the size of the price change, the price elasticity of demand, and expenditure on this good as a percentage of total income. The smaller the price change and the smaller the proportion of income spent on the good, the smaller is S/M. It can readily be shown that[13]

$$\frac{|S|}{M} \leq \frac{|\Delta P|}{P} \frac{P \cdot X}{M} \tag{5}$$

This shows that, for example, for a good absorbing 50 percent of total income and for a 100 percent price change, S/M cannot exceed 0.5, while for a 10 percent price change for a good absorbing 10 percent of income, S/M will be less than 0.1. Thus condition (2) is likely to be satisfied except for very large price *increases* for goods with low price elasticities which also absorb a large proportion of the total budget.

As for the first condition, the smaller that consumer surplus is as a percentage of income, or the smaller that the income elasticity of demand is, the more likely (1) is to be satisfied. For example, if consumer surplus is 5 percent of income, the income elasticity of demand can be as high as 2.0 and still satisfy (1). If S/M just barely satisfies condition (2), the income elasticity can not exceed .11 to satisfy (1).

Assuming that conditions (1) and (2) hold, let us turn to the rules of thumb. First, according to (1), the maximum error involved in using S as an approximation for either CV or EV is 5 percent. Second, the smaller the *change* in income elasticity over the range being considered, the more precise are (3) and (4) as statements of the error involved in using S rather than CV or EV. If the income elasticity of demand does not change with the range being considered ($E_m = E_m$), (3) and (4) become equalities and are exact statements of the error. Finally, as the income elasticity of demand for the good decreases, the differences among ordinary consumer surplus, $CV,$ and EV decrease, disappearing as E_m goes to zero.

In summary, Willig's analysis provides a strong justification for using the empirically observable consumer surplus measure of welfare change as a valid approximation for either of the theoretical measures EV or CV. Each of the latter has conceptual and theoretical problems

---

[13] From a given initial situation, S is largest when the demand curve is perfectly inelastic. Then $|S| = X\Delta P$. Condition (5) follows readily.

in its interpretation in some circumstances, but these appear to be relatively minor at the practical level.

WELFARE EFFECTS OF CHANGES
IN FACTOR PRICES

If the quantity of the factor the individual supplies to the market is unaffected by changes in its prices, the price change affects only income. And the income change is an exact measure of the welfare effect of the price change. But if the change in factor price affects the quantity supplied—for example, by altering the choice between labor and leisure—then the welfare measure must reflect both changes in income and changes in the utility derived from the quantity of the factor withheld from the market. CV and EV measures of welfare change can be defined in a manner consistent with the preceding analysis of product price changes. The relationship between these measures and the area above the individual's factor supply curve is similar to the relationship between CV, EV, and S for product price changes.[14]

Consider the supply of labor where the individual allocates time between income-producing work and utility-yielding leisure. The individual's labor supply function can be derived from his underlying utility function given other prices, and the like. As is well known, the labor supply curve can be backward bending, at least over some range, if the positive income effect on the demand for leisure outweighs the negative substitution effect of more expensive leisure. See figure 6. For any initial equilibrium, for example, at a wage rate of w', it is possible to derive a compensated supply curve that shows the quantities supplied at various prices assuming income has been adjusted to maintain the individual at his initial utility level. The compensated supply curve can also be derived by differentiating an expanded version of the expenditure function

$$E = E(P, w, U^0); \; (P = p_1, \ldots, p_i, \ldots, p_n)$$

with respect to w. Because the compensated supply curve represents

---

[14] See Mishan (1959) for a discussion of the CV and EV measures, consumer surplus, and economic rent.

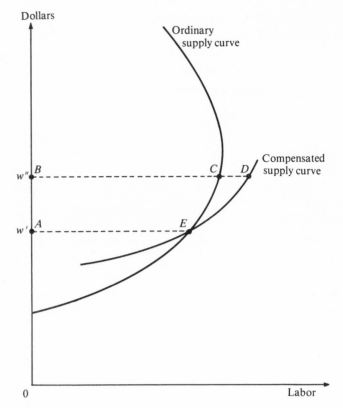

Figure 6. The compensating variation for a factor price increase

only the substitution effect between work and leisure, it is always upward sloping and more elastic than the ordinary supply curve.

If w increases, say to w'', the CV measure of welfare gain is the integral of the derivative of the expenditure function with respect to w. Geometrically this is the area to the left of the compensated supply curve between the two price levels, that is, $ABDE$ in figure 6. This is greater than the area between the prices bounded by the ordinary supply curve. There is also another compensated supply curve defined for the new utility level after the price change. It goes through point C. The EV measure of welfare change is the area to the left of this curve (not shown in figure 6) between the price levels. Unless the income elasticity of demand for leisure is zero, CV is greater than EV for wage increases, while EV is greater than CV for wage decreases.

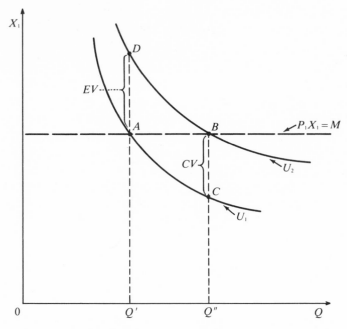

Figure 7. Compensating and equivalent variations for a change in quantity

WELFARE EFFECTS OF A QUANTITY CHANGE

Many environmental policy proposals involve changes in the quantity of an environmental good or service rather than changes in the price of a marketable good. From the individual's point of view the most important characteristic of some environmental goods is that they are available only in fixed, unalterable quantities at a zero price. In this section, it is shown that the CV and EV measures of welfare change are applicable in principle to unpriced goods whose quantities change. Figure 7 shows a preference mapping for an individual where Q is the environmental good and x_1 is the private composite good. x_1 is also used as the numeraire. The vertical line Q' represents the initial fixed quantity of the environmental good. The horizontal line shows the level of consumption of x_1, which exhausts income M, given p_1.

Now assume that a pollution control policy increases the level of the environmental good to Q''. The individual is shifted from his equilibrium position at point A to point B on a higher indifference curve. The CV measure asks what quantity of x_1 must be taken away in order to bring the individual back to the initial indifference curve. This is the quantity $B-C$. Since it is not possible to adjust the level of Q, the CV measure is identical to the CS measure defined in the first section of this chapter. The EV measure asks what change in x_1 given the initial level of Q is equivalent to the change in Q. The EV is given by the vertical distance $A-D$ in figure 7. Again, since variation in Q is precluded, the EV and ES measures coincide. But the EV and CV measures will not be the same unless the income elasticity of demand for Q is zero. For normal goods, EV exceeds CV for quantity increases, while CV exceeds EV for quantity reductions.

The CV and EV measures can also be derived from the expenditure function. When utility is a function of private goods X and an environmental good whose quantity is exogenous to the individual, the expenditure function is

$$E = E(P, Q, U^0)$$

The partial derivative of this function with respect to Q gives the amount that expenditure or income must change to hold utility at the specified level as Q changes. This traces out a marginal willingness to pay or compensated inverse demand curve. The CV and EV measures correspond to areas under the inverse demand functions compensated to the appropriate utility level.

The extension of this analysis to in-kind transfers of goods with a market value, for example, housing, medical care, or food, is straightforward in principle but sometimes difficult in practice. So long as there are no restrictions on resale of the transferred goods or if the transferred quantity is less than the individual would have purchased at the market price, the welfare value of the transfer is simply quantity times market price. However, if the transfer leaves the individual in a position where he would prefer to consume less of the good, given prices and his real income, the welfare change is less than the market value of the transfer. Measurement of the welfare change requires knowledge of the underlying demand function or utility function.[15]

INDIVIDUAL WELFARE CHANGES: A SUMMARY

The comparison and evaluation of the CV and EV as alternative welfare measures has shown that they both have limitations in principle.

[15] For further discussion, see Schmundt, Smolensky, and Stiefel (1975).

The *EV* measure is not unique when there are price changes for more than one good. The *CV* measure is unique in this case, but may not provide consistent rankings of two or more possible policy alternatives.

However, we have seen that both measures are close to the ordinary consumer surplus in most empirically relevant cases. Thus, there is a strong argument for using the ordinary consumer surplus as an empirical approximation to the theoretically correct *CV* or *EV* measures. In order to implement the *CV* or *EV* measure correctly, there is a need to know the expenditure function or utility function. And this requires the estimation of a complete set of demand functions for all goods. The ordinary consumer surplus measure can be estimated from demand functions for single goods in a partial equilibrium setting, assuming they are properly specified.

The discussion has focused primarily on goods which do pass through markets. For nonmarketed goods—for example, public goods—the market does not provide observations on prices and quantities, that is, the demand curve. This is a fundamental problem for applied welfare analysis. Economists must resort to various indirect market and non-market approaches to inferring public goods demands. These approaches are the subject of the next two chapters.

AGGREGATION AND SOCIAL WELFARE

Assume that we have obtained measures of the welfare change, either plus or minus, for all individuals. How can we use this information to make choices about public policy alternatives? Or to put the question in its most profound sense, what is the appropriate relationship between the welfare of individuals and the social welfare? In the literature on welfare economics, there are basically four ways to approach this question.[16]

The first approach to the problem is the so-called Pareto criterion, which states that no policy change shall be accepted unless at

---

[16] What follows is a very brief review of alternative social welfare criteria. Since the main concern of this book is with measurement, the question of social welfare criteria, that is, how to use the measures, is off the main track. For more extensive discussions of the problem, see Mishan (1960, especially section III). Haveman and Weisbrod (1975) provide a more up-to-date discussion of the concept of benefits and their role in the analysis of social welfare.

least one person is made better off (that is, has a positive welfare change) and no individual is made worse (that is, has a negative welfare change). This criterion deliberately rules out any attempts to add up or otherwise make commensurable the welfare measures of different individuals. Since most actual public policy proposals impose costs on at least some individuals, most policy actions by the state could not be accepted under this criterion. This would be particularly true in the environmental area where environmental management costs are often channeled through the production sector while benefits accrue to households in the form of increased levels of environmental services. It is highly unlikely that this would result in a pattern of incidence of benefits and costs in which no one would lose.[17] This limiting feature of the Pareto criterion has stimulated an ongoing search for a welfare criterion that would justify the state doing certain things that at least some people feel it should be able to do.[18]

The second approach to the problem was proposed independently by Hicks (1939) and Kaldor (1939). It states that a policy should be accepted if those who gain by the policy could fully compensate for the welfare losses of those who lose by the policy. The Hicks-Kaldor test would be satisfied if the sum of all individual welfare changes were greater than zero. The criterion is essentially one of *potential* Pareto improvement, since if the compensation is actually paid, no one loses.[19] Should the compensation actually be paid? If you think the answer should be yes, then the Hicks compensation test is transformed into a variation of the Pareto criterion in which the state serves to enforce the taxes and transfer payments that are necessary to ensure that no one actually experiences a welfare loss. If you think the answer should be no, you are, in effect, assuming that all individual welfare changes are commensurate and can be added or aggregated into a sum. This is the efficiency criterion of the new welfare economics.[20] According to the

[17] See for example, Gianessi, Peskin, and Wolff (1977).

[18] However, for a strong defense of the Pareto criterion on classical liberal grounds, see Peacock and Rowley (1975).

[19] Scitovsky noted the possibility that a compensation test could favor a move from position *A* to *B*; yet from the vantage point of position *B*, a return to position *A* could pass a compensation test based on the new relative prices and incomes. See Scitovsky (1942). However, it does not seem likely that this paradox would occur for the relatively small changes in resource allocation that constitute most public choices.

[20] See Haveman and Weisbrod (1975).

efficiency criterion, the objective of social policy is to maximize the value of the output of goods and services broadly defined.[21] Value is to be measured in terms of individual preferences as reflected in markets. The Hicks-Kaldor criterion measures changes in the value of output.[22]

You might believe that whether compensation should be paid or not depends upon who has to pay and who gets the benefits. This requires a consideration of the equity or fairness in the distribution of income as an element in the evaluation of social policy. The third approach to the question of social welfare criteria, proposed by Little (1957), makes explicit the concern for equity. He proposed a twofold test. First, does the policy pass the Hicks-Kaldor test? And second, does the resulting change improve the distribution of income? The Little criterion legitimizes a concern with the distributional effects of changes in resource allocation, but it does not resolve the question of what constitutes an improvement.

The fourth approach involves an attempt to make specific social judgments regarding equity and to introduce equity considerations systematically into the evaluation of social policy. The most common proposal calls for the establishment of a set of weights or a social welfare function which gives different weights to individual welfare changes according to the relative deservingness of the different individuals.[23] Of course, the main problem with the social welfare weight approach is the determination of the weighting function.[24]

Nevertheless, the willingness to make explicit value judgments about equity makes it possible to consider a wider range of policy choices. For example, if one opts for the Pareto criterion, or the potential compensation version of Hicks-Kaldor, one rules out the possibility of accepting a project which has a sum of individual welfare changes

---

[21] This definition is meant to be broad enough to include such things as leisure, environmental services, and nonmarket production that are not measured by the conventional gross national product (GNP) accounts.

[22] One justification for the Hicks-Kaldor potential compensation test is that a large number of efficient projects will spread benefits sufficiently widely so that everyone is a net gainer from the set of projects taken as a whole, even though some might be losers on individual projects. This argument assumes, of course, that there is no systematic bias in the distribution of benefits and costs across projects. The validity of the assumption is an empirical question.

[23] See, for example, Eckstein (1961). For a more extended discussion of this approach, see Haveman and Weisbrod (1975, pp. 61–64) and references therein.

[24] See, for example, Freeman (1971).

that is less than zero but which would substantially improve the distribution of income. An example of such a policy would be one which imposes a welfare loss of $1,000 on a millionaire while bringing benefits of $99 to each of ten impoverished orphans. A welfare-weighting function could approve negative sum policies like this provided that the weights given to the beneficiaries were sufficiently greater than the welfare weights of the losers. In addition, neither of these criteria would reject a project which imposes costs on no one but distributes benefits only to the richest of our society. Some might make the value judgment that that, in itself, is undesirable. A social welfare function that included some measure of inequality of the aggregate distribution as an argument might reject inequality-creating projects like this. And it would also be likely to accept negative sum projects that reduced inequality.

AGGREGATION AND MEASUREMENT

The preceding discussion has been based on the assumption that the analyst has knowledge of each individual's welfare change as measured from individual demand curves. But this is not likely to be the case. Thus we must confront the problem of obtaining consistent estimates of aggregate welfare changes from market data in the form of aggregate demand curves. The problem is that a unique aggregate demand curve for a good may not exist. Suppose that for a given set of prices of other goods, given preferences of individuals, and given individual incomes, the individual demand curves are estimated and added horizontally to form a market demand curve. Any transfer of income from one individual to another will result in shifts in the individual demand curves. If these shifts do not net to zero, the aggregate demand curve is shifted. In fact there may be as many aggregate demand curves as there are possible income distributions.

In order for there to be a consistent aggregation of individual demand curves into a unique market demand curve, one of two conditions must be satisfied. One condition is that there be no changes in the distribution of the income associated with the data from which the market demand curve is estimated. Furthermore, to use the aggregate demand curve to measure welfare changes, the policy being considered must not alter the distribution of income. The alternative assumption is that the income elasticity of demand for the good in question be the same for all individuals.

Since neither condition is likely to hold, the analyst seeking to obtain consistent measures of welfare change is left in an uncomfortable position. One prescription would be to forego aggregation of demand curves and to estimate separate demand curves for each individual. But this places unrealistic demands upon the data base. The only alternative for the analyst is to assume that income elasticities are not very different among individuals and that changes in the income distribution have not been large. Then the analyst may be justified in hoping that any distortions of his measures of welfare change caused by inconsistent aggregation are small.

The question of income distribution affects the validity of measurements of welfare change in another sense, too. The relative prices from which the CV or EV are measured are themselves a function of the distribution of income. If the underlying distribution of incomes is rejected as being unfair, the observed relative prices and measures of welfare changes which are derived from them must logically be rejected as a basis for making social policy judgments.

There are two mechanisms by which changes in the income distribution can lead to changes in the measures of welfare change. First, even though relative prices do not change, if individuals have different income elasticities of demand, the changes in quantity demanded and in each individual's CV or EV measures would not necessarily net out to zero. Thus, the aggregate welfare measure would not be independent of the income distribution.

The second mechanism is demand-induced changes in relative prices when supply curves are not perfectly elastic. Consider a redistribution which reduced income inequality. The aggregate demand for Cadillacs might shift to the left while the aggregate demand for Volkswagens shifts to the right. If supply curves are not perfectly elastic, there will be changes in the relative prices of Cadillacs and VWs.

Again the analyst is left in the uncomfortable position of having to make one of two types of assumptions. Either he must accept the present distribution of income as the basis for deriving measures of social value,[25] or he must make some assumption regarding the significance of the two mechanisms by which changes in income distribution affect the magnitude of welfare measures. He could assume identical income elasticities of demand for all individuals, or he could assume that all goods are produced at constant cost.

---

[25] If he makes this assumption, he is logically precluded from using social welfare weights or some version of the Little "improvement" test in choosing among policies.

To summarize the main points of the last two sections, the analyst may wish to measure aggregate welfare changes by calculating areas under aggregate market demand curves for the goods in question. To do so, the analyst must satisfy himself (and others) on three sets of questions. First, are the conditions concerning the relationships among alternative welfare measures satisfied so that differences between the *CV* and *EV* measures can be reasonably assumed to be small enough to be ignored? Second, since measuring the area under an aggregate demand curve implicitly weights the welfare changes of all individuals equally, does the analyst accept the value judgment that the welfare changes of all individuals are commensurate without individualized weights? And third, is the analyst willing to assume that the conditions for the existence of a unique aggregate demand curve are at least approximately satisfied?

When considered together, these questions may give rise to misgivings about proceeding to the estimation of welfare changes from aggregate data. But if aggregate data are all that are available, and the analyst is not willing to give affirmative answers to all these questions, then there is little that he can say about the policy change. I believe it is better to use the data at hand in the best way possible and to be as frank and explicit about the limitations, errors, and biases of the data and technique, than to forego the opportunity to shed perhaps a little light on a policy issue because the data were not perfect.

SUMMARY

In this chapter, I have explained the derivation of the *EV* and *CV* measures of individual welfare change and examined the conditions under which precise measurement of these terms is possible. We have found that the conditions are quite restrictive. We require knowledge of the Hicks-compensated demand curves; and these can only be derived from consistent econometric estimates of complete sets of demand functions for all goods estimated separately for each individual. But we have seen that the ordinary consumer surplus measure, the area under the individual's ordinary demand curve, is a very close approximation to the theoretically precise measurement under most conditions. Thus consumer surplus can be accepted as a useful approximation to the desired measure of welfare change.

I have also examined the ways in which welfare measures for individuals can be used to make choices about policies which affect many individuals simultaneously. We have found that unless policymakers are willing to adopt some convention for making welfare changes of individuals commensurate so that an aggregate welfare change can be defined, they must reject any policy change which imposes a welfare loss on any individual—no matter how small the loss nor how large the gain to others. The rule for aggregation can specify equal weights for all individuals (the Hicks-Kaldor compensation criterion) or assign different weights on some ethical basis.

Finally, I have examined the conditions under which aggregate welfare measures can be estimated from market demand curves and found these conditions to be restrictive. But again, I have emphasized a pragmatic approach to the problem. It seems likely that the errors that arise because the conditions are not fully satisfied will be small enough so that the measures obtained will still be useful for public policy.

The welfare measures described in this chapter presume the existence of markets for all goods. Yet we have seen that changes in the available quantity of nonmarketed goods can affect individual welfare, that is, can create benefits. The purpose of the next two chapters is to show under what conditions and in what ways it is possible to use information from the market and from nonmarket processes to estimate the implicit demands for nonmarketed, nonpriced public goods such as environmental quality.

REFERENCES

Currie, John M., John A. Murphy, and Andrew Schmitz. 1971. "The Concept of Economic Surplus," *Economic Journal* vol. 81, no. 324 (December) pp. 741–799.

Diamond, Peter A., and Daniel McFadden. 1974. "Some Uses of the Expenditure Function in Public Finance," *Journal of Public Economics* vol. 3, pp. 3–21.

Eckstein, Otto. 1961. "A Survey of the Theory of Public Expenditure Criteria," *Public Finances: Needs, Resources, and Utilization* (Princeton, N.J., Princeton University Press).

Freeman, A. Myrick III. 1971. "Project Design and Evaluation with Multiple Objectives," in R. Haveman, and J. Margolis, eds., *Public Expenditures and Policy Analysis* (Chicago, Markham).

Gianessi, Leonard P., Henry M. Peskin, and Edward Wolff. 1977. "The Distributional Effects of the Uniform Air Pollution Policy in the United

States," unpublished Discussion Paper D-5 (Washington, D.C., Resources for the Future) in press, *Quarterly Journal of Economics*.

Hause, John C. 1975. "The Theory of Welfare Cost Measurement," *Journal of Political Economy* vol. 83, no. 6 (December) pp. 1145–1182.

Haveman, Robert H., and Burton A. Weisbrod. 1975. "The Concept of Benefits in Cost–Benefit Analysis: With Emphasis on Water Pollution Activities," in Henry M. Peskin and Eugene P. Seskin, eds., *Cost–Benefit Analysis and Water Pollution Policy* (Washington, D.C., The Urban Institute).

Hicks, John R. 1939. "The Foundations of Welfare Economics," *Economic Journal* vol. 49.

Kaldor, Nicholas. 1939. "Welfare Propositions of Economics and Interpersonal Comparisons of Utility," *Economic Journal* vol. 49, pp. 549–552.

Krutilla, John V. 1967. "Conservation Reconsidered," *American Economic Review* vol. 57, no. 4 (September) pp. 777–786.

Little, I. M. D. 1957. *A Critique of Welfare Economics,* 2nd ed. (Oxford, Clarendon Press).

Mäler, Karl-Göran. 1974. *Environmental Economics: A Theoretical Inquiry* (Baltimore, Johns Hopkins University Press for Resources for the Future).

Mishan, Ezra J. 1959. "Rent as a Measure of Welfare Change," *American Economic Review* vol. 49, no. 3 (June) pp. 386–394.

———. 1960. "A Survey of Welfare Economics, 1939–1959," *Economic Journal* vol. 70, no. 278, pp. 197–256.

———. 1976. "The Use of Compensating and Equivalent Variations in Cost–Benefit Analysis," *Economica* vol. 43 (May) pp. 185–197.

Mohring, Herbert. 1971. "Alternative Welfare Gain and Loss Measures," *Western Economic Journal* vol. 9, no. 4 (December) pp. 349–368.

Moss, William G. 1976. "Some Uses of the Expenditure Function in Public Finance: A Comment," *Journal of Public Economics* vol. 5, no. 3, pp. 373–379.

Peacock, Alan T., and Charles K. Rowley. 1975. *Welfare Economics: A Liberal Restatement* (London, M. Robertson).

Schmundt, Maria, Eugene Smolensky, and Leanna Stiefel. 1975. "When Do Recipients Value Transfers at Their Costs to Taxpayers?" in I. Lurie, ed., *Integrating Income Maintenance Programs* (New York, Academic Press).

Scitovsky, Tibor. 1941. "A Note on Welfare Propositions in Economics," *Review of Economic Studies* vol. 9, pp. 77–88.

Silberberg, Eugene. 1972. "Duality and the Many Consumer's Surpluses," *American Economic Review* vol. 62, no. 5 (December) pp. 942–952.

Willig, Robert D. 1976. "Consumers' Surplus Without Apology," *American Economic Review* vol. 66, no. 4 (September) pp. 589–597.

CHAPTER 4

Measuring Benefits From Market Data

Benefits, or positive welfare changes, have been defined in terms of the area under the demand or inverse demand curve for the good or service. In principle, benefits are measured by the area under the appropriate Hicks-compensated demand curve for the CV or EV definitions of benefits. In practice, benefits can be approximated by the area under the ordinary demand curve. These demand curves exist even for public goods and nonmarketed goods such as the services of the environment. But they cannot be estimated from direct observations of transactions in these goods. Given the absence of markets in the public good or environmental good, how can information on demand and benefits be obtained?

There are basically three approaches to obtaining demand or benefit information. The first two rely on nonmarket mechanisms for generating information. The first approach is to ask individuals to reveal directly their willingness to pay or their demand for stated levels of the public good or service or the quantity they would demand at a stated price. Interviews or surveys could be conducted. The main difficulty with this approach lies in the possible incentives for individuals to attempt to influence the outcome of the process by misstating their true preferences. Chapter 5 will address some of the problems involved in direct revelation of preferences through questioning.

The second approach is to pose the question of the level of public good supply as a referendum issue, and to see whether benefits and preferences are revealed through the voting process. Under certain assumptions about voting behavior and the shape of preference functions of individuals, the voting process may lead to a level of public good provision which equates marginal benefits and marginal costs. The approach of using data derived from voting schemes for determining public goods demands will also be examined in chapter 5.

The third approach is to exploit the relationship between private marketed goods and public goods (either through production or consumption activities) and to use information generated by the related private goods markets to draw inferences about public goods demand. In the remainder of this chapter, we shall explore some of the possible relationships between public and private goods in an effort to determine under what circumstances the demand for the public good can be inferred from information on market transactions for the related private good. It must be assumed that there are no market imperfections (other than the environmental externality) which distort these market prices. But given the assumption, the exploitation of public good–private good relationships leads to several empirical techniques for estimating public goods demand. These techniques satisfy the following three criteria: (1) they are consistent with the basic theory of demand and consumer preferences; (2) they provide an estimate of the area under a demand curve; and (3) they are practical in the sense of imposing realistic data and computational requirements.

In the remainder of the chapter, Q will be used to denote some parameter of environmental quality. The problem is to estimate in monetary terms the changes in individuals' welfares associated with changes in Q. The basic thesis of this chapter is that the degree to which inferences about the benefits of increases in Q can be drawn from market observations and the appropriate techniques to be used in drawing these inferences, both depend on the way in which Q enters individual utility functions. There are two broad categories. Q can produce utility indirectly as a factor input in the production of a utility-yielding good. Or Q can produce utility directly by being an argument in individuals' utility functions. In this latter case, a variety of substitution and complementarity relationships between Q and some private good are possible. The next section explores the case where Q is a factor of production. The remainder of the chapter investigates the case where Q enters directly into individuals' utility functions.

ENVIRONMENTAL QUALITY AS A FACTOR INPUT

When Q is a factor of production, changes in Q lead to changes in production costs which in turn affect the price and quantity of output or the returns to other factor inputs or both. The benefits of changes in Q can be inferred from these changes in observable market data. There are several examples where Q can be interpreted as a factor input. The quality of river water diverted for irrigation affects the agricultural productivity of irrigated land. The quality of intake water may influence the costs of treating domestic water supplies or the costs of production in the industrial operations utilizing water for processing purposes. Agricultural productivity is impaired by some forms of air pollution. And to the extent that air pollution causes materials damages, it can affect the cost of production for a wide variety of goods and services.

Assume that good x is produced with a production function

$$x = x(K, L, \ldots, Q)$$

where K and L are capital and labor respectively, and where the marginal product of Q is positive. Since Q affects the production and supply of a marketable good, the benefits of changes in Q can be defined and measured in terms of changes in market variables related to the x industry. A change in Q will cause shifts in both cost curves and factor demand curves. The consequences of these shifts depend on conditions in factor and product markets. There are two channels through which changes in Q can produce benefits. The first is through changes in the price of x to consumers. The second is through changes in the incomes received by owners of factor inputs used in x production.

To illustrate the first channel, assume that x is produced in a competitive industry under conditions of constant cost, that is, factor supplies to this industry are infinitely elastic. Assume that the change in Q affects the cost curves of a significant proportion of producers in the market. As a result the supply curve shifts downward, causing a fall in the price and an increase in total quantity. The benefit of the price reduction accrues to consumers and can be measured by the area to the left of the demand curve bounded by the two prices.[1]

The second channel is through changes in the incomes received by factors of production. Consider only one producer who is a price taker in the output market. If the change in Q affects only this producer, output price will not be changed. Since the change in Q affects the marginal costs of production, the firm's marginal cost and supply curves are shifted down, as shown in figure 8. The benefit is equal to the area $ABCE$. This measure consists of two components. The area $ABDE$ is the reduction in the cost of producing the original level of output. The second component (the area BCD) is an inframarginal rent on the increase in output. Who receives the benefits and how they are measured depend on how factor prices are affected by the change

---

[1] Recall the discussion in chapter 3 of the assumptions which must be made in order to interpret areas under aggregate demand curves as measures of individuals' welfare changes.

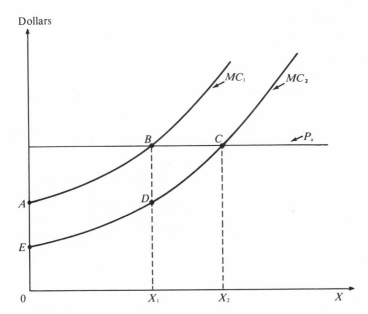

Figure 8. Benefits with output price unchanged

in Q. If the producer is a price taker in the markets for all variable factor inputs, then the benefit will accrue to the owner of a fixed factor, land for example, or to the residual income claimant as profit. In this case, benefits can be measured by changes in profits and fixed factor incomes. However if the producers affected by changes in Q face less than perfectly elastic factor supply curves, at least some of the benefits will be passed on to factors through changes in factor prices and incomes. The factors' shares of benefits can be approximated by the areas to the left of factor supply curves as discussed in chapter 3.

Usually if the output change is large enough to cause changes in variable factor prices, there will also be changes in product price. This case is shown in figure 9. Where the industry experiences increasing costs, but the change in Q shifts cost and supply curves down to the right, there will be changes in surpluses to both consumers and factors. Benefits are equal to the net change in the sum of the surpluses, or the area $ABCE$.[2]

Implementation of these measures requires knowledge of the effects of changes in Q on the cost of production, the supply conditions for output, and the ordinary demand curve for good x. There are two

---

[2] This is the measure advocated by Harberger (1971).

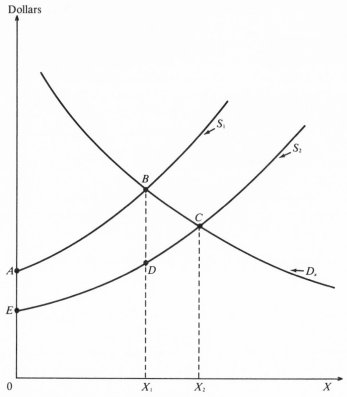

Figure 9. Benefits with changing output price

special cases which make estimation of benefits relatively straightforward.

Perfect Substitutes

Where Q is a perfect substitute for other inputs in the production of a good, an increase in Q leads to a reduction in factor input costs. If the substitution relationship is known, the decrease in per unit production costs is readily calculated. For example, if water quality improvement results in a decrease in chlorination requirements for drinking water supplies, the decrease in chlorination costs per unit of output can be readily calculated.

Where the change in total costs does not affect marginal cost and output, the cost saving is a true measure of the benefits of Q. If the change in Q affects variable and marginal costs, the cost saving measure should include the effect of lower cost on output. This would be the areas *BCD* in figures 8 and 9 above. However, if the percentage reduction in marginal costs were small, or the marginal cost curve were inelastic, or both, the corresponding increase in output would be relatively small. Thus, the simple saving measure could still be used to provide a lower bound and approximate estimate of true benefits.

Net Factor Income

Where knowledge of cost, demand, and market structure suggests that benefits of a change in Q will accrue to producers, benefits may be estimated from observed or predicted changes in the net income of certain factor inputs. If the production unit in question is small relative to the market for the final product, and small relative to the market for variable factors, it can be assumed that product and variable factor prices will remain fixed after the change in Q. The increased productivity then accrues in the form of a profit or in the form of a surplus income or quasi-rent to the fixed factors of production.

With sufficient knowledge of the operation of the production unit in question, it could be possible to use plant engineering or economic data to estimate the changes in factor incomes. In the case of agricultural production, agronomic data may be used to determine the relationship between salinity of irrigation water or air quality on the one hand and crop yields on the other. Farm budget and farm practice studies can be used to estimate the changes in factor incomes that would be associated with changes in air or water quality. If the crop in question is one for which there is no federal intervention to support prices, the change in gross farm income is equal to the change in crop yield multiplied by the market price. Changes in expenditures for other inputs must be netted out to determine the change in net farm income. The major pitfall to be avoided is the possibility that the price used to value the output may overstate the true social value of the crop if price support policies are in effect. Where the fixed factor is land, observed changes in land rent, or changes in land value (the capitalized present value of changes in rents) can be taken as estimates of factor income benefits.

The net income approach is also applicable to the case of commercial fisheries. Again, if the fishery in question is small relative to the total market for that fish product, it can be safely assumed that product price will be unchanged. Data on the relationship between biological productivity and water quality can be used to determine the increase in net physical yield associated with the pollution control program. If a fishery is being appropriately managed to maximize net economic yield, the benefit of the increase in water quality is equal to the market value of the increased yield, net of any changes in the expenditures on other variable factors of production.[3]

AN INDIVIDUAL'S DEMAND FOR ENVIRONMENTAL QUALITY

In order to analyze those cases where Q affects individuals directly, we first outline a basic model of individual preference and demand which incorporates environmental quality as an argument in the utility function. We then consider the implications of different forms of utility functions for estimation of the demand for Q. We consider only one individual so that the problem of consistent aggregation to market demand curves can be ignored. Assume a utility function of the following form

$$U = U(X, Q)$$

where X is the vector of private goods quantities ($X = x_1, \ldots,$ $x_i, \ldots, x_n$). By entering environmental quality as an argument in the utility function, we are assuming that the individual perceives at least the effects of changes in environmental quality. For example, if high oxidant levels cause eye irritation, the individual must be aware of the irritation, so that he feels "better" when it is reduced. He need not know the cause of the irritation or the actual levels of air pollution. However, if the individual is not aware of the effects of changes in Q, the individualistic welfare approach to benefit estimation can not be applied, at least not directly. For example, individuals may not perceive

---

[3] The assumption of maximizing net economic value is not likely to be valid. The economic benefit of the improvement of quality can be considered as an increase in the economic rent attributable to the fishery resource. But in an unregulated, free access fishery, this rent accrues in the short run to the existing fishermen, and raises their income above their opportunity costs. The short-run profits attract additional resources to the fishery, and ultimately this dissipates the rent to zero (Gordon, 1954; Crutchfield and Pontecorvo, 1969).

the effects of long-term exposure to air pollutants on mortality rates of large populations.

Maximizing utility subject to a budget constraint

$$\sum_i p_i x_i = M$$

where M is money income, and taking Q as given to the individual, we can derive a set of ordinary demand functions

$$x_i = x_i(P, M, Q)$$

where P is the vector of private goods prices ($P = p_1, \ldots, p_i, \ldots, p_n$). Note that in general it is possible that the level of the public good could be an argument in private goods demand functions. We will return to this point below.

The dual to the utility maximization problem can be stated as follows: minimize expenditures ($\sum_i p_i x_i$) subject to the constraint that utility equal or exceed some stated level, say U^0. The solution to this problem gives the expenditure function

$$E(P, Q, U^0) = M \tag{1}$$

The expenditure function has a number of useful properties for applied welfare analysis. First as was shown in chapter 3, the derivative of the expenditure function with respect to any price gives the Hicks-compensated demand function for that good, that is,

$$x_i^* = \partial E/\partial p_i = E_{p_i}(P, Q, U^0)$$

Similarly the derivative of (1) with respect to Q (with the appropriate change of sign) gives the Hicks-compensated *inverse* demand function or marginal willingness to pay for changes in Q. Let w be the marginal willingness to pay or marginal demand price for Q. Then

$$w = -\partial E/\partial Q = -E_q(P, Q, U^0) \tag{2}$$

The benefit to the individual for a nonmarginal increase in the supply of Q is

$$b = -\int_{Q'}^{Q''} E_q(P, Q, U^0) \, dQ \tag{3}$$

This is either a *CV* or *EV* measure of welfare change depending on the level of utility at which (3) is evaluated. The question to be discussed in the next section is whether there are any circumstances in which information about (2) or (3) can be derived from observations of market prices and quantities for private goods.

One of the considerations that will prove useful in the analysis is whether or not the utility function is separable. Since the concept of separability plays an important role in the discussion which follows, I digress for a moment to provide more rigorous definitions of two forms of separability.[4] Separability refers to the possible effect of partitioning the goods entering into the utility function into subsets and relationships among these subsets. Assume that the set of all goods can be partitioned into three subsets with the following notation

$U = U(X, Y, Z)$

$X = x_1, \ldots, x_i, \ldots, x_m$

$Y = y_1, \ldots, y_i, \ldots, y_n$

$Z = z_1, \ldots, z_i, \ldots, z_p$

$m, n, p \geq 1$

A utility function is weakly separable if the marginal rate of substitution between any pair of goods within a partition or subset is independent of the quantities of goods in any other subset. The following utility function is weakly separable

$$U = V[u^1(X), u^2(Y), u^3(Z)]$$

This means that the demand functions for goods in one subset can be written as independent of the prices of goods in any other subset. Thus, if separability can be assumed, it simplifies the task of econometric estimation of demand functions.[5]

A utility function is strongly separable if the marginal rate of substitution between two goods in different subsets is independent of the quantity of any good in any other subset. Thus, $MRS_{x_i y_i}$ is independent of z_i. The following utility function is strongly separable

$$U = V[u^1(X) + u^2(Y) + u^3(Z)]$$

[4] See Goldman and Uzawa (1964) or Katzner (1970).
[5] See Katzner (1970), p. 80.

If the utility function is nonseparable, there are no restrictions on the terms that are arguments in marginal rates of substitution or demand functions for individual commodities. The marginal rate of substitution between any pair of goods depends on the quantities of all goods. And the demand function for any good depends upon the prices of all goods.

EMPIRICAL APPROACHES

Our primary strategy will be to use a priori assumptions to impose certain restrictions on the form of the utility functions and demand functions. Different types of restrictions and specifications have different implications for the measurability of public goods demands. Our first assumed restriction leads to a situation in which it is impossible to estimate the demand for the public good from market data.

A Hopeless Case

Suppose that the utility function is strongly separable, with Q as the single argument in one of the subsets. In other words

$$U = V[u^1(X) + u^2(Y) + u^3(Q)]$$

where X and Y are subsets of marketable goods. Strong separability means that the marginal rates of substitution between any x_i and y_i are independent of Q. Changes in Q have no effect on marginal rates of substitution of any of the marketable goods. Q can be excluded as an argument in all of the market demand functions. Although changes in Q affect utility, they leave no record of this impact in the data on market transactions. In principle it is not possible to estimate the demand for Q from observable market data on transactions in x_i or y_i when the utility function is strongly separable in Q.

Strong separability is a property of two of the most commonly used functional forms for utility functions—the Cobb-Douglas

$$(U = a \prod_i x_i^\alpha Q^\beta)$$

and the *CES*

$$U = a \left(\sum_i \alpha_i x_i^{-\rho} + \beta Q^{-\rho} \right)^{-1/\rho}$$

This can be seen by writing them in their log transformations. Separability may be a characteristic of an important class of benefits. For example, those amenities of the urban environment which are not directly associated with private goods consumption may be separable. The option value associated with the preservation of unique natural environments is also likely to be separable.[6]

Weak Complementarity

For some forms of utility functions, the private goods demand functions contain Q as arguments

$$x_i = x_i(P, Q, M)$$

Suppose that this system of demand equations has been estimated econometrically and that the system satisfies the Slutsky Conditions for integrability.[7] Is it then possible to integrate this system to solve for the underlying utility function and expenditure function? If the answer is yes, then it would be possible to compute demand or willingness to pay functions for Q from market data whenever private good demand functions had this form.

The answer is that in general it is not possible to solve completely for the utility and expenditure functions with the information given. Mathematically the result of the integration contains unknown terms which are themselves functions of Q and the constants of integration.[8] It is necessary to impose additional conditions on the problem in order to solve for the unknown terms and determine the constants of integration. The additional conditions involve what Mäler (1974, pp. 183–189) has called "weak complementarity."

Weak complementarity is defined by Mäler to occur if when the quantity demanded of a private good x_1 is zero, the marginal utility or

---

[6] For discussion of the option value concept, see Cicchetti and Freeman (1971).

[7] See Hurwicz (1971).

[8] For a more detailed discussion and proof, see Mäler (1974), pp. 183–189.

marginal demand price of Q is zero. The weak complementarity assumption would seem to apply to a number of useful situations. For example, the marginal value of water quality in a particular lake could be assumed to be zero for those persons who did not use the lake for recreation. The marginal value of air quality over a particular residential site would be zero for those who did not live at that site.

Mathematically weak complementarity involves two conditions:
(a) that there be a price, $\hat{p}_1$, for x_1, such that

$$x_1(\hat{p}_1, P, Q, M) = 0$$

and (b) that for the expenditure function

$$E = E(\hat{p}_1, P, Q, U^0)$$
$$\partial E/\partial Q = 0$$

Conditions (a) and (b) together establish an initial position for the individual that is used to determine the constants of integration.[9] It is interesting to note that these conditions describe a position for the individual which satisfies the first order conditions of a utiltiy maximization problem in which the individual can choose the quantities of all goods, including Q, at given prices including a zero price for Q.

Since direct application of the weak complementarity method as described here would require the econometric estimation of complete systems of demand equations, it would appear to be of relatively limited practical significance. Fortunately the weak complementarity conditions also permit the estimation of the demand price for Q without solving for the underlying utility and expenditure functions. This latter method requires only information on the demand for x_1.

Assume that for a given level of Q, the demand curve for x_1 has been estimated econometrically. This demand curve is labeled D_Q in figure 10. Assume that the price of x_1 is given at p_1' and does not change throughout the analysis. The ordinary consumer surplus associated with the use of x_1 is the area ABC under the demand curve. Now assume that quality is improved to Q^*. The increase in the quality associated with the use of x_1 is assumed to increase the demand for x_1, thus shifting the demand curve

---

[9] For proof and a demonstration with a numerical example, see Mäler (1974), pp. 183–189. Results quite similar to Mäler's have been obtained more recently by Bradford and Hildebrandt (1977).

outward to D_Q^*. The calculation of the benefit associated with this change is straightforward and can be divided into three steps.

1. Given the old demand curve of D_Q, postulate a hypothetical increase in price from p_1' to p_1''. In order to leave the individual no worse off, he must be compensated by the area ABC.
2. Now postulate the improvement in quality and the shift in the demand curve to D_Q^*. Given the weak complementarity assumption, utility is unaffected since the consumption of x_1 is zero. Therefore there is no need for compensation, either positive or negative.
3. Now postulate a return to the old price of p_1'. The individual is made better off by the area ADE. In order to restore the individual to his original welfare position, he must be taxed by this amount. The net effect of these changes is a gain to the individual (in the absence of the hypothetical compensating payments) of the area $BCED$ ($= ADE - ABC$). This is the benefit of the change in Q.

If weak complementarity did not hold, there would be a positive benefit associated with the increase in Q even though the quantity demanded of x_1 were zero in step 2 above. In this case, the area $BCED$ would be an underestimate of the benefits of increasing Q.

If D_Q is the Hicks-compensated demand curve, this area ($BCDE$) is an exact measure of the CV or maximum willingness to pay for the increment to Q. If an expression can be formulated for this area as a function of Q, the derivative of this function with respect to Q is the marginal demand price for Q. Typically D_Q is an ordinary demand curve, not a Hicks-compensated demand curve. The analysis by Willig (1976) outlined in chapter 3 can be used. He showed the conditions under which areas under ordinary demand curves can be taken to be close approximations of the precise compensating or equivalent variation measures. A straightforward extension of Willig's analysis shows that if the income elasticity of demand for x_1 is constant over the range of variation, his conditions also apply to areas between ordinary demand curves as in figure 10. Thus for practical purposes, the technique described here can be applied to market data. The primary empirical requirement for utilizing this technique is that we be able to obtain econometric estimates of the demand function for the private good as a function of Q as well as prices and income. This requires observations of the market for x_1 under different quantities of Q. If Q has never changed, there is no possibility of identifying the partial relationship between Q and the demand for x_1.

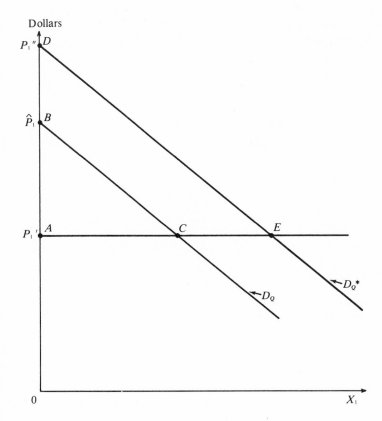

Figure 10. Benefits with weak complementarity

Substitutes and Complements

Mäler (1974, pp. 116–118) has shown that the marginal demand price of Q can be expressed in terms of the price of any private good and the marginal utilities of that good and Q. The expression is

$$w = -\frac{\partial E(P, Q, U^0)}{\partial Q}$$

$$= -P_i \left(\frac{\partial U/\partial Q}{\partial U/\partial x_i}\right)$$

$$= -P_i MRS_{Qx_i} \tag{4}$$

This would be a useful practical result if it were possible to derive simple expressions for the marginal rates of substitution. One set of possibilities involves substitution and complementarity relationships.

Consider another case where separability is used to isolate Q and a good z.[10] Suppose the utility function is weakly separable and is of the following form

$$U = V\{u^1(X), u^2(Y), [cz^{-\rho} + (1 - c)Q^{-\rho}]^{-1/\rho}\}$$

Given the separability assumption, the marginal rate of substitution between z and Q is independent of the quantities of x_i and y_i. The *MRS* is

$$MRS_{zQ} = \frac{c}{1 - c}\left(\frac{Q}{z}\right)^{\rho-1}$$

$$= \frac{c}{1 - c}\left(\frac{Q}{z}\right)^{1/\sigma}$$

where σ is the elasticity of substitution, which is constant. From (4) we have

$$w = -P_z\left(\frac{c}{1 - c}\right)\left(\frac{Q}{z}\right)^{1/\sigma}$$

Substitutes. In general, to use this formulation, we need to know both the elasticity of substitution, σ, and "c." There is one special case where the expression reduces a usable term. If z and Q are perfect substitutes in consumption, the elasticity of substitution between them is infinite, and the expression for the demand price of Q reduces to $P_z r$, where r is the equivalence or substitution ratio between z and Q.[11] If perfect substitutability can be assumed, r (or c) should be computable from known or observable technical consumption data.

The perfect substitutability assumption lies behind the "defensive expenditures" technique for estimating benefits. Defensive expenditures are expenditures made to prevent or counteract the adverse effects of pollution. If defensive expenditures are a perfect substitute for reductions in the level of pollution effects experienced, then an individual can effectively purchase the optimal amount of Q through defensive outlays. In practice, defensive outlays which would be perfect substitutes for Q would be rare. There is no such thing as a perfect defense. There are some disutilities associated with pollution that cannot be prevented by further spending. This is equivalent to saying that σ is less

---

[10] The following discussion is based on Mäler (1974), pp. 178–183.

[11] $r = c/(1-c)$. For example, if $c = .75$, then $r = 3$. This means that one unit of Q is a perfect substitute for three units of z.

than infinite. Hence, changes in defensive outlays are likely to give underestimates of the true benefits of the changes in Q. Nevertheless, recognizing this limitation, analysis of changes in defensive outlays related to pollution could substantially narrow our range of ignorance about benefits.

The purchase of perfect substitutes and less than perfect defensive expenditures are examples of what Zeckhauser and Fisher (1976) have called averting behavior. Averting behavior is defined to include all activities that people undertake to avoid or mitigate the adverse effects of externalities. Averting behavior can involve expenditures of time and other resources as well as dollars. When Q increases, the need for averting behavior decreases; averting behavior substitutes for Q in individuals' utility functions. A full consideration of averting behavior suggests the practical difficulties of using the substitute assumption to estimate benefits. First as mentioned above, averting behaviors are not likely to be perfect substitutes for Q. So the reduction in averting behavior costs will understate the benefit in Q by not accounting for the improvement in utility. And second, in many instances there is a variety of modes of averting behavior. Individuals are likely to utilize several modes simultaneously. Unless the analyst can identify and measure the reductions in all modes of averting behavior, the benefit of increases in Q will be underestimated.

Complements. If the elasticity of substitution is zero, z and Q are perfect complements. For a given quantity of Q the demand for z is a decreasing function of P_z up to some level, call it z', after which the marginal utility of z becomes zero and the demand curve for z becomes perfectly inelastic. The quantity of z at which the demand becomes zero depends on the complementary relationship between z and Q. For P_z greater than P'_z, the price–income constraint prevents the individual from purchasing enough z to fully utilize the given level of Q. Hence, the marginal utility and demand price of additional Q are zero. For prices below P'_z, the individual would purchase more z if he could obtain more Q to go with it. Hence, the marginal utility and demand price of Q is greater than zero.

Mäler has shown that if the demand function for z and for other marketed goods is known, it is possible to compute the expenditure function and the demand price for Q when P_z is less than P'_z.[12] The ex-

---

[12] See Mäler (1974), pp. 180–183.

act expression for the demand price for Q depends upon the specification of the true demand curves. There is no simple generalization of
the technique.

Hedonic Prices of Public Goods

The techniques described so far have been developed for the case
where the level of public good provision or environmental quality is
fixed and the same for all individuals. Although this represents the
textbook version of the public goods problem, it is not descriptive of all
possible cases involving public goods or environmental quality. Individuals can choose the level of consumption of local public goods
through their choice of a jurisdiction to reside in. There are important
cases where individuals have some freedom to choose their effective
consumption of the public good or environmental quality (Q) through
their selection of a private goods consumption bundle. Where these
choices are possible, information on public good demand is embedded
in the prices and consumption levels for private goods. For example,
if air quality varies across space in an urban area, individuals may
choose their exposure to air pollution through their residential location
decisions. Residential housing prices may include premiums and dis-
counts for locations in clean or dirty areas. It may be possible to estimate the demand for public goods such as clean air from the price
differentials revealed in private markets. The demand function for the
public good is estimated through a two-step procedure in which first
the implicit price of Q is estimated by the application of the hedonic
price technique, and then the implicit prices are regressed against observed quantities to estimate the demand function itself.

The hedonic technique is a method for estimating the implicit
prices of the characteristics which differentiate closely related products
in a product class.[13] For example, houses constitute a product class
differentiated by characteristics such as number of rooms and size of
lot. In principle, if there are enough models with different combina-

---

[13] The hedonic price technique was developed by Griliches and others initially for the purpose of estimating the value of quality change in consumer
goods. See Griliches (1971). Rosen (1974) has used the hedonic price concept
to analyze the supply and demand of the characteristics which differentiate products in competitive markets. For discussion of the application of the concept to
measuring the demand for environmental quality characteristics, see Anderson
and Crocker (1972), Bishop and Cicchetti (1975), and Freeman (1974).

tions of rooms and lot size, it is possible to estimate an implicit price relationship which gives the price of any model as a function of the quantities of its various characteristics. The coefficients of the characteristics are the implicit prices. For example, the difference in price between two models with different numbers of rooms but identical in all other respects is interpreted as the implicit price of additional rooms.

More formally, let X represent a product or commodity class. Any unit of X can be completely described by a vector of its characteristics. Continuing with the housing example, let c_i represent the specific characteristics of a structure and its lot, and Q_j represent neighborhood and environmental characteristics such as quality of schools and air quality levels. Then for any unit of X, and say x_1,

$$P_{x_1} = P_x(c_{11}, \ldots, c_{1i}, \ldots, c_{1n}, Q_{11}, \ldots, Q_{1j}, \ldots, Q_{1m}) \qquad (5)$$

where c_{1i} is the quantity of the ith site characteristic in unit x_1, and Q_{1j} is the quantity of the jth environmental characteristic. The function P_x is the hedonic or implicit price function for X. If P_x can be estimated from observations of the prices and characteristics of different models, the price of any possible model can be calculated from knowledge of its characteristics.

The implicit price of a characteristic can be found by differentiating the implicit price function with respect to that characteristic. That is

$$\partial P_x / \partial Q_j = P_{Qj}(c_{11}, \ldots, c_{1i}, \ldots, c_{1n}, Q_{11}, \ldots, Q_{1j}, \ldots, Q_{1m}) \qquad (6)$$

This gives the increase in expenditure on X that is required to obtain a model with one more unit of Q_j, *ceteris paribus*. If (5) is linear in the characteristics, then the implicit prices are constants for individuals. But if (5) is nonlinear, then the implicit price of an additional unit of a characteristic depends on the quantity of the characteristic being purchased. Equation (5) need not be linear. Linearity will occur only if consumers can "arbitrage" activities by untying and repackaging bundles of attributes (Rosen, 1974, pp. 37–38). For example if individuals are indifferent between owning two six-foot-long cars and one twelve-foot car, *ceteris paribus*, they can create equivalents of twelve-foot cars by repackaging smaller units. If both sizes exist on the market, the larger size must sell at twice the price of the smaller one, and the implicit price function will be linear in length. The example suggests that nonlinearity will not be uncommon.

Under some circumstances it may be possible to use the information contained in the implicit price function to identify the demand relationship for a characteristic—even if the characteristic is a public good such as environmental quality. First assume that each individual purchases only one unit of X, or if he purchases more than one, they are identical models. Otherwise the individual facing a nonlinear hedonic price function might be observed to act upon two different implicit prices for the same characteristic. Also assume that the utility function is weakly separable in X and its characteristics. This makes the marginal rate of substitution between any pair of characteristics of X independent of the consumption of any good other than X. Without separability, the demand for a characteristic would in fact be a function of the consumption levels of other goods, and the estimation of the second stage demand function would require additional price and quantity data beyond that derived from the hedonic price function.

For each individual, the quantity of Q_j purchased is known by observation and its implicit price is known from (6). This point (Q'_j, P'_{Qj}) can be interpreted as a utility-maximizing equilibrium for this individual resulting from the intersection of his inverse demand or marginal willingness-to-pay function and the locus of opportunities to purchase Q_j as defined by the marginal implicit price function. This is shown in figure 11. Individuals can be viewed as moving out along P_{Qj} as long as their willingness to pay exceeds the marginal implicit price. Thus P_{Qj} is a locus of individual equilibrium marginal willingnesses to pay.

Can individuals' marginal willingness-to-pay functions be identified from the observations described in figure 11? The answer depends on the circumstances of the case. If the implicit price function is linear in Q_j, then it is not possible to identify a demand curve for Q_j. The price observation is the same for all individuals. However P_{Qj} can be interpreted as the marginal willingness to pay or marginal benefit for small changes in Q_j for each individual.

If equation (5) is nonlinear, the ability to identify the demand curve depends on the specification of the underlying model. Four cases can be considered. First, if all individuals have identical utility functions and incomes, and therefore have identical demand functions for Q_j, equation (6) is the inverse demand function. Assuming all individuals are in equilibrium, (6) gives the equilibrium implicit price of Q_j, given Q_j for each individual. It is a point on each individual's

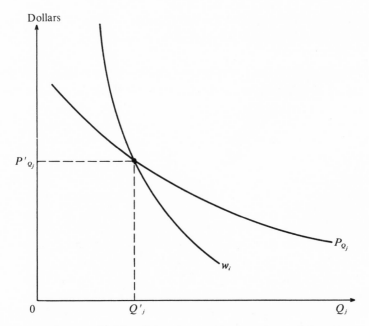

Figure 11. The marginal implicit price and inverse demand functions

inverse demand curve. And given identical demand functions, all observations of P_{Q_j} (Q_j) lie on the same inverse demand curve.

Second, if the supply of models of given bundles of characteristics is perfectly elastic at the observed prices, then the implicit price function can be taken as exogenous to individuals. A regression of observed quantities of Q_j against the observed implicit prices as defined by (6), incomes, and other socioeconomic characteristics of individuals should identify a demand function for Q_j

$$Q_j = Q_j(P_{Qj}, M, \ldots)$$

Third, if the available quantity of each model is fixed, individuals can be viewed as bidding for models with desired bundles of characteristics. A regression of the implicit prices against quantities of Q_j, incomes, and other variables should identify an inverse demand function

$$w = P_{Qj}(Q_j, M, \ldots)$$

Finally if both the quantities demanded and quantities supplied of characteristics are functions of prices, a simultaneous equation approach can be used.[14]

If inverse demand functions for individuals can be identified via one of the techniques outlined here, benefits of changes in Q_j can be calculated by taking areas under the demand curves bounded by the old and new levels of Q_j. Since these are not income-compensated demand curves, the areas are approximations of the true compensating variation measure as discussed in chapter 3.

SUMMARY

We have reviewed the conceptual basis for empirical techniques that attempt to take advantage of market information. Where Q is an input into the production of marketed goods and services, our techniques focus on the effects of changes in Q on output and factor markets, not on the utility of Q per se. We have found that there is a valid theoretical basis for examining changes in factor incomes such as land rents, costs savings in production, and changes in consumer surplus associated with the private good outputs.

When Q is a consumption good and enters directly into the utility function, the problems are more severe. One of the more promising techniques is based on the concept of weak complementarity. Benefits are measured in terms of shifts in the demand curve for the private complementary good. The approach may be applicable to estimating recreation benefits due to the water quality changes.

Where the public good is a perfect substitute for a private good, benefit estimation is straightforward if the substitution ratio and the price of the private good are known. Defensive expenditures and measures of additional costs (for example, for household cleaning, or medical care and drugs in the case of health) are examples of estimates that are based on approximations of the perfect substitute assumption. The less perfect the defense, the more inaccurate is the estimate based upon the perfect substitute assumption.

Another promising case is where Q varies across space, as in air pollution, or as a characteristic embodied in some private good. Then individuals can choose different Qs by varying residential locations or

---

[14] For further discussion of this case, see Rosen (1974), pp. 48–51.

by choosing different private good models. The hedonic price approach can be used to measure the implicit price of Q; and under some circumstances the demand curve for Q can be identified.

REFERENCES

Anderson, Robert J., and Thomas D. Crocker. 1972. "Air Pollution and Property Values: A Reply," *Review of Economics and Statistics* vol. 54, no. 4 (November) pp. 470–473.

Bishop, John, and Charles Cicchetti. 1975. "Some Institutional and Conceptual Thoughts on the Measurement of Indirect and Intangible Benefits and Costs," in Henry M. Peskin and Eugene P. Seskin, eds., *Cost Benefit Analysis and Water Pollution Policy* (Washington, D.C., The Urban Institute).

Bradford, David F., and Gregory G. Hildebrandt. 1977. "Observable Preferences for Public Goods," *Journal of Public Economics* vol. 8, no. 2 (October) pp. 111–131.

Cicchetti, Charles J., and A. Myrick Freeman III. 1971. "Option Demand and Consumer's Surplus: Further Comment," *Quarterly Journal of Economics* vol. 85, no. 3 (August) pp. 528–539.

Crutchfield, James A., and Giulio Pontecorvo. 1969. *The Pacific Salmon Fisheries: A Study of Rational Conservation* (Baltimore, Johns Hopkins University Press for Resources for the Future).

Freeman, A. Myrick III. 1974. "On Estimating Air Pollution Control Benefits from Land Value Studies," *Journal of Environmental Economics and Management* vol. 1, no. 1 (May) pp. 74–83.

Goldman, S. M., and Hirofumi Uzawa. 1964. "A Note on Separability in Demand Analysis," *Econometrica* vol. 32, no. 3 (June) pp. 387–398.

Gordon, H. Scott. 1954. "The Economic Theory of a Common Property Resource: Fisheries," *Journal of Political Economy* vol. 62, no. 2 (April) pp. 124–142.

Griliches, Zvi, ed. 1971. *Price Indexes and Quality Change* (Cambridge, Mass., Harvard University Press).

Harberger, Arnold C. 1971. "Three Basic Postulates for Applied Welfare Economics: An Interpretive Essay," *Journal of Economic Literature* vol. 9, no. 3 (September) pp. 785–797.

Hurwicz, Leonid. 1971. "On the Problem of Integrability of Demand Functions," in John Chipman and others, eds., *Preferences, Utility, and Demand* (New York, Harcourt Brace Jovanovich).

Katzner, Donald W. 1970. *Static Demand Theory* (New York, MacMillan).

Mäler, Karl-Göran. 1974. *Environmental Economics: A Theoretical Inquiry* (Baltimore, Johns Hopkins University Press for Resources for the Future).

Rosen, Sherwin. 1974. "Hedonic Prices and Implicit Markets: Product Differentiation in Pure Competition," *Journal of Political Economy* vol. 82, no. 1 (January/February) pp. 34–55.

Willig, Robert D. 1976. "Consumers' Surplus Without Apology," *American Economic Review* vol. 66, no. 4 (September) pp. 589–597.

Zeckhauser, Richard, and Anthony Fisher. 1976. "Averting Behavior and External Diseconomies" (mimeo).

CHAPTER 5

Measuring Benefits from Nonmarket Data: Surveys and Voting

In this chapter my purpose is to examine the conditions under which it is possible to estimate welfare gains through nonmarket means such as surveys, questionnaires, bidding games, and voting. As we saw in chapter 4, there are some circumstances in which it is not possible to derive benefit measures from activities of the market. In such cases, the nonmarket approaches are all that is available to the analyst. But even when market-related measures of benefits are available, estimates derived from nonmarket techniques may be useful as a check on the consistency of the estimating procedures.

The problem is to induce people to reveal directly or indirectly their preferences for the provision of public goods. I will examine three basic approaches to the problem of revelation of preferences. The first is to ask individuals to state in one form or another their "willingness to pay" to obtain some specified level or change in the level of a public good. There is a variety of ways in which questions can be posed to individuals but they all have in common the elicitation of a money value, or in effect, a bid for some specified quantity.

The second approach is to ask individuals how much of the public good they would demand at a given price or under given conditions of taxation. The price or repayment is taken as given or to be determined according to some stated rule or procedure. The individual is asked to behave as he would in the market for a private good by specifying a quantity demanded conditional on the price or repayment.

The third approach relies on a voting mechanism in which two parties or candidates compete for votes by specifying alternative programs for the provision of the public good. A variation on the voting mechanism is the referendum on a specific proposal for provision of the public good. Individuals may vote either yes or no.

In principle, any of these procedures could be carried out either with a random sample or with the universe of affected individuals. A survey or questionnaire could be administered to the whole population. Or a sample could be drawn and asked to participate in a voting scheme. The question of sampling versus universal participation is in part one of administrative cost. The accuracy of benefit estimates obtained from subsets of the total population is essentially a question of statistical sampling theory.[1] Even when evidence is garnered from actual elections where everyone is eligible to vote, the question of the representativeness of the sample must be considered. This is because participation in elections is usually substantially less than 100 percent. Moreover, there is good reason to believe that the "self-selected" sample of voters will be nonrepresentative. Voting participation varies among ethnic groups, and by income and educational level.

Before turning to a discussion of the three approaches, it should be made clear that I am not concerned with the optimization properties or dynamic characteristics of voting and bidding schemes coupled with resource reallocation rules. Some of these schemes posit complicated voting and resource allocation mechanisms that are quite unrealistic in terms of existing institutions for resource allocation and social choice. For example, several recent articles have examined the optimization properties of systems where planners are assumed to post certain data on prices or quantities and tax shares or both, individuals are asked to reveal their marginal rates of substitution between the public good and a private good conditional on this information, and prices and quantities are adjusted by the planner on the basis of individuals' responses.[2] My concern is solely with the ability of a given technique to provide information on individuals' demand curves for the public good and the welfare gains which are measured by areas under these demand curves.

REVEALING WILLINGNESS TO PAY

The question to be discussed in this section is: can the answers provided by the members of a group to questions concerning the will-

---

[1] Green and Laffont (1977) have analyzed demand-revealing processes from this perspective.

[2] See Malinvaud (1972), Dreze and de la Vallée Poussin (1971), and Groves and Ledyard (1977).

ingness to pay for a public good provide reliable information about the group's demand curve for that good? And if so, under what conditions can the demand curve be identified? There are two kinds of problems that arise in deriving demand information from willingness-to-pay questions. The first is that the way the questions are asked and the way in which respondents expect the answers to be used can create incentives for strategic behavior on the part of respondents. Respondents may be induced to provide distorted or biased information in an effort to influence some aspect of the outcome of the process. It is possible to design questions in which there is no apparent incentive for strategic behavior or biased responses. But this leads to the second type of problem: there may be no positive incentive to provide accurate responses. And if a respondent must devote time and mental energy to considering this response, positive incentives may be required to elicit the necessary effort to provide accurate information.

I shall discuss the problem of strategic behavior first. The difficulty in inducing individuals to provide unbiased responses concerning their demands for public goods has played a prominent role in the literature on public goods theory. But we must bear in mind that the absence of incentives to provide biased responses does not necessarily mean that there is a positive incentive for correct responses.

Strategic Behavior

Questions concerning willingness to pay can be framed in one of two ways.[3] An individual could be asked his total willingness to pay to receive a specified quantity of the public good rather than do without it entirely. His answer, if it is unbiased, is a compensating variation (CV) measure of the welfare gain if the public good is provided in the specified quantity. In other words, it is the integral of the Hicks-

---

[3] There are several procedures for eliciting values. Individuals could simply be asked to state their willingness to pay. Or they could be asked to indicate whether a value proposed by the questioner is too high or too low. In this case the proposed values are adjusted by some rule until the individual indicates that the value is neither too high nor too low. See for example Brookshire, Ives, and Schulze (1976) and Randall, Ives, and Eastman (1974). These bidding games may be subject to problems such as starting-point bias. To indicate relative preferences among several types of public goods, individuals could be asked to allocate a fixed budget of scrip or coupons among the alternatives in accordance with their preferences. See Pendse and Wyckoff (1974) and Strause and Hughes (1976).

compensated demand curve for the public good which holds utility constant at the level associated with zero public goods supply. Alternatively, individuals could be asked for their marginal willingness to pay for an additional unit of the public good given that it is presently supplied at some specified level Q^0. The answer to this question is the marginal demand price for the public good, or the derivative of the expenditure function with respect to the public good, Q.

Suppose that an individual is asked about his total willingness to pay for Q^0 of the public good. Assume that individuals will not be required to make any payment for the public good. If the individual prefers Q^0 over $Q = 0$, and if he believes that his answer might affect the decision about whether to supply the public good or not, the rational individual will select his response so as to maximize the likelihood of the good being provided. His best response has no relationship to his preferences or willingness to pay; rather, it is the highest figure that he thinks will be believed by the authorities collecting the data. It will be an overstatement of his true willingness to pay.

If the question concerned his marginal willingness to pay, and there were no repayment obligation, his response would be an overestimate or underestimate of the true marginal willingness to pay, depending upon whether the individual's marginal utility for Q at Q^0 was greater or less than zero. In either case, the individual selects his answer on the basis of his expected influence on the decision about whether to supply the public good.

If the individual is asked his total willingness to pay and is informed that his repayment obligation will be linked to his answer, the incentives governing his response are different. The individual might be told that if the public good is supplied, his required payment will be equal to his stated willingness to pay, or perhaps that the total cost will be shared in proportion to the respondents' willingnesses to pay. Then the individual must weigh the effect of his answer on the likelihood that the good will be supplied against the effect of his answer on his repayment obligation. In general, if the number of respondents is large, the latter effect will predominate. And the individual will understate his willingness to pay.[4]

Efforts to provide a solution to the problem of strategic behavior have generally taken one of two avenues. One is to attempt to measure the bias and adjust actual responses according to the measured degree

---

[4] For a proof, see Mäler (1974), pp. 161–164.

of bias. The other is to structure questions so as to eliminate the incentives for strategic behavior.

Kurz has shown that under certain circumstances, if the functional relationship between the true willingness to pay and the actual biased response can be specified (the bias function), it is possible to estimate the coefficients of this function and compute the true willingness to pay from the actual biased responses (Kurz, 1974). While Kurz's work can be regarded as opening up a fruitful avenue for further research, it does not provide an operational procedure. In Kurz's analysis, it is possible to identify the bias function only for particular specifications of the functional relationships between actual responses and true willingness to pay, and only when the bias function is the same for all respondents. As was shown in the preceding discussion, the degree of bias is influenced by individuals' expectations of the impact of their answers on both public good supply and repayment obligation. And we do not have a model of this aspect of subjective behavior on the part of individuals which could provide an a priori justification for any particular specification of the bias function.

The other avenue of approach is to design an experimental situation or a specific set of questions that would eliminate the incentives for strategic behavior. Several researchers have asked respondents to reveal their willingness to pay in what were clearly hypothetical situations. In one case, respondents were explicitly told that their answer would have no effect on supply (Hammack and Brown, 1974). In other cases, respondents knew that the interviewers were not acting in an official capacity; thus they could infer from the context that their responses would have no direct effect either on public good supply or their repayment obligation.[5] By removing the two elements of the real world situation which encouraged strategic behavior, it was hoped that the incentives for bias responses were eliminated.

However there are two difficulties with this approach. The first is that an individual could conceivably look beyond the specific experimental context and attach some positive value to the likelihood that the survey (and therefore his answer) could influence general policy toward the provision of this public good. Thus the survey instrument provides the individual with a costless way of influencing public goods policy in the broader sense. The other problem is that individuals may

[5] See, for example, Acton (1973), Brookshire, Ives, and Schulze (1976), Cicchetti and Smith (1976), Knetsch and Davis (1966), and Randall, Ives, and Eastman (1974).

see no advantage to giving careful thought to their answers. Thus while there may be no incentive to provide biased responses, there is no incentive to provide accurate responses either. We will return to the problem of accuracy below.

Peter Bohm has advocated a way of asking willingness-to-pay questions which deals more directly with an individual's expectations as to how his answer influences his repayment obligation (Bohm, 1971). Bohm suggests that the individual be left uncertain as to how, if at all, his response might affect his liability to pay and, further, suggests how the uncertainty should be conveyed:

> If the willingness-to-pay exceeds the given construction costs, . . . the plant will actually be constructed. Moreover, they *may* be called upon to pay exactly the amount they stated. They are, however, also informed that the actual payment may not be equal to this amount, that, for example, it may be proportional to the amount stated. . . . Furthermore, it is possible that the costs of the plant will be partly or completely financed by the federal government and thus only partially or not at all by the people in the region concerned. It is made clear that, at the moment of the "referendum," the actual distribution of payment is unknown (pp. 95–96).

Bohm then argues that the rational individual will be unable to perceive any clear advantage either to overstating or understating his willingness to pay, and therefore may decide that honesty is the best policy:

> The individual consumer knows that, if he states his true willingness-to-pay, he *may* end up in a situation in which he pays more than "necessary" for the given public good output. But neither can he neglect the fact that he may have *some* influence on the final decision on whether to produce the good or not *and* that he may have to pay very little, perhaps nothing, for this influence. It is hard to predict his behavior under these circumstances. . . . Once it is clear that there is no open-and-shut case for the individual when considering under- or overstatement of his preferences, the choice of strategy may well seem so complicated to him that he prefers to state his true willingness-to-pay. (p. 98)

Bohm's argument is more hopeful than rigorous on this point. Mäler has carried Bohm's analysis one step further by showing that when uncertainty as to the repayment obligation is present, correct revelation of willingness to pay is a max–min strategy for the individual (Mäler, 1974, pp. 174–175). However, it is not a unique max–min strategy. We cannot be sure that individuals when confronted with uncertainty will adopt a max–min decision rule. And even if they do, we cannot be sure that they will necessarily follow a strategy of correct revelation.

Tideman has provided a more carefully worked out scheme in which the distribution of the tax burden for a proposed project is specified as part of the questionnaire, but individuals are asked to indicate their willingness to pay for marginal changes around the specified level (Tideman, 1972). He suggests that each individual be questioned as follows:

> The city is thinking about building a $50,000 park in your neighborhood. If the plan goes through, your share of the cost will be $28 per year. No final decision will be made until the value of the project is checked. In case a $45,000 park or a $55,000 park is built, how much would a $5,000 change in the expenditure on the park be valued in terms of your benefits? Whatever figure you give will be used in adjusting your taxes. For instance, if you say an additional $5,000 of park is worth $3 per year to you, your bill for the $55,000 park would be $31, and for the $45,000 park would be $25.

> Would a respondent reveal his true marginal value benefit? That would depend on his expectations. If he expected the level of expenditure to be revised upward, then it would be in his interest to understate his benefits, so that his taxes would be reduced by more than his loss of benefits. If the possibility of lower expenditure just balances the possibility of higher expenditure . . . then neither an overestimate nor an underestimate of his benefits will involve expected gain. (p. 113)

Tideman's conclusion is clearly based on the assumption that the individual believes that he cannot influence the outcome by his bid, that is, that his subjective probabilities are independent of the magnitude of his bid. Also, it is necessary to Tideman's conclusion that the individual attach equal probabilities to an increase in supply and a decrease in supply. This can be shown as follows.

The expected payoff E for an individual is

$$E = p(w - b) + (1 - p)(b - w)$$

where p = subjective probability that supply will be increased

w = true marginal willingness to pay for an increase

  = welfare gain from increased supply of public good

b = actual bid

With $p = .5$, the expected payoff reduces to

$$E = .5(w - b) + .5(b - w)$$
$$= .5(b - b) + .5(w - w) = 0$$

The individual cannot affect his expected payoff by his choice of a bid. However if the individual does not attach equal probabilities to an increase or decrease in public goods supply, there is an incentive to bias his bid. Rearranging, the expected payoff is

$$(2p - 1)(w - b)$$

For $p > .5$, expected payoff is maximized with zero bid. With $p < .5$, expected payoff increases with higher bids without limit. For there to be a finite optimum bid, the individual must be assumed to be risk averse, that is, to make decisions so as to maximize expected utility and to have a decreasing marginal utility of income.[6]

In the equal probability case the individual cannot increase his expected payoff by distorting his bid. But there is no benefit in terms of expected payoff to true revelation of preferences. However, while expected payoff is independent of the bid, the variance of the outcomes is reduced as the difference between true willingness to pay and the bid becomes smaller. The variance is zero with true revelation. In the unequal probability case, both the expected payoff and its variance decrease as the difference between the true willingness to pay and the bid decrease. In general, the best that can be said for true revelation under Tideman's proposal is that it is a max–min strategy.

If they were unbiased, the responses to Tideman's question would indicate the appropriate direction of change in the level of public goods supply, but not how large the change should be. The procedure could not be repeated for successive increments in public goods supply for two reasons. The first is the practical reason of feasibility: the procedure is based on the assumption of actual tax payments or compensations. And second, even if people attach equal probabilities to the two outcomes in the first experiment, and hence give unbiased responses, they are likely to use the information from the first round to adjust their subjective probabilities. Individuals are more likely to give biased responses on successive iterations of the procedure.

To determine the magnitude of the change in public goods supply, Tideman proposes that each individual be asked to reveal the elasticity of his marginal willingness-to-pay schedule along with his actual marginal willingness to pay for the specified change. He would

---

[6] Finite nonzero optimum bids can also arise if the individual's subjective probability is positively related to his bid. The same incentives to provide biased bids are present.

be told that the *median* response would be used as representative for all individuals. Since strongly biased responses would not affect the median, the individual would perceive no incentive to provide biased responses. Tideman concludes that at least under a fairly wide range of possible conditions and assumptions, the incentives will not be biased and the rational individual will maximize his gain or minimize his potential loss by stating his true marginal preferences and elasticity.

Tideman's suggestion is intriguing. But at the practical level it appears to require an individual of unusual sophistication to perceive accurately the incentive structure built into the questions. In addition, the assumptions about subjective probabilities (that is that they are equal and independent of the bid) are quite restrictive.

Kurz has also proposed a type of question which employs individuals' subjective probabilities to derive an expected payoff function for each individual (Kurz, 1974, pp. 341–347). Although Kurz describes his procedure only in terms of asking for total willingness to pay, the payoff function can be adapted for questions about marginal willingness to pay as well. Kurz's procedure has the advantage of eliminating the bias when individuals attach unequal probabilities to the two alternative outcomes: supply versus no supply in the case of the total willingness-to-pay question, and increase versus decrease in the case of the marginal willingness-to-pay question. There are two steps in the procedure. The first is to ask each individual to indicate his subjective probability that the project will be implemented (or that supply will be increased in the marginal case). Let the stated subjective probability be p. Then the individual is asked to reveal his willingness to pay for the stated level of the public good under the condition that if the good is supplied, individuals will be required to pay an amount proportional to their stated willingness to pay. However, if the public good is not supplied, individuals will be compensated in the following amount

$$t[p/(1 - p)]b$$

where t is the stated proportion. If p is a true revelation of the subjective probability, the expected payoff is

$$E = p(w - tb) + (1 - p)t[p/(1 - p)]b$$
$$= pw$$

In other words, if individuals reveal true or unbiased subjective probabilities, their expected payoffs are independent of their bids. So as in Tideman's procedure, although there is no incentive to provide biased responses to willingness-to-pay questions, there is no positive incentive for accuracy. In fact in this case, true revelation does not even affect the variance of the outcomes.

If the procedure is used to ask for total willingness to pay, it only reveals one point on each individual's demand curve for the public good. But the procedure could not be repeated for alternative proposed levels of the public good, since individuals would learn something of the structure of the game and perceive incentives to provide biased estimates of their subjective probabilities.[7]

To summarize, both Tideman and Kurz propose procedures in which individuals are forced to balance the possible gains from a biased answer if one contingency occurs with the possible cost of that bias if another contingency occurs. They have developed types of questions in which the individual who maximizes expected payoffs will see no positive incentive to distort his revealed willingness to pay. But the problem is that the payoff function contains no positive incentive to take the time and effort to determine and reveal the correct willingness to pay.[8]

---

[7] See Newbery (1974). In fact Bohm (1977) has argued that people would be unlikely to cooperate in the first round unless they were told of the nature and purpose of the exercise. But if this information is revealed before the first round, the incentives for misrepresentation are present from the outset.

[8] In the Tideman and Kurz models, if the public good is provided, each individual's tax depends in some way on his own bid. There is another class of models in which the tax burdens depend in some way on the revealed preferences of others, and individuals are motivated to provide correct bids. In the Tideman-Tullock model of what they call "the demand revealing process," if an individual's bid is decisive in the sense that it changes the outcome, his payment depends in part on the costs he imposes on all others by changing the outcome. See Tideman and Tullock (1976). In the Groves-Ledyard "optimal allocation model," each individual's payment is his proportional cost share *less* the reported consumer surpluses of all others. See Groves and Ledyard (1977). For further discussion of this class of models, see *Public Choice* (1977). While these models are of considerable analytical interest, they represent radical departures from presently used public choice mechanisms and do not offer operational solutions to the preference revelation problem, given present political institutions.

There is another aspect of the Tideman and Kurz proposals that deserves comment. Both proposals are based on the assumption that actual payments and compensations will be made. And Kurz explicitly proposes that the question will be asked only of a sample of the population. If the project passes, the sample is required to pay according to the payoff function. This might be perceived as an unfair distribution of the fiscal burden of the public good provision or the social choice mechanism or both. If the project is not passed, the sample group is

How serious is the problem of bias in practice? Are the biases large enough to call into question most survey work? Or is the bias problem like the difference between the *EV* and *CV* measures of welfare change —that is, likely in practice to be so small relative to other errors of specification and measurement that it can be safely ignored in empirical work? The literature reviewed here has been largely theoretical and deductive in nature; it has assumed maximizing behavior on the part of individuals and deduced qualitative hypotheses concerning their behavior given the incentive structure of the social choice mechanisms and the nature of the questions asked. There has been relatively little empirical work in an experimental setting designed to shed light on the significance of strategic behavior.

The most serious attempt to estimate the magnitude of bias is by Bohm (1972). In Bohm's experiment, subjects were instructed about the nature of the experiment and then asked to indicate their willingness to pay to see a video tape of a television program. They were told that if the sum of their stated willingnesses to pay was greater than the cost of showing the program (and the cost was known to the subjects), the program would be shown to the group. Different groups were told that they would be subject to different repayment requirements. The five repayment plans were:

1. Each person's payment would be equal to his stated willingness to pay
2. Each person would pay an amount proportional to his stated willingness to pay, the proportion being the same for all members of the group and determined so that total payments would just cover total cost
3. Payment would be in accordance with one of several possible alternatives, but the choice of payment plan would be made later. This alternative was meant to test Bohm's earlier proposal that respondents be left uncertain as to whether overstatement or understatement would be to their advantage (Bohm, 1971)
4. The payment would be a fixed stated fee, the same for all members of the group

---

compensated according to the payoff function, and the revenues must be raised somewhere. In fact Kurz is concerned with the cost of these experiments. And he proposes a variation of the procedure outlined above that he shows to have lower experimental cost.

5. There would be no payment required. Costs would be cov-
ered from other revenue sources.

In addition, respondents were given information on the strategic elements of the repayment plan that they were subject to. They were given
information on both the advantages and disadvantages to themselves
of alternative strategies, as well as some discussion of the "moral
obligation" to reveal true preferences. The main finding of the experiment is that there is no significant difference in the mean stated willingness to pay among the groups subjected to the five alternative experimental repayment situations. Thus, the one major experiment designed to test the hypothesis of strategic behavior cannot reject the
null hypothesis that strategic behavior is absent when individuals are
asked questions in an explicitly public choice setting.[9]

Brookshire, Ives, and Schulze surveyed local residents and three
categories of recreationists in the Grand Canyon National Recreation
Area to estimate their willingness to pay to prevent the scenic and
aesthetic degradation associated with a proposed power plant siting on
Lake Powell. This was a hypothetical situation in that respondents
knew that the survey administrators were not acting in an official capacity, that the survey would not directly determine whether the public
good—scenic amenity—would be provided, and that there was no provision for payment or compensation. One element of the research was
to try to determine whether strategic behavior or biased responses were
present. Brookshire, Ives, and Schulze hypothesized that if strategic
behavior were important, nonenvironmentalists would bias their answers
toward zero and that environmentalists would bias their willingness-
to-pay answers upward. They deduced that if strategic behavior were
important, the frequency distribution of willingness-to-pay answers
would be relatively flat, with a large number of zero responses and a
large number of high responses. While they conducted no statistical
test of the hypothesis, they argued that a visual inspection of the frequency distribution does not support the hypothesis of strategic behavior. The highest bids were quite small relative to the mean income
of the sample group, and the modal bid was in the range of $2–$4 for
all sample groups.

[9] As will be discussed below, Bohm also asked the willingness-to-pay question in an experimental setting where respondents knew that the exclusion principle would be applied. Responses in this setting were significantly higher than
those in one of the public goods settings.

Accuracy

An accurate response to a question about willingness to pay is one which is consistent with the underlying preference ordering or utility function and with the behavior that would be revealed if the public good could be offered in a market where exclusion was possible. The concept of accuracy as defined here is somewhat different and more broad than the usual use of the term in the survey research literature. There, response error is defined as the difference between the true value and the reported value.[10] The implicit assumption is that the true value is an objective magnitude that can be observed independently for purposes of verification or measurement of response error. But the essence of the problem of preference revelation is that the true value is subjective and typically cannot be observed independently.

There are two sets of factors that govern the accuracy of individuals' responses. The first is the ability of an individual to make an accurate determination of his preferences in what is essentially a hypothetical situation. In an explicitly economic framework, it could be said that accuracy is costly in terms of the time and mental energy that must be used to gather information, process it, and reach a conclusion about willingness to pay. If accuracy is viewed as an output, its cost is an increasing function of the degree of accuracy.

The second set of determinants of accuracy is the incentive to be accurate, or the demand for accuracy. Suppose an individual has a true demand function for a private good, $x = D(p)$. If he chooses the quantity to purchase in accordance with some different demand function, say $x = D^*(p)$, he would suffer a utility loss. The individual has an incentive to behave "correctly" so as to avoid this potential loss. But if an individual is asked a hypothetical question about his willingness to pay for the public good, he does not have to act on his response or live with its consequences. He incurs no actual utility loss for an inaccurate response. There is no incentive to be correct.

In summary, it is hypothesized that learning how to respond in accordance with one's preferences is costly, and resources are devoted to increasing the accuracy of responses only so long as the marginal net utility gain to greater accuracy is positive. If the hypothesis is accepted, we must examine questions designed to elicit willingness-to-pay information not only in terms of the incentives to bias, but the incentives

[10] See Lansing and Morgan (1971) or Moser and Kalton (1972).

to or the benefits from accuracy. But we saw in an earlier section that those questions which were most successful in avoiding the problem of bias also eliminated any incentive for accuracy. This problem has either been explicitly assumed away or not addressed at all in the theoretical literature on preference revelation.[11]

A few of the researchers actually asking questions of individuals have explicitly considered the circumstances which might make it easier for individuals to provide accurate responses.[12] The factors that are discussed primarily involve efforts to reduce the cost of accuracy for individuals. For example, the experimental situation should ask the individual to place himself in a realistic or credible position. The experiment should not require that the individual imagine himself in an unfamiliar role or situation. The individual should be provided with specific concrete data and accurate descriptions of alternatives. At least up to some point, the more information of a descriptive sort that is provided to an individual, the less effort he must make to imagine the consequences of his responses. If the questions concern hypothetical alternatives, the alternatives should have attributes which are familiar to the individual and are within his range of experience. In other words, the individual should easily be able to visualize the alternative situations.

Since the problem of accuracy has been almost totally ignored in the economics literature, there is almost no empirical evidence concerning the magnitude of the problem. There are just two small, inconclusive pieces of evidence that I have been able to find. The first comes from Peter Bohm's experiment described above. He asked the members of a sixth group to state their maximum willingness to pay to watch the television show after telling them that only the ten highest bidders would actually be admitted, and that those admitted would actually have to pay the amount of their bid. The responses of the group faced with the possibility of exclusion showed on average a greater willingness to pay than those of all of the groups for which individual exclusion was ruled out. However the only pair-wise comparison for which the difference was significant at the 5 percent level

---

[11] Kurz (1974) explicitly assumes that "in the absence of any reward or loss due to the revelation of true preferences, individuals have the *intrinsic* desire to tell the truth and thus be prepared to reveal their true demands" (p. 333) [emphasis added].

[12] See, for example, Bohm (1972), Knetsch and Davis (1966), and Randall, Ives, and Eastman (1974).

was that with group three (that is, the repayment plan would be determined later). Thus there is some weak evidence to support the proposition that the possibility of exclusion gave people an incentive to devote more thought to their response and thus provide more accurate responses.[13]

On the other hand, in 1966 Knetsch and Davis compared the responses to the willingness-to-pay question with an alternative market-based measure of demand based upon travel cost behavior and found the two measures to be in rough agreement or correspondence. In all, however, the evidence must be considered inconclusive.

Conclusions

Where surveys are actually used to make policy, simple questions about willingness to pay provide incentives for strategic behavior at least in principle. However the evidence on actual strategic behavior from those experiments designed to reveal it is inconclusive concerning its quantitative importance. It is possible to construct questions which eliminate the incentives for biased responses in principle. But such questions also give no incentive to provide accurate responses.

Where hypothetical situations have been posed to individuals in experimental situations, there is little incentive for strategic behavior since neither the public goods supply nor individual repayment obligations are directly linked to the outcome of the survey. However while incentives for strategic behavior may be weak or absent, there is also little or no incentive to be accurate in responses. The design of questions and the experimental setting are both important because not only do they influence incentives for strategic behavior, but they influence the cost of accuracy as well.

Finally, given the problem of accuracy of individual responses, it is probably appropriate to interpret responses as being subject to a measurement error. An important question is how the measurement error is distributed. If it is possible to assume that the error term is normally distributed with a zero mean, then properly designed experiments could provide data on sample means and variances; and the population mean and confidence level could be estimated. But we have no evidence on this question.

---

[13] Bohm suggests, on the other hand, that the answers may reflect elements of competitive behavior and "auction fever" (Bohm, 1972, p. 126).

REVEALING PREFERRED QUANTITIES

Instead of asking individuals to indicate their willingness to pay for a given quantity of the public good, a group of individuals could be asked to indicate their preferred quantity or level of supply of the public good given a specified payment obligation or tax share. Bowen (1943) provided the classic analysis of this procedure. Bowen's objective was to show that decisions based on such a voting scheme could lead to the optimum level of provision of the public good.[14]

If all individuals share equally in the cost of public good provision, and if voters' preferences are distributed so that the preferred quantity of the median voter is also the mean of preferred quantities for the group, then the preferred quantity of the median voter will also be the efficient level of public goods supply. The condition for efficient public goods supply is

$$\sum w_i(Q) = MC(Q)$$

where $w_i(Q)$ = the ith individual's marginal willingness to pay, or demand price for Q

  $MC(Q)$ = marginal cost of Q

Each individual chooses his quantity bid so that his marginal willingness to pay equals his marginal cost, that is, his tax share. Since the tax burden is distributed equally, his tax share is $MC(Q)/N$. Thus for the median voter we have

$$w_m = MC(Q)/N$$

where w_m is the median voter's marginal willingness to pay. If the median coincides with the mean, we have

$$N \cdot w_m = \sum w_i = MC(Q)$$

which corresponds to the efficiency condition.[15]

[14] For a discussion of the applicability of Bowen's model to problems of allocating resources to pollution control, see Portney (1975).

[15] The assumption of equal tax shares is unnecessarily restrictive. With unequal tax shares, the median voter's preferences will be the efficient quantity if the net benefits (marginal willingness to pay minus marginal tax share) for each individual are distributed so that the median net benefit is zero. See Tideman (1972). However, the assumption that the median and mean preferences are equal is more troublesome. Where the preferred quantity is a function of income, or where the mean preference is close to zero, the mean is likely to be above the median. See Bohm (1977, p. 188).

One virtue of the median voting procedure is that incentives for strategic behavior and the revelation of biased quantities are weak or nonexistent. Since the tax share is given, an individual can affect his payment obligation only if he can affect the median quantity. But the ability of an individual to shift the median quantity through a distorted vote is extremely limited, and the payoff for doing so may be small or even negative. If the individual expects the median quantity to be less than his preferred quantity, he could only shift the median by offering a distorted vote below the median. But this would shift the median away from his preferred quantity, not toward it. The payoff for strategic behavior in that instance would be negative. However it must also be pointed out that these same characteristics of the median voting procedure provide only limited incentives for accurate revelation of quantities.

The objective is not to examine the optimization properties of different voting or preference revelation schemes, but to determine what information can be derived concerning the underlying demand curves for the public goods. What does quantity revelation tell us about demand? First, since each individual states a quantity that equates his marginal willingness to pay with the stated price or tax share, the quantity revelation procedure yields one point on each individual's marginal willingness to pay, or demand schedule. Thus the information content of the quantity revelation scheme is similar to that of the hedonic price function discussed in chapter 4.

Second, if the quantities revealed by individuals were regressed against those socioeconomic variables (including income) which were hypothesized to influence preferences and demand, the regression equation could be used to derive a cross-sectional estimate of the income elasticity of demand for the public good.

To determine other points on each individual's demand or willingness-to-pay function, it would be necessary to repeat the quantity revelation procedure at alternative prices or tax shares. However if this is done, the problem of strategic behavior arises once again. Our finding that incentives for strategic behavior are absent in the median voting procedure is based on the assumption that each individual believes that the outcome of the voting will be used only to determine the quantity of the public good in accordance with the median voting rule. If an individual understands that the information from the voting procedure will be used for other purposes, for example to estimate his demand curve and willingness to pay, then he does have incentives to distort the willingness-to-pay information that the procedure provides.

However if different sample groups were drawn and each were asked to reveal their preferred quantities for different prices or tax shares, and if each group believed that its own public good supply would be determined by the median voting rule, then it might be possible to estimate the demand curves for subsets of individuals with similar socioeconomic characteristics. The data set for each individual would include the price or tax share at which the public good was offered to him, his preferred quantity, his income, and other relevant socioeconomic characteristics. The data for all sample groups could be pooled. Multiple regression analysis would reveal the effect of price on quantity demanded, holding income and other socioeconomic characteristics constant. Demand curves would thereby be identified.

VOTING

In the real world, voting is seldom if ever conducted in the ways described in the preceding sections. Voters are not asked to write down a preferred quantity or a willingness to pay. Rather they are asked to vote for one or another candidate for a specific office or to vote yes or no on a specified proposal, for example a budget level for the provision of a public good. This section will focus on the binary, yes–no votes as typified by referenda on public goods supply. The amount of information about benefits and demands that can be derived from real world voting schemes depends in large part on how the issues are framed, and what determines the actual public spending proposals brought to the voters in referendum. If the political process can be assumed to work so that referendum issues or the platforms of candidates for office tend to cluster around the preferences of the median voter, then the actual choices made through the political process can be assumed to represent points on the demand curve of the median voter. If outcomes for a number of political jurisdictions can be observed, where cost conditions, median incomes, and so forth, differ across jurisdictions, then it may be possible to estimate the demand function for the public good.[16]

Assume that local political jurisdictions exist only for the purpose of supplying a single public good and collecting the taxes to finance its provision. If the decision about the quantity of the public

[16] The principal examples of this line of research are Barr and Davis (1966), Borcherding and Deacon (1972), and Bergstrom and Goodman (1973).

good is made by elected officials, they must run for office on a platform stating their position regarding the preferred level of public good supply. Competition among candidates should lead to a clustering of platforms around the preferences of the median voter. The most successful candidate, that is, the winner, will be the one who places his platform closest to the median voter.

Where public good supply decisions are made by referendum, voters can only say yes or no on a proposed level of public good supply. A no vote means that $Q = 0$ is preferred to the referendum proposals. Referendum proposals are formulated by the party in power. If the party wishes only to maximize the probability that the referendum will pass, it will tend to propose quantities smaller than those preferred by the median voter. However a rational party should be more foresighted. A party conducting such a successful referendum could be replaced at the next election by another party which announced as its platform that it would conduct a referendum on a larger proposal—one which was closer to the preferences of the median voter. Thus in the long run, referendum proposals should tend to cluster around the median voter preference.

If the outcomes of elections or referenda in a large number of jurisdictions are observed simultaneously, it can be assumed that they approximate the median preferences in each jurisdiction; and any divergence between actual outcomes and median preferences for a particular jurisdiction can be assumed to be small and to average to zero. Given these assumptions, each jurisdiction can be taken as a sample unit. And the data on public good quantity, price or tax share, median income, and socioeconomic characteristics for each jurisdiction can be pooled and analyzed by multiple regression.

This general approach has been used by Bergstrom and Goodman to estimate the price and income elasticities of demand for general municipal expenditures, police, and parks and recreation (Bergstrom and Goodman, 1973), and by Borcherding and Deacon to estimate price and income elasticities of demand for eight categories of local public services including education, highways, police, and fire protection (Borcherding and Deacon, 1972).

While these two studies suggest the feasibility of obtaining information on the demand for some kinds of public services from observations of political choices, the approach appears to be of limited applicability to environmental services and the benefits of pollution control in particular. The voting procedures of this and the preceding sections require that the choice of a quantity, a referendum, or a platform be coupled somehow with an obligation to share in some way in the cost of providing that public good. Therefore, these procedures would be capable of generating information on the demand for pollution control only in those cases where the costs of pollution control will be financed from revenues raised within the political jurisdiction.

Many of the important pollution control problems for which benefit data are desired do not fit this description, at least in the United States. If some portion of pollution control costs is borne by the private sector, then the link between a vote on quantity and tax share or price is broken. And the vote cannot be interpreted as revealing anything about the economic demand for pollution control. Also, the voting approach would only be applicable where both the benefits and costs of the pollution control program fall entirely within the applicable political jurisdiction. If pollution spills across jurisdictional boundaries, some of the benefits of pollution control will be realized outside the jurisdiction. No voting measure could capture these interjurisdictional spillovers.

SUMMARY

In this chapter I have examined in general terms three nonmarket techniques for determining demands for public goods such as environmental quality—asking about values, asking about quantities, and voting on proposals. I have reviewed the well-known incentives for strategic behavior or biased responses that are present when individuals are asked to reveal their values or marginal willingness to pay in a real world setting. Aside from Peter Bohm's experiment with Swedish television programs, we have almost no empirical evidence on the practical importance of these problems. Most of the empirical work on demand revelation by questionnaire has been based on hypothetical situations where the individual knows his responses will have no effect on either his payment obligation or the quantity of the public good actually to be supplied. I have argued that there are no apparent incentives to provide accurate responses. Thus, in the absence of evidence showing that people can and do make accurate assessments of their preferences in these situations, the results of these surveys should not be given great weight by decisionmakers.

Asking people to reveal their preferred quantity of the public good, given the payment obligation, can, given Bowen's assumptions, produce unbiased estimates of the optimal quantity. But when the procedure is used in hypothetical situations, the question of accuracy must be raised. And in any event the procedure provides estimates of only one point on the aggregate inverse demand curve for the public good.

Referenda results do provide observations on preferences taken from real rather than hypothetical settings. If political competition is successful in pushing referendum proposals toward the median voter position, demand functions for public goods can be identified by combining results across jurisdictions with different combinations of price or tax and quantity.

But all in all, the potential for nonmarket techniques as applied to the demands for air and water quality seems quite limited. Levels of air and water quality are seldom decided by referendum *and* financed by taxes. And surveys are of doubtful accuracy—at the present state of the art.

REFERENCES

Acton, Jan P. 1973. *Evaluating Public Programs to Save Lives: The Case of Heart Attacks* (Santa Monica, Calif., Rand Corporation).

Barr, James L., and Otto A. Davis. 1966. "An Elementary Political and Economic Theory of the Expenditures of Local Government," *Southern Economic Journal* vol. 33, no. 2 (October) pp. 149–165.

Bergstrom, Theodore C., and Robert P. Goodman. 1973. "Private Demands for Public Goods," *American Economic Review* vol. 63, no. 3 (June) pp. 280–296.

Bohm, Peter. 1971. "An Approach to the Problem of Estimating Demand for Public Goods," *Swedish Journal of Economics* vol. 73, no. 1 (March) pp. 94–105.

———. 1972. "Estimating Demand for Public Goods: An Experiment," *European Economic Review* vol. 3, pp. 111–130.

———. 1977. "Estimating Access Values," in Lowdon Wingo and Alan Evans, eds., *Public Economics and the Quality of Life* (Baltimore, Johns Hopkins University Press for Resources for the Future and the Centre for Environmental Studies).

Borcherding, Thomas E., and Robert T. Deacon. 1972. "The Demand for Services of Nonfederal Governments," *American Economic Review* vol. 62, no. 5 (December) pp. 891–901.

Bowen, Howard R. 1943. "The Interpretation of Voting in the Allocation of Economic Resources," *Quarterly Journal of Economics* vol. 58, pp. 27–48 (reprinted in Kenneth J. Arrow and Tibor Scitovsky, eds. 1969. *Readings in Welfare Economics* [Homewood, Ill., Richard D. Irwin,] pp. 115–132).

Brookshire, David S., Berry C. Ives, and William D. Schulze. 1976. "The Valuation of Aesthetic Preferences," *Journal of Environmental Economics and Management* vol. 3, no. 4 (December) pp. 325–346.

Cicchetti, Charles J. and V. Kerry Smith. 1976. *The Costs of Congestion: An Econometric Analysis of Wilderness Recreation* (Cambridge, Mass., Ballinger).

Dreze, J. H., and de la Valleé Poussin. 1971. "A Tatonnement Process for Public Goods," *Review of Economic Studies* vol. 38, pp. 133–150.

Green, Jerry, and Jean-Jacques Laffont. 1977. "Imperfect Personal Information and the Demand Revealing Process: A Sampling Approach," *Public Choice* vol. 29, no. 2 (Supplement to Spring) pp. 79–94.

Groves, Theodore, and John Ledyard. 1977. "Optimal Allocation of Public Goods: A Solution to the 'Free Rider' Problem," *Econometrica* vol. 45, no. 4 (May) pp. 783–809.

Hammack, Judd, and Gardner M. Brown, Jr. 1974. *Waterfowl and Wetlands: Toward Bioeconomic Analysis* (Baltimore, Johns Hopkins University Press for Resources for the Future).

Knetsch, Jack L., and Robert K. Davis. 1966. "Comparisons of Methods for Recreation Evaluation," in Allen V. Kneese and Stephen C. Smith, eds., *Water Research* (Baltimore, Johns Hopkins University Press for Resources for the Future).

Kurz, Mordecai. 1974. "An Experimental Approach to the Determination of the Demand for Public Goods," *Journal of Public Economics* vol. 3, pp. 329–348.

Lansing, John B., and James N. Morgan. 1971. *Economic Survey Methods* (Ann Arbor, Mich., Institute for Social Research, University of Michigan).

Mäler, Karl-Göran. 1974. *Environmental Economics: A Theoretical Inquiry* (Baltimore, Johns Hopkins University Press for Resources for the Future).

Malinvaud, Edmund. 1972. "Prices for Individual Consumption, Quantity Indicators for Collective Action," *Review of Economic Studies* vol. 39, pp. 385–406.

Moser, C. A., and G. Kalton. 1972. *Survey Methods in Social Investigation,* 2nd ed. (New York, Basic Books).

Newbery, David. 1974. "Experimental Approach to the Determination of the Demand for Public Goods: A Comment," *Journal of Public Economics* vol. 3, pp. 425–429.

Pendse, Dilip, and J. B. Wyckoff. 1974. "Scope for Valuation of Environmental Goods," *Land Economics* vol. 50, no. 1 (February) pp. 89–92.

Portney, Paul R. 1975. "Voting, Cost–Benefit Analysis, and Water Pollution Policy," in Henry M. Peskin and Eugene P. Seskin, eds., *Cost–Benefit Analysis and Water Pollution Policy* (Washington, D.C., The Urban Institute).

Public Choice. 1977. Vol. 29, no. 2 (Special Supplement to Spring).

Randall, Alan, Berry Ives, and Clyde Eastman. 1974. "Bidding Games for Evaluation of Aesthetic Environmental Improvement," *Journal of Environmental Economics and Management* vol. 1, no. 2 (August) pp. 132–149.

Strauss, Robert P., and G. David Hughes. 1976. "A New Approach to the Demand for Public Goods," *Journal of Public Economics* vol. 6, no. 3 (October) pp. 191–204.

Tideman, T. Nicolaus. 1972. "The Efficient Provision of Public Goods," in Selma J. Mushkin, *Public Prices for Public Products* (Washington, D.C., The Urban Institute).

————, and Gordon Tullock. 1976. "A New and Superior Principle for Collective Choice," *Journal of Political Economy* vol. 84, no. 6 (November-December) pp. 1145–1159.

CHAPTER 6

Property Values
and Benefit Estimation

Economic theory has long recognized that the productivity of land differs across sites. The classical theory of rents holds that productivity differentials will yield differential rents to land and therefore differential land values. Where land is a producer's good, competition and free entry are sufficient to ensure that productivity differentials are fully reflected in the land rent structure. For any property where the land rent is less than the productivity, the activity occupying that land must be earning a profit. Some potential entrant will be willing to bid above the going rent in order to occupy that site and reap the rewards of a superior productivity. It is this competition which bids up land rents to eliminate the surplus or profit.

Some environmental characteristics such as air or water quality may affect the productivity of land either as a producer's good or consumer's good. Where this is so, the structure of land rents will reflect these environmentally determined productivity differentials. Rent differentials will be equal to productivity differentials where land is used as a producer's good and competition and mobility eliminate profits. But where the principal use of land is as a consumer good or an input into the household production function for housing services, the above result will not necessarily hold. The differences in preferences among households may result in some households reaping an economic surplus, that is, being able to occupy the land at a rent which is less than their maximum willingness to pay for it, at the same time as no other household is willing to outbid them to occupy that parcel of land.

These results from classical rent theory have aroused considerable interest among economists in the possibility of using land rent or land value information for residential properties to measure the benefits to households brought about by changes in environmental characteristics such as air or water quality. Ronald Ridker (1967) was the first economist to attempt to use residential property value data as the basis for estimating the benefits of changes in measures of environmental quality such as air pollution. He reasoned as follows:

> If the land market were to work perfectly, the price of a plot of land would equal the sum of the present discounted streams of benefits and costs derivable from it. If some of its costs rise, (e.g., if additional maintenance and cleaning costs are required) or if some of its benefits fall (e.g., if one cannot see the mountains from the terrace) the property will be discounted in the market to reflect people's evaluation of these changes. Since air pollution is specific to locations and the supply of locations is fixed, there is less likelihood that the negative effects of pollution can be significantly shifted on to other markets. We should therefore expect to find the majority of effects reflected in this market, and we can measure them by observing associated changes in property values. (p. 25)

Ridker employed both time-series and cross-sectional data in his efforts to measure the influence of air pollution on residential property values. Since Ridker's work, time-series studies have not been common because of the difficulties in controlling for other influences on property values over time. But there have been many cross-sectional studies relating the variation in property values across a single urban area (and one among eighty-five SMSAs) at a point in time to differences in air pollution levels and other explanatory variables. Many of these studies are summarized and briefly compared in the appendix to this chapter. With three exceptions, these studies have all found significant correlations between residential property values and air pollution levels within the urban areas studied, thus providing support for the hypothesis that the amenity value of cleaner air is capitalized into the value of land.[1]

Since the publication of Ridker's book and the article reporting on his cross-sectional study of St. Louis (Ridker and Henning, 1967), an extensive literature has developed on the proper interpretation of air pollution–property value data. Many authors have followed Ridker's initial insight, quoted above, by examining how and under what circumstances changes in property values over time could be predicted and used as an estimate of benefits. More recently several researchers have designed their empirical studies as applications of the hedonic price technique for estimating the implicit prices of attributes such as air quality from cross-sectional data. By this approach, benefit measures

---

[1] The exceptions are Wieand (1973), Steele (1972), and Smith's (1976) study of intercity property value differences. Also, for a skeptical view of the feasibility of measuring the property value–air pollution relationship and using it to estimate benefits, see Lester Lave (1972).

are based on property value differences at a point in time. It has been shown that hedonic price relationships can be used directly to compute the marginal benefit of improved air quality, that is, the benefit associated with marginal improvements in air quality over all parts of the urban area. It has also been shown that the hedonic price data can be used as an input into a second stage of analysis to estimate individual inverse demand or marginal willingness-to-pay functions for air quality.[2]

The next section of this chapter will briefly review and summarize the main conclusions of the early debate about the correct interpretation of property value studies. Specifically this section will address the question of how and under what circumstances changes in property values in an urban land market can provide an accurate measure of the benefits of changes in air quality in that city. The answer depends on the degree of interurban mobility of the population. Mobility plays a key role in the simple models in ensuring that differences in amenity levels between cities are reflected in land values. But interurban migration can also affect and be affected by wage levels. In the following section the analysis is expanded to consider the interactions among wage levels, amenity levels, and land values in a many-city model linked by population mobility and trade.

Subsequent sections will present discussions of the theoretical and empirical aspects of the hedonic price technique as an approach for estimating the demand for air quality improvements. Finally, the applicability of property value techniques for estimating benefits from and demands for other forms of amenities, such as absence of noise and access to water bodies, will be discussed.

CHANGES IN PROPERTY VALUES AS A
MEASURE OF BENEFITS

In this section three questions are considered. First, given the standard definition of benefits—that is, as surpluses measured by areas under appropriate demand curves—can the aggregate benefits caused by changes in air quality be measured by the associated changes in aggregate property values? It should be noted that property value changes are merely the discounted present value of anticipated changes in the flow of rents. Since benefits are normally defined as a flow, that is, dollars per

[2] See Freeman (1974).

year, the real question is whether benefits are accurately reflected in rents. But since property values are often more easily observed than rents (for example, for owner-occupied housing), the empirical part of the argument will usually proceed in terms of property values. It is assumed that the appropriate discount rate for translating flows to stocks and vice versa is known.[3] Under certain conditions, the capitalized value of benefits will be fully reflected in property value changes, but these conditions are fairly restrictive. In fact measures of property value changes are not likely to be useful as measures of benefits.

The second question involves the prediction of property value changes on the basis of cross-sectional data on the property value–air quality relationship. Suppose that the equation giving the price of a residential property as a function of its air quality and other variables is known.

$$R_i = R(Q_i, \ldots) \; i = 1, \ldots, n \tag{1}$$

where R_i = price of ith property

Q_i = air quality of ith property

If there is a change in air quality over any or all of the sites in an urban area, can equation (1) be used to determine the new property values? The answer depends on the nature of urban land markets. The conditions under which an affirmative answer can be given are again rather restrictive.

The third question is: can equation (1) be used in any way to provide information on the demand for air quality and the benefits of air quality improvements? The answer depends on the model from which equation (1) is derived, its specification, and the other variables included in the equation. One such model will be discussed later in this section. The other model, the basis for the hedonic technique, will be discussed in a subsequent section. I consider the answers to each of these questions in more detail now.

Property value changes measure benefits accurately only when some mechanism exists to ensure that all potential surpluses are eliminated by higher land rents. If potential land users are forced to bid against each other for the use of a parcel of land with improved air quality, rents and property values will rise until land users are indif-

---

[3] Property taxation can affect the capitalization of rents. This will be dealt with in a later section.

ferent between improved parcels at higher rents and more polluted parcels at lower rents. Then, land users' willingness to pay for cleaner air is completely captured by land owners as rent. Thus the answer to the first question involves a consideration of the circumstances under which surpluses can be shown to be necessarily eliminated.[4]

Whether surpluses are eliminated depends on the pattern and determinants of demand for land and whether the land market under consideration is part of a larger open economic system. Let us first consider the case where land is used only as an input into some production process, for example, agricultural production. The demand for land is a derived demand and depends on the demand for agricultural output and the agricultural production function. Assume a valley with homogeneous agricultural land, but where land in the south is exposed to air pollution which reduces agricultural productivity. In equilibrium, rents in the south will have adjusted downward so that producer's returns *net* of rent are equalized throughout the valley.

Let us suppose that air pollution is eliminated in the south, raising the productivity of land so that it is equal to land in the north. If the increased output from south land is sufficient to depress agricultural prices, at least some of the benefits of air quality improvement accrue to consumers of agricultural products in the form of surpluses. These benefits are not captured by changes in land rents. Thus a necessary condition for land rent changes to measure benefits is that there be no changes in output prices or prices of other inputs. If there are no changes in these other prices, rents in the north are unaffected by the improved air quality in the south. Land in the south now has the same productivity as north land—both in a physical sense and, because prices are unchanged, in the economic sense. Thus rents in the south must rise to equal rents in the north. The rise in rents accurately measures the benefits of improved air quality.

In this example it has been assumed that there is only one activity, farming, located in the relevant land market. It would be more realistic to consider the case where many different types of activities occupy sites within the valley. When the elimination of air pollution in the south disturbs the original equilibrium, some activities

[4] Actually surpluses can exist in the initial position provided that there is no change in these surpluses associated with the air quality improvement. It is easier to envisage economic mechanisms that would assure that surpluses are eliminated than it is to envisage mechanisms that would guarantee no changes in an existing pattern of surpluses.

might relocate within the valley; some might vanish; while other entirely new activities might enter the valley. Presumably all the relocations, even those away from the improved land, were motivated by an improvement in profit given the new pattern of land rents, prices, and the like. Do all of these changes have to be taken into account to measure benefits properly?

Lind (1973) has established two important conclusions. The first is that even though some activities relocate, the benefit of the air quality improvement can be at least approximated by measuring the total net increase in productivity of only those activities that choose to locate on the improved land. In other words, as a first approximation, one need not be concerned with effects on activities locating on unimproved sites. The second conclusion is that if it can be assumed that all profits and surpluses are eliminated or captured by land owners in the form of rents, these productivity increases can be approximated by the increase in land rents on only the improved properties.

This conclusion appears to contradict the widely cited Strotz Paradox, according to which benefits are measured by the sum of the absolute values of rent changes for the improved *and unimproved* lands (Strotz, 1968). In other words, if rents fall in the north, in our example, this is also a benefit which must be added to the rent increase in the south.[5] But both the paradox and contradiction disappear on a closer examination of Strotz's and Lind's papers.

Let there be a total of n parcels of land that are identical except that $s(< n)$ of these are polluted while the remainder are clean. Let r_2 and r_1 represent the rents of the clean and polluted parcels respectively. Lind has shown that if pollution is eliminated so that all parcels are identical, benefits are approximated by

$$B = s(r_2 - r_1) \tag{2}$$

In other words, benefits can be estimated from rent *differentials* ob-

---

[5] As Strotz put it:
Suppose rents in the [south] increase by $1,000,000 and that rents in the [north] fall by $700,000. To a first approximation . . . , will a dollar measure of the public benefit to the entire community of the improvement . . . be $1,000,000 or must we subtract the $700,000 decrease in rents in the [north] to obtain a measure of only $300,000? The answer is, Neither. Instead, we should add the $700,000 decrease to the $1,000,000 increase and estimate the benefit . . . as $1,700,000. The loss of rents in the [north] is as much a benefit as the gain in rent in the [south] (1968, p. 176).

served before the improvement in air quality.[6] This result does not depend on the zero surplus assumption, and it takes into account possible relocations of activities that might result from the air quality improvement.

Now to relate (2) to the Strotz Paradox, let r_3 $(r_2 \geq r_3 \geq r_1)$ represent rents on all parcels after the air quality improvement. Strotz's measure of benefit is

$$B = (n - s)|r_3 - r_2| + s(r_3 - r_1) \tag{3}$$

By adding terms to (2) we have

$$B = s(r_2 - r_3) + s(r_3 - r_1) \tag{4}$$

If as in our simple example of agricultural land, rents in the south rise to equal rents in the north $(r_2 = r_3)$, (2), (3), and (4) all coincide. On the other hand if rents in the north fall, we have $r_2 > r_3 > r_1$. Strotz's measure is consistent with (4) and (2) only if north and south are of equal size, that is, if $(n - s) = s$.[7] In other words, Strotz's measure is fully consistent with Lind's generalized rent differential measure (2), given its own special assumptions.

So far we have established that rent changes can be used as benefit measures only if there are no surpluses. Given that condition, it is possible to ignore relocations of economic activity and to focus only on changes in the rent of directly affected properties. And despite the Strotz Paradox, in general it is not proper to count changes in rents of unaffected properties since these changes imply the existence of surpluses.

These conclusions for land as a productive input closely parallel those reached by Polinsky, Rubinfeld, and Shavell in a series of papers analyzing the relationship between air quality, residential land use, and urban land rents.[8] Assume a city on an open plain with a business district at its center. The land surrounding the city is used for the resi-

---

[6] See Lind (1973), especially p. 203, Freeman (1975), and Lind (1975). This result is consistent with the hedonic price technique discussed below.

[7] Of course, Strotz recognized this and made it clear at the end of the paper. But the "paradox" has been more memorable than the qualifications and generalization which followed.

[8] The first paper (Polinsky and Shavell, 1975) dealt primarily with the question of predicting property value changes. In the second paper (Polinsky and Shavell, 1976), their model was developed more fully and used to answer all three of the questions posed at the beginning of this section. In the third paper (Polinsky and Rubinfeld, 1977), their model was implemented empirically to develop estimates of benefits for St. Louis. The following discussion is based on these three papers.

dences of those who work in the central business district (CBD). Each family head makes a fixed number of trips per unit of time to work at the CBD at a money cost, *T*, which depends on the distance, *d*, from the CBD. Air quality, *Q*, is also an increasing function of distance, *d*.

All individuals are assumed to have identical utility functions and fixed money income levels.[9] Households are assumed to choose their consumption of a composite good, consumption of housing services, and residential location subject to a budget constraint in which commuting cost and the rental price of housing are functions of *d*. In other words, they choose *X*, *H*, and *d* so as to

maximize $U = U(X, H, Q)$

subject to $M = r(d)H + X + T(d)$ (5)

where X = composite consumption good with price at unity

    H = quantity of housing services

    Q = air quality at the residence

    r = rental price of housing services

    M = money income

Demand functions for *X* and *H* can be derived from the solution to this problem. Substituting the demand functions into (5) gives the indirect utility function

$$U = V[r(d), M - T(d), Q(d)] \qquad (6)$$

Since all individuals have the same utility function and the same money income and since individuals are free to move from one location to another to increase their utility, an equilibrium in residential choice can only occur when all individuals have the same utility, say U^*. There is a pattern of land rents which will sustain this equilibrium that is such that all individuals have the same utility, U^*. Given the utility function and given expressions for the supply of land at each distance from the CBD, the equilibrium rent function can be derived.[10]

$$r(d) = f[U^*, M - T(d), Q(d)] \qquad (7)$$

This determines the form and the specification of the rent function for econometric estimation.

---

[9] If wage rates are endogenous to the model, the following conclusion will be modified. Models with endogenous wage rates are discussed in the next section.

[10] For example, see Polinsky and Shavell (1976), pp. 121–123.

Now assume that there is a change in the pattern of air quality over the city so that at least at some distances, air quality is improved, other things being equal. Can the new rent at any distance, say *d*, be predicted from equation (7)? This depends on the degree of population mobility in and out of the city. If there is no migration into or out of the city, the answer is no. Those who reside where air quality has improved initially experience an increase in utility. This triggers a series of adjustments and relocations until a new equilibrium is attained in which all individuals realize a new higher level of utility, U^{**}. Since the utility level is an argument in the rent function, the new rents can not be predicted from (7) unless it is possible to compute separately the new level of utility, U^{**}.

However, if the city is open, that is, migration among cities is costless, the increase in utility in this city will trigger in-migration. Migrants will bid up land rents, driving the utility level in this city back down to U^*, the common exogenous utility level for the economy as a whole. In this open city model, U^* is exogenous and constant. Thus equation (7) can be used to compute the new rent for any distance, given a change in air quality at that distance.

The identity between benefits and changes in land rents also requires the open city assumption with its exogenous utility level. Since utility levels are unchanged in the open city, each household's increased utility associated with the air quality improvement is just offset by its increased expenditure on rents. The benefits actually accrue to land owners; and the increase in land rents is a compensating variation measure of these benefits. However in the closed city, since utility levels actually change, changes in land rents do not measure the necessary compensating variation.

The third question posed at the beginning of this section was whether a rent function such as equation (7) could provide information on the underlying structure of demand for air quality. Polinsky and Shavell (1976) have shown that for at least one form of utility function, the parameters of the underlying utility function can be identified from the empirically estimated version of (7). They demonstrate this for the Cobb-Douglas form of utility function. Specifically, assume that the utility function is the following form

$$U = A X^\alpha H^\beta Q^\delta$$

where $\alpha, \beta, \delta < 1$

and $\alpha + \beta = 1$

The procedure is to solve first for the indirect utility function and then for the equilibrium rent function

$$r(d) = C^{1/\beta}[M - T(d)]^{1/\beta}Q(d)^{\delta/\beta}$$

where $C = A\alpha^{\alpha}\beta^{\beta}/U^{*}$

This expression is linear in the logs and can be estimated as follows

$$\log r = b_0 + b_1 \log [M - t(d)] + b_2 \log Q(d) \qquad (8)$$

where $b_0 = 1/\beta \log C$

$b_1 = 1/\beta$

$b_2 = \delta/\beta$

Estimates of b_1 and b_2 are sufficient to solve for δ and β. And $\alpha = 1 - \beta$. Thus the utility function is identified. This is true even for the closed city since changes in the common utility level affect only the intercept term of equation (8). Benefits due to changes in air quality can be calculated directly from the utility function.

In an empirical application of this procedure, Polinsky and Rubinfeld (1977) assumed that individuals have identical Cobb-Douglas utility functions but different incomes. Different incomes lead to different utility levels for each income class. From the derivation of equation (8), it can be seen that variation in income and utility levels affects only the intercept term for (8). Polinsky and Rubinfeld estimated a single equilibrium property value schedule of this form incorporating dummy variables to account for the effect of different income levels on the intercept term. After identifying the parameters of the utility function, Polinsky and Rubinfeld used the utility function to compute the change in income that is required to compensate for postulated changes in air quality for each household.[11]

[11] Polinsky and Rubinfeld used the same estimated property value equation to calculate the present value of the benefit stream by two other methods as well. One is to use the property value equation to predict the change in aggregate property values on the assumption that the city is "open." If the city is in fact not open, this calculation underestimates benefits. The second approach, discussed in a later section, computes a marginal willingness to pay for air quality for each household and assumes that this is constant for nonmarginal changes in air quality. If marginal willingness to pay is in fact diminishing with improvements in air quality, this second approach leads to an overestimate of benefits. However Polinsky and Rubinfeld find that this approach leads to a smaller estimate than the aggregate change in property values. Moreover, both approaches lead to estimates which are substantially less than the estimate based on the utility function.

The Polinsky-Rubinfeld empirical study is noteworthy in that it is the only cross-sectional study of the air pollution–property value relationship that is explicitly based on a model other than the hedonic price model discussed in a later section of this chapter. A major limitation to the approach is the necessity for making some assumption about the precise form of the utility function. There is no a priori basis for choosing a particular functional form to represent household behavior. Functional forms for utility functions are typically chosen on the basis of analytical and econometric convenience. To the extent that the true utility function differs from the form chosen for estimation, benefit estimates derived from this technique will be biased in an unknown direction.

I conclude by summarizing the answers to the three questions posed at the beginning of the section. First, property value changes accurately measure benefits only if some mechanism such as interurban population mobility exists to assure that there are no economic surpluses associated with the air quality change. Second, the elimination of surpluses is also necessary but not sufficient if changes in property values are to be predicted from econometric rent equations. If the form of the utility function can be specified, it may be possible to identify its parameters from the estimated coefficients of the rent functions. If so, benefits could be calculated directly from the utility function independently of changes in property values.

This analysis has been based on the assumption of fixed money income so that differences in air quality were the only motivation for migration—and migration did not affect relative wage rates across cities. If wage rates are made endogenous to the model, then one can explore the possibility that differences in air quality and other amenities would be reflected in wage rate differentials. I turn to this possibility now.

PROPERTY VALUES, AMENITIES, AND INTERURBAN WAGE DIFFERENCES

In a national economy with many separate urban centers, the prices of both goods and factors of production in the several cities may

---

They suggest possible biases in their econometric estimations and computations which could explain these anomalies. See Polinsky and Rubinfeld (1977), pp. 173–174.

be linked by the movement of goods between cities in trade, by inter-urban factor mobility, or both. The theory of international trade can be used to help in understanding the basic economic forces at work.

The first conclusion of trade theory is that in the absence of re-strictions such as tariffs or quotas, the prices at which goods are traded in different cities will differ only by the magnitude of transportation costs between exporting and importing cities. For simplicity, assume that transportation costs are zero, and therefore prices are equalized by trade. A second conclusion is that under certain conditions, goods price equilization implies the equalization among cities of the factor prices used in the production of traded goods, even if factors are not mobile between cities. The most important and relevant conditions are:

— identical production functions in all cities
— constant returns to scale in the urban economy
— the number of traded goods must equal or exceed the number of factors used to produce tradable goods
— no qualitative difference in factors across cities
— competition in all markets.[12]

In a model with trade in goods but no factor mobility between cities, trade equalizes the prices of both goods and factors. Differences in the levels of environmental amenities can not affect wage rates.[13] These features are similar to the "closed city" model discussed in the preceding section. Will changes in amenity levels affect land rents as in the earlier models? That depends on the details of the production func-tion. If land is an input into the production of traded goods as well as housing, factor price equalization holds for land rents as well. Rents are unaffected by amenity levels. Changes in amenities affect only util-ity. But if land is an input only in the production of nontraded goods such as housing, trade does not equalize patterns of land rents across cities. Changes in amenity levels can result in changes in land rents. But as in the simple closed city model, there is no mechanism for eliminating economic surpluses. And in general changes in aggregate land rents do not accurately measure benefits.

Now consider an economic system with both free trade and cost-less mobility of labor among cities. Assume that households have iden-

---

[12] For a proof and discussion of the assumptions, see an international trade text, such as Caves and Jones (1973), or Heller (1973).

[13] If pollution is a negative externality to production, it could affect factor prices through its effect on productivity, product prices, and equilibrium trade flows.

tical utility functions and labor skills. Equilibrium across cities requires that utilities be equalized. Consider the indirect utility function

$$U = V(W, P_x, P_h, Q)$$

where P_x is the price of the composite good, and P_h is the price of the nontraded good, housing services. Housing services are produced from inputs of land, labor, and capital. Trade in goods ensures that P_x is the same in all cities. Therefore if there are differences in amenity levels across cities, there must be compensating differences in wage levels, or housing prices, or both. But again if the conditions for factor price equalization are satisfied, wage differentials cannot exist. Thus amenity differences must be reflected in differences in the price of housing and ultimately land rents. Even this requires that land is not also an input in the production of traded goods. Otherwise factor price equalization applies to rents as well. Then there can be no equilibrium unless rising population decreases amenities or there are decreasing returns to urban scale (which is inconsistent with factor price equalization).

For wage differentials to persist, there must be some violation of the conditions leading to factor price equalization. One possibility is that transportation costs or trade barriers prevent the equalization of goods prices. Then wages and housing prices will adjust to compensate for both differences in amenities and in price levels. If a "cost of living" index is formed by the appropriate weighting of the prices of goods and housing and the index is used to deflate money wages, then differences in these real wages among cities can be attributed to differences in amenity levels.

Factor price equalization might also fail for other reasons, for example, qualitative differences in natural resource endowments or nonconstant returns to scale. Then the wage differentials that are necessary to equate utilities across cities, that is, to compensate for amenity differences, can persist in equilibrium.[14] Will changes in wages in one city measure the value of changes in amenity levels? Assume that factor price equalization has not occurred, say because of decreasing returns to scale, and that wage differentials exist in the initial equilibrium. If amenities are improved in one city, this will trigger changes in both wages and housing prices. Migration of labor to the city will push down wages. Increased demand for housing will raise the price of housing and land rents. With labor mobility (the open city model) this

---

[14] See Meyer and Leone (1977) for an empirical study of wage differentials and urban amenities.

goes on until utilities are again equalized across cities. Households have experienced no change in utility. With lower wages, businesses experience transient profits. But competition eventually eliminates them, either through reductions in goods prices or increases in returns to nonmobile factors, especially land used for goods production. If goods prices are held constant by trade, then the only beneficiaries are landowners. Their benefit is measured by the sum of increased residential land rents and rents from land used in goods production. In other words, increases in productive land rents must be added to increases in residential land rents if benefits are to be measured accurately when wages change.[15] Since the increase in rents to productive land should be equal to the decrease in aggregate wage payments, an equivalent measure of benefits is the sum of the absolute values of the changes in wage payments and residential land rents.

HEDONIC PRICES AND THE DEMAND FOR AIR QUALITY

The basic theory of hedonic price estimation was outlined in chapter 4. Here the theory will be briefly reviewed in the context of estimating the implicit price of air quality as a characteristic of residential property. Assume that, as in equation (5), each household's utility is a function of its consumption of a composite commodity, X, amenities, Q, and its flow of housing services, H. H is itself a function of three sets of variables

$$H = H(S, N, Q) \tag{9}$$

where S represents a set of structural characteristics of housing such as size, number of rooms, age, type of construction; N represents a set of characteristics of the neighborhood in which the house is located, for example, quality of local schools, accessibility to parks, stores, or work place, or crime rates; and Q is the level of air quality at the site.[16]

---

[15] This is the conclusion reached by Polinsky and Rubinfeld (1977).

[16] An alternative interpretation of (9) can be based on the household production framework. Households obtain utility from final service flows which they produce utilizing a household technology. Households purchase intermediate goods and services in markets and use them as inputs into a set of household production functions to produce final service flows such as H. Under this interpretation, the function H is the household production function for housing services. At the practical level there are no essential differences between the two interpretations. See V. Kerry Smith (1976), chapter 6.

Any large area has in it a wide variety of sizes and types of housing with different locational, neighborhood, and environmental characteristics. An important assumption of the hedonic technique is that the urban area as a whole can be treated as a single market for housing services. Individuals must have information on all alternatives and must be free to choose a housing location anywhere in the urban market. It is as if the urban area were one huge supermarket offering a wide selection of varieties. Of course, households cannot move their shopping cart through the supermarket. Rather their selection of a residential location fixes for them the whole bundle of housing services. It is much as if shoppers were forced to make their choice from an array of already filled shopping carts. Households can alter the level of any characteristic by finding an alternative location alike in every respect but offering more of the desired characteristic. It must be assumed that the housing market is an equilibrium, that is, that all households have made their utility-maximizing residential choice given the prices of alternative housing locations, and that these prices just clear the market given the existing stock of housing and its characteristics.

Given these assumptions, the price of the ith residential location can be taken to be a function of the structural, neighborhood, and environmental characteristics of that location. In other words

$$R_i = R(S_i, N_i, Q) \tag{10}$$

As explained in chapter 4, this relationship can be linear in a characteristic if repackaging of that characteristic is possible. But in general this need not be the case. Two living rooms with 6-foot ceilings are not equal to one living room with a 12-foot ceiling. Where repackaging is not possible, (10) will be nonlinear.

The first step of the hedonic technique is to estimate an hedonic function like (10) which explains the prices of individual houses as a function of their structural, neighborhood, and environmental characteristics. Alternatively, with the appropriate discount rate, (10) can be converted to an expression which gives the annual rent as a function of the same variables

$$r_i = r(S_i, N_i, Q) \tag{11}$$

It is interesting to compare this equation with the rent function (7) derived from the Polinsky-Shavell model discussed earlier. Equations

(10) and (11) are functions only of the characteristics of housing and its neighborhood, while (7) includes terms in utility and in household income. The hedonic theory treats the price function as exogenous to the household, so that it is independent of household characteristics such as income.

Assume that (11) has been estimated for an urban area. The partial derivative with respect to any of its arguments, for example Q, gives the implicit marginal price of that characteristic, that is, the additional amount that must be paid by any household to move to a bundle with a higher level of that characteristic, *ceteris paribus*. If (11) is non-linear, the marginal implicit price of a characteristic is not constant, but depends on its level and perhaps the levels of other characteristics as well. If the household is assumed to be a price taker in the housing market, it can be viewed as facing an array of implicit marginal price schedules for various characteristics. A household maximizes its utility by simultaneously moving along each marginal price schedule until it reaches a point where its marginal willingness to pay for an additional unit of that characteristic just equals the marginal implicit price of that characteristic. If a household is in equilibrium, the marginal implicit prices associated with the housing bundle actually chosen must be equal to the corresponding marginal willingnesses to pay for those characteristics.

Now let us consider only the implicit price of Q. Panel a in figure 12 shows the partial relationship between r and Q as estimated from (11). Panel b in figure 12 shows the partial derivative of r with respect to Q, $r'(Q)$. This is the marginal implicit price of Q. It also shows the inverse demand or marginal willingness-to-pay curves for two households, $w_i(Q)$ and $w_j(Q)$, and the equilibrium positions for these two households. Each household chooses a location where its marginal willingness to pay for Q, $w_i(Q)$ is equated with $r'(Q)$.

The rent function shown in figure 12 is concave from below, and the implicit marginal price function is downward sloping. Although in principle the rent function could take any form (concave, convex, or linear), there are a priori reasons for expecting the rent function to be concave from below. Q is an inverse function of the concentrations of pollutants in the atmosphere. As pollutant concentrations approach zero, Q approaches some upper limit. If the rent function were concave upward, this would imply that as pollutant concentrations approach zero, the marginal purchase price of Q approaches its maximum. This in turn would mean that those who have obtained the highest available Q

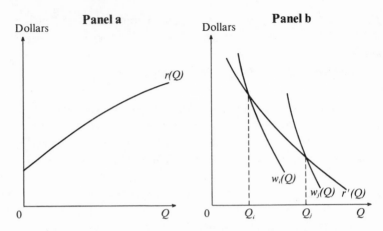

Figure 12. The hedonic price function, marginal implicit price function, and individual willingnesses to pay

would also have the highest marginal willingness to pay for additional Q. If the rent function were concave from below, those households with high marginal willingness-to-pay curves and which already experience high levels of Q would have a low willingness to pay at the margin for additional Q.

The first stage just described develops a measure of the price of Q but does not directly reveal or identify the inverse demand function for Q. The second stage of the hedonic technique is to combine the quantity and implicit price information in an effort to identify the inverse demand function for Q.[17] Assume that each individual purchases only one housing bundle. If more than one were purchased, it would be necessary that they be identical or that the hedonic price function be linear in all characteristics. This is so that there can be only one marginal implicit price recorded for each individual for each characteristic.

It is hypothesized that the household's demand price or willingness to pay for Q is a function of the level of Q, income, and other household variables that influence tastes and preferences. In addition, since there may be substitute and complementary relationships among characteristics, willingness to pay for Q may depend on the levels (or marginal implicit prices) of other characteristics. It is convenient to assume that the utility function is weakly separable in housing so that

[17] Recall the discussion in chapter 4.

prices of other goods can be omitted in the specification of the willing-ness-to-pay function. Given these assumptions we have

$$w_i = w(Q_i, S_i, N_i, M_i, \ldots) \qquad (12)$$

Each household's observed r_i' (Q_i) is taken to be a measure of w_i. Can this inverse demand function be identified with the information at hand? Recall that we have only one set of observations for each house-hold. Thus it is necessary to group the observations of a number of households. As is the case for all demand function estimation from cross-sectional data, we must assume that all households included in the data set have utility functions that are identical except for observable characteristics such as age, education, or family size, which can be parameterized and entered as arguments in the willingness-to-pay func-tion.

There are two special cases to be considered. First, if the rent func-tion is linear in Q, identification of the inverse demand function is not possible. This is because the implicit marginal price is constant when the rent function is linear. With no variation in price across the data set, nothing is revealed about the relationship between implicit price and Q.[18] However as shown in the appendix to this chapter, most of the empirical studies have found nonlinear forms to give more satisfac-tory econometric results.

The second special case arises when all households are identical in all respects—incomes, utility functions, and the like. In this case equation (11) is the inverse demand function. Recall that the marginal implicit price curve is a locus of points on households' marginal will-ingness-to-pay curves. With identical incomes and utility functions, these points all fall on the same marginal willingness-to-pay curve.

If neither special case applies, then the supply side of the implicit market for the characteristic must be examined. There are three possi-bilities. First, if the supply of houses with given bundles of characteris-tics is perfectly elastic at the observed prices, then the implicit price function of a characteristic can be taken as exogenous to individuals. While this might be an appropriate characterization of the short-run supply behavior of price setting in an oligopolistic market such as auto-mobiles, it does not appear to be applicable to housing. Second, if the available quantity of each model is fixed, individuals can be viewed as

---

[18] However even in this case, the income elasticity of willingness to pay can be estimated.

bidding for fixed quantities of models with the desired bundles of characteristics. Third, if both the quantities demanded and quantities supplied of characteristics are functions of prices, a simultaneous equation approach can be used.

Two views have been expressed in the literature concerning which one of the latter two supply side models is appropriate. Harrison and Rubinfeld (1978) assume that the supply of air quality is perfectly inelastic with respect to price or willingness to pay at each residential location. In other words at a given location, air quality is independent of households' willingness to pay. Thus equation (12) can be interpreted as a fully identified inverse demand curve.

Nelson (1978b) has taken a different view. He argues that there is a supply side effect on the implicit price of air quality.

> Taking the total supply of land for all uses in a metropolitan area as fixed at a point of time, the supply of land to the residential housing industry is simply this fixed amount less the effective demand for land for all other uses. . . . *Ceteris paribus,* suppliers of residential housing will have higher bid prices [to bid land away from nonresidential uses] for a given unit of land and improvements, the higher the associated level of environmental quality (p. 365).

Thus, offer prices for residential land will be higher, the higher the air quality. Nelson specifies a two-equation model. The demand side equation is (12). The supply side equation is

$$O_i = O(Q_i, \text{Density}, d)$$

where O_i = offer price

d = distance from CBD

Nelson argues that the two-stage least squares estimation of this system identifies both bid (demand) and offer (supply) functions for air quality.

Unfortunately neither paper has clearly and correctly stated the case for their position. The issue is one of short-run *versus* long-run equilibrium in the market for housing. But neither paper provides a fully satisfactory treatment of what adjustments are assumed to take place in response to market forces. Harrison and Rubinfeld assume that air quality at given locations is unresponsive to the implicit price for air quality. This would be true in both the short run and long run. But the relevant supply variable is not air quality at given sites; it is the number of sites with a given air quality. For example, the larger the number of clean air houses, the lower their price relative to other types of houses, *ceteris paribus,* and the lower the marginal implicit price of clean air derived from the hedonic price equation. The number of houses of a given air quality can be increased either by an improvement in air quality over the urban area, or by increasing the number of houses available in the region of given air quality. With present institutional arrangements, the former can be assumed to be unresponsive to price; but the latter is likely to be somewhat price elastic. This is the type of adjustment mechanism hypothesized by Nelson. However he focused on switching land between industrial and residential land use rather than on changes in residential density.

The question of which assumption, exogenous or endogenous supply, is more appropriate boils down to the speed of the supply side adjustment to price changes relative to the speed at which housing prices adjust to changes in supply. In order to use the hedonic price approach at all, it is necessary to assume that the observed housing prices approximate equilibrium prices, that is, those prices which just make everyone willing to hold the existing stock of houses. In other words the assumption of rapid price adjustment is basic to the technique. On the other hand since supply adjustments typically require changes in land use patterns, including replacing old structures and adding to overhead capital, they are likely to proceed slowly—at speeds measured in years. This is an argument for treating the supply side as exogenous. But it is recognized that the question is an empirical one. And there may be instances, for example in rapidly growing regions, where the short-run assumption would be inappropriate. But in general it seems reasonable to treat air quality as exogenous, that is, independent of its implicit price, and to assume that ordinary least squares estimation of (12) identifies the inverse demand curve for Q.

In summary, in this section we have outlined the hedonic theory of implicit price estimation as applied to urban residential housing markets. We have shown that the implicit prices of nonmarketed attributes such as air quality can be derived from the hedonic price function. Furthermore, with reasonable assumptions, it is possible to use implicit price and quantity information to identify the inverse demand functions.

Once the household marginal willingness-to-pay function has been identified, benefit estimation is straightforward. If air quality improves over the urban area, the household's benefit is the integral of the marginal willingness-to-pay function between the old and new levels of Q

at that site. To find aggregate benefits, sum over all households. Specifically

$$B = \sum_{i=1}^{n} \int_{Q_{i1}}^{Q_{i2}} w_i(Q) \, dQ$$

Since the willingness-to-pay curves (12) are not compensated to a constant utility level, this does not give a precise *CV* or *EV* measure. But if Willig's conditions are satisfied, then this estimate can be accepted as a close approximation.[19] This form of benefit measure is appropriate provided that the prices of other characteristics do not change at the same time. Individuals may alter the quantities purchased of other attributes; demand curves for other attributes may shift back and forth because of complementary and substitution relationships among housing attributes. But all this is irrelevant for benefit estimation provided that the prices of other attributes do not change. If the implicit prices of other attributes do change, then we have the well-known problem of evaluating welfare gains with multiple price changes.[20] And we need to

---

[19] See chapter 3. Harrison and Rubinfeld (1978) have reported data which make possible a check on these conditions. They report (p. 89) that a middle-income household ($11,500 per year) would be willing to pay $2,200 for a house yielding a 1 pphm improvement in nitrogen dioxide levels when the actual level is 9 pphm. Income elasticities are about 1.0 (p. 90). Using a 10 percent discount rate, this is about $220 per year. Willig's first condition is that

$$\left| \frac{S}{M} \cdot \frac{Em}{2} \right| \leq .05$$

We have $S = \$220$
$M = 11{,}500$
$Em = 1$

and

$$\left| \frac{S}{M} \cdot \frac{Em}{2} \right| \simeq .01$$

His second condition is that:

$$\left| \frac{S}{M} \right| \leq .9$$

Other values from this study as well as others surveyed in the appendix to this chapter are broadly consistent with these figures.

[20] Again see chapter 3.

know the new hedonic price function to know how the marginal implicit prices of other attributes have changed.

APPLYING THE HEDONIC TECHNIQUE TO AIR QUALITY

In this section we will discuss a number of question relating to the hedonic price model, its specification, measurement of variables, estimation, and interpretation.

Air Pollution Versus Air Quality

The model has been developed using air quality, Q, as a good with a positive price. Yet air quality is not regularly measured. Rather the data come in the form of pollution measurements. It might be tempting to create a measure of Q out of pollution data through some transformation, for example, $Q = 1/P$, where P is a measure of pollution. The major pitfall with this approach is that the transformation has the effect of imposing a particular functional form on the pollution-implicit price relationship. If this functional form is inappropriate, the result is a misspecification of the empirical model. The best alternative is to treat pollution as a bad. It enters the model with a negative price. In all respects, its treatment is symmetrical with that of Q. The resulting demand curves represent the demand for pollution reduction.

Land Value or Property Value

One question is whether the dependent variable to be explained should be pure land rent (site value) or the price of housing. The latter is a measure of total expenditure on the site and its improvements. Since air quality is a characteristic of the site rather than of its structural improvements, the former measure seems desirable on a priori grounds.[21]

[21] Some researchers have used various approaches to construct measures of site value from available data on housing expenditures. See Wieand (1973), Steele (1972), and B. Smith (1978). Crocker (1970) had both sales price (expenditure) and appraiser's estimates of land value for individual transactions.

The importance of the choice between site value and expenditure depends upon the model chosen as the basis for the estimating technique. If a general land value and location model such as that employed by Polinsky and Shavell (1976) is chosen, then it is important to obtain measures of site value. In the most carefully worked out version of that model, Polinsky and Rubinfeld (1977) allowed for substitution between land and capital in producing housing services. The model showed that if air quality improved, the change in land value would be less than the change in property value or expenditure due to factor substitution. And it is land value changes rather than property value changes which measure benefits in the Polinsky-Rubinfeld-Shavell open city model.

If the hedonic price model is employed, the problem could be handled through the choice of variables to be included in the implicit price function. This function seeks to explain the price or expenditure on a unit of housing as a function of the size and characteristics of housing structure and other improvements to the site, the size of the site, and various locational characteristics (neighborhood, distance from the place of work, and air quality). If all of these variables are properly controlled for, the coefficient on Q measures the implicit price of the air quality of that location independently of other attributes such as lot size, housing structure, and the like. No special effort is required to construct or measure a separate land value variable.[22]

Measuring Property Value

Another question is the source of data on housing expenditures and values. Data on actual market transactions are preferable. For rental housing there is a regular monthly "market transaction," and fairly accurate data could be gathered on housing rents from this. However the majority of residential housing is owner occupied. And only a very small percentage of the total owner-occupied housing stock is exchanged through the market each year. Collecting an adequate sample of market transactions for an urban area is a major task.

A second best source of property value data would be professional appraisals of individual properties for taxation or other purposes. Some

---

[22] However where the unit of observation is the census tract rather than individual transactions, controlling for structural characteristics and lot size may be more difficult. See below.

jurisdictions have developed computer-based systems of appraisals and assessments that include data not only on appraised values but also on a variety of structural and site characteristics. As these systems are developed and extended, they can provide a valuable data source for further property value studies. However, the appraisals must be used with caution. At least in some jurisdictions they may be systematically biased for political or other reasons.[23]

The most commonly used source of data in property value–air pollution studies is the U.S. Census of Population and Housing. The census asks each owner to estimate the value of his property. The census also gathers other data on structural characteristics as well as socioeconomic data on occupants. These data are aggregated by census tracts and reported as means or medians. Although the census tract observations represent a convenient source of data for property value studies, there are two kinds of problems with them.

The first concerns the degree of accuracy of individual owner estimates of values. Nelson (1978a) was able to compare median owner estimates with median professional assessments by census tracts for Washington, D.C. He found that owner estimates were systematically higher by between 3 and 6 percent, while zero-order correlation coefficients were approximately 0.9 or better. He concluded that as long as errors in owners' estimates are random, statistical estimates of price functions will be unbiased.

The second problem is the loss of detail and reduced ability to control for relevant housing and location characteristics, both because of the limited number of variables reported and because of aggregation of individual data by census tract. Census tract boundaries are chosen in an effort to construct relatively homogeneous units in terms of housing and socioeconomic characteristics. If within-tract variation is relatively small compared to the variation among tracts, then relatively little is lost by aggregating a given set of observations to census tract units before undertaking the statistical analysis. But even within generally homogeneous communities there may be substantial variation in relevant characteristics such as number of rooms. The effect of these variables on individual property values would be masked by aggregation.

Furthermore, the list of variables collected and reported at the census tract level is not as extensive as one would like to have in exam-

---

[23] See Berry and Bednarz (1975).

ining air pollution effects. As noted above, a major question is the ability to control for the structural and lot size components of housing expenditure while isolating that part of total housing expenditure related to locational characteristics such as air quality. The 1970 census of housing and population reported the following structural variables.

Number of housing units:
    Lacking plumbing
    Having own kitchen
    By number of rooms
    By year built
    By form of heat
    With basement
    With more than one bathroom
    With air conditioning.

Other individual characteristics that may be important include:
    Structural material, e.g., brick, wood
    Swimming pool
    Lot size
    Average room size
    Location on street—corner vs. mid-street,
        main thoroughfare vs. side street.

Of course the omission of any variable can bias parameter estimates in regression analysis. But there is an additional problem which can be seen by taking a broader view of the underlying rationale for using property value data to estimate the demand for air quality. In a very insightful paper, Zeckhauser and Fisher (1976) characterized the way people respond to externalities as "averting behavior." This refers to the various actions that people take to avoid or mitigate the adverse effects of externalities. When averting behavior is present, it can help the analyst to identify and measure benefits of air quality improvement. For example, averting behavior may be viewed as a substitute for improvements in air quality. With perfect substitutability, expenditures on averting behavior provide a measure of the benefits of an equivalent improvement in air quality. People may attempt to avoid air pollution by purchasing residences in clean air areas. It is this behavior, and its impact on housing prices, which makes possible the use of the hedonic implicit price technique.

But averting behavior can complicate the process of estimating benefits from property value data. If averting behavior is unrelated to the physical characteristics of the house itself, for example, buying gas masks, then the necessity for averting behavior reduces the net stream of services from the house. This would be reflected in a lower housing price. Property value differences and expenditures on averting behavior would provide alternative measures of the same effect. Actually property values would be superior if averting behavior could not fully protect against any utility loss associated with pollution. Property values would reflect both the averting behavior and the utility loss.

However if averting behavior involves changes in the physical characteristics of the house itself, for example using air conditioning or corrosion-resistant exterior paints, then its protective service enhances the value of the house for any given level of pollution. In these cases the hedonic price function must include terms for these attributes of housing. This is possible if the data base consists of prices and characteristics for individual housing units. But it is a disadvantage of the census tract data that they do not capture some of the attributes of housing related to averting behavior.

Rents, Taxes, and Property Values

It is typically the market price of a property that is observed; and inferences about the streams of rents and of benefits are drawn by converting observed present values to annual streams. The institutions of income and real property taxation affect the way in which the market capitalizes rents (and changes and differentials in rents) into market prices for properties. These effects must be properly understood if the process of retracing these steps to infer rents from property value observations is to be successful.

In the simplest case of a stream in perpetuity and with no taxes, the conversion of property value to rent is given by

$$r = Ri$$

where i is the appropriate discount rate. We proceed by examining first the effects of the two forms of taxation separately, then their combined effects. Our conclusion is that unless the analyst takes account of the effects of taxation, the use of property values is likely to lead to an overestimation of benefits.

Ad valorem taxation of property is a device for capturing some of the rent of land for the government. Since taxation affects the net return to the property owner, it should affect the market value of property as an asset.[24] An individual would purchase a property as an asset only if its market price, R, is equal to or less than the discounted present value of the rental stream net of property taxation. Market forces would establish the following relationship between property values and rents

$$R = (r - tR)/i \tag{13}$$

where t is the ad valorem tax rate.

If property values are known, the rental stream they represent can be computed by rearranging (13)

$$r = R(i + t) \tag{14}$$

Assume that the property value–air pollution relationship, $R(Q)$, has been estimated. The marginal benefit of a change in Q at a site is:

$$\begin{aligned} w_i(Q_i) &= r'(Q_i) \\ &= (i + t)R'(Q_i) \end{aligned} \tag{15}$$

where primes represent partial derivatives.
The present value of this stream of benefits is

$$\frac{w_i(Q_i)}{i} = \left(1 + \frac{t}{i}\right) R'(Q_i) \tag{16}$$

In other words when the hedonic price function is defined in terms of property value, ignoring the effect of property taxation on the capitalization of rents can lead to the underestimation of benefits. The term (t/i) is a measure of the percentage error resulting from omitting the tax term in the calculation of benefits. For a discount rate of 10 percent

---

[24] The effects of property taxation on benefit estimation were first discussed by Niskanen and Hanke (1977). While the following argument is based on the use of property value differentials, similar points can be made with respect to using property value changes to measure benefits.

and an effective tax rate of 10–20 mils per dollar of market value (1–2 percent), the error is between 10–20 percent. Niskanen and Hanke (1977) estimate a substantially larger error. They argue that since the tax revenues go to municipal governments, the relevant discount rate to apply to the government's "share" of benefits is the municipal bond rate net of any inflationary premium. They find that this rate has ranged from 1–2.4 percent. Thus they estimate percentage errors of 69–99 percent for the benefit estimates of Ridker and Henning (1967), Anderson and Crocker (1971), and Zerbe (1969). However Niskanen and Hanke have chosen an inappropriate discount rate for the task at hand. The market has placed observable prices on the unobserved streams of rents—and benefits. The present task is to retrace this process, that is, to calculate the rents and benefits from the observed market values. Thus we should use the same discount rate that was used by the market originally.

But this is not the whole story. The income tax code treats the imputed rental income of homeowners differently from the rental income of landlords. The absence of a tax liability for imputed rent further complicates the task of inferring annual rents and benefits from observations of (capitalized) market prices for housing assets. This is because the market will place different values on two assets with the same rental stream if one is subject to income taxation while the other is not.

Assume two perpetual assets with equal annual rents or returns. The return to the first asset, r, is taxable at the rate g percent, while the return to the second asset, r^* $(= r)$, incurs no tax liability. If i represents the marginal opportunity cost of capital, the two assets will be priced so as to equalize the after tax rate of return

$$R = r/i$$

and

$$R^* = \left(\frac{1}{1-g}\right)\frac{r^*}{i} > R$$

If R^* is observed, the tax free rental stream can be computed from

$$r^* = i(1 - g)R^*$$

As in (15) and (16), marginal benefits to homeowners and their present value are

$$w_i(Q_i) = i(1 - g)R^{*\prime}(Q_i) \tag{17}$$

$$\frac{w_i(Q_i)}{i} = (1 - g)R^{*\prime}(Q_i) \tag{18}$$

Ignoring the effects of income taxation leads to an overestimation of benefits.[25]

The tax code confers an additional benefit on homeowners by allowing them to deduct property tax payments in calculating taxable income. This lowers the real cost of the property tax by g percent.[26] Combining all these effects, ad valorem taxation, deductibility, and exemption of imputed rental income, we have

$$R^* = [r^* - (1 - g)tR^*]/i(1 - g) \tag{19}$$

Solving for r^* gives

$$r^* = (i + t)(1 - g)R^*$$

and marginal benefits are calculated by

$$w_i(Q_i) = (i + t)(1 - g)R^{*\prime}(Q_i) \tag{20}$$

and

$$\frac{w_i(Q_i)}{i} = \left(1 + \frac{t}{i}\right)(1 - g)R^{*\prime}(Q_i) \tag{21}$$

The effects of ignoring taxation in calculating benefits depend on the magnitudes of g and t/i. The higher the marginal income tax rate, the more likely benefits would be overstated if taxes were ignored. For an

---

[25] The discount factor $i(1 - g)$ is analogous to the municipal bond rate, and it arises for the same reason. However where the marginal tax rate is itself a function of income, g varies across households; and (17) and (18) must be computed separately for each household.

[26] The code also permits the deduction of mortgage interest. But since the interest cost (either out-of-pocket or opportunity cost) of holding an asset does not enter in the calculation of the present value of its stream of returns, except as shown below, this feature of the code does not affect the capitalization equations.

example, suppose the marginal income tax rate is 30 percent, the opportunity cost of capital is 10 percent, and the property tax rate is 2 percent. Then the terms in parentheses come to 0.84. Ignoring tax effects would lead to an overstatement of benefits by almost 20 percent.[27]

Measuring Pollution

The first question the investigator must answer is which pollutants are of interest. The most commonly investigated pollutant has been suspended particulates (or sometimes dust-fall). This is perhaps the most readily perceptible of the six common air pollutants. Its effects in terms of soiling and reduced visibility are readily apparent. Various measures of sulfate pollution have also been found to be significant in some studies.[28] The effects of sulfur pollution on materials and vegetation may also be perceptible. Photochemical oxidants (smog) have perceptible effects in the form of eye and respiratory irritation and

---

[27] Sonstelie and Portney (1977) suggest as an alternative approach that the appropriate variable for the hedonic equation is user cost or what they call gross rent. This variable captures the full cost of owning (and using) an asset such as a house. User cost would include property taxes and the opportunity cost of capital plus any change in the market price of the asset over the interval, say a year. It would be calculated as follows

$$u = (i + t + m)R$$

where m is the percentage rate of depreciation in market value.

The user cost approach differs from that outlined here in two respects. The first is the inclusion of depreciation or change in market value over time. R could be changing because of general price inflation, changes in the price of housing relative to other goods, or changes in the variables defining R. See equation (19). Only the latter changes have relevance for benefit estimation and they would be captured by a modified version of (20) and (21), which generalized from the assumption of constant streams in perpetuity. However, the depreciation term might be useful in empirical work as an approximation of expected changes in these variables, provided that it were adjusted to net out general price level effects.

The second difference arises in considering the effects of some provisions of the income tax code on user cost. First, the tax exemption for imputed rent does not affect the user cost of holding a house, since user cost is an opportunity cost. Second, the tax deductibility of mortgage interest does affect user cost, but it does not affect the market capitalization of streams of benefits. If user cost is used to compute benefits, the net result of these two effects is to overstate benefits in comparison with equations (20) and (21).

[28] See the appendix to this chapter for references and more details.

reduced visibility. However, oxidants have been used in relatively few studies, probably because of the scarcity of good data on the spatial distribution of oxidants over urban areas.

Empirical studies are likely to encounter the problem of multicollinearity in the pollution variables in one form or another. If only one pollution variable is utilized, estimates of the pollution coefficient are likely to be biased in that they will include the effects of omitted but collinear pollution variables.[29]

Another question in measuring pollution is how the temporal variation in the concentrations of a pollutant is to be summarized and reported.[30] Most of the studies cited in the appendix to this chapter have used annual averages or annual geometric means. However, some studies have resorted to averages struck over shorter time periods, primarily because they were the only data available. There is evidence that for a given averaging period, pollutant readings follow a log normal distribution (Larsen, 1971). If this is the case, the temporal variation in pollutant concentrations can be completely summarized by the geometric mean and geometric variance of this distribution. Thus only these two variables are required to describe a time series of air quality readings. Rubinfeld (1978) reports that this may not be an important problem in practice. In the Harrison-Rubinfeld (1978) Boston study, geometric variances were reported to be approximately constant across space, even though geometric means showed substantial spatial variation. However, this is a question which still deserves further study, particularly since the Harrison-Rubinfeld data were generated from an atmospheric dispersion model, not from actual observations.

Income as an Explanatory Variable

As with other questions, the answer to whether income should be included as an explanatory variable in the equation explaining property values depends on the model from which the equation is derived. In the Polinsky-Rubinfeld (1977) general model, income net of transportation cost is an argument in the rent function which is derived mathematically

---

[29] For further discussion of multicollinearity see chapter 2. See also Ridker and Henning (1967), pp. 251–253, and Nelson (1978a).

[30] For further discussion of this point see chapter 2.

from the model. If estimation is based on models of this general class, then income logically should be included as a variable.

The hedonic price technique seeks to explain price or expenditures on housing in terms of its own characteristics. Since income is a characteristic of households rather than housing, the logic of the technique dictates that income of the purchaser not be included in the regression equation. However, there is a rationale for using an income aggregate such as census tract median income. Median income of a census tract could be taken as a proxy for socioeconomic dimensions of neighborhood quality. The inclusion of census tract income could be justified on this basis either where the unit of observation is the census tract or individual properties.

Controlling for Other Variables

In specifying a hedonic price equation for estimation, care must be taken to provide adequate controls by including other variables thought to influence housing prices. The omission of any variable correlated with pollution can bias the estimate of the implicit price of pollution. It is particularly important to control for other variables which vary systematically across space, for example, accessibility to employment centers or airport or traffic noise.

Functional Form

The choice of the functional form for the estimating equation is not only a matter of econometric convenience. There are interesting economic implications of alternative functional forms. Assume a property value equation as follows

$$R_i = R(P_i, \ldots)$$

where P_i = air pollution at the ith location.

By hypothesis, the marginal implicit price of pollution, $\partial R_i / \partial P_i$ is negative. But there are two additional questions about the properties of this function which have economic implications. The first is whether the

Table 1. Some alternative functional forms for hedonic price functions

Rent function	Second derivative	Sign of second derivative[a]
Linear $R = a + bP$	0	Zero
Quadratic $R = a + bP + cP^2$	$2c$	Positive for $c > 0$ Zero for $c = 0$ Negative for $c < 0$
Log $R = aP^b$	$(b - 1)b\dfrac{R}{P^2}$	Positive
Semi-log $\log R = a + bP$	$b^2 P$	Positive
Inverse Semi-log $R = \log a + b \log P$	$-b/P^2$	Positive
Exponential $R = a + bP^c$ where $c\ (>0)$ is an unknown parameter	$(c - 1)\dfrac{cbP^c}{P^2}$	Positive for $c < 1$ Zero for $c = 1$ Negative for $c > 1$
Semi-log exponential $\log R = a + bP^c$ where $c\ (>0)$ is an unknown parameter	$2be^{a + bP^c}[1 + 2bP^c]$	Negative if $2bP^c > 1$
Box-Cox transformation $\dfrac{R^c - 1}{c} = a + bP$ where c is an unknown parameter	$(1 - c)b^2 R^{1 - 2c}$	Positive for $c < 1$ Zero for $c = 1$ Negative for $c > 1$

[a]Assuming $b < 0$

marginal implicit price of pollution is independent of the levels of other housing attributes. Of the eight functional forms shown in table 1, only the log and the Box-Cox transformation make the implicit price of pollution depend on the levels of other characteristics. The others all impose independence.

The second question is whether the marginal implicit price depends on the level of pollution, and if so, in what way? Specifically the question concerns the sign of the second derivative of the property value function. The property value function could be convex from below, linear, or concave, with the signs of the second derivative being positive, zero, and negative respectively. As already noted, if the property value function is linear, the implicit marginal price of pollution is con-

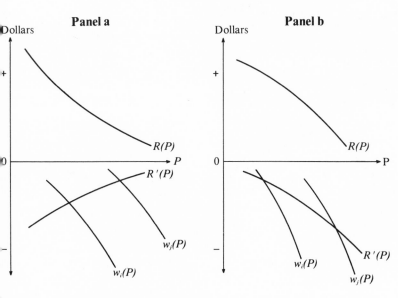

Figure 13. Alternative functional forms

tant, and estimation of demand curves for air quality or pollution abatement is not possible. However most researchers have found non-linear functional forms to give better fits.

If the property value function is convex from below as shown in panel a of figure 13, the implicit (negative) price of pollution is an increasing function of P. This is shown in the lower quadrant of panel a. In economic terms, this means that the marginal damage due to pollution is a decreasing function of pollution levels; and marginal willingness to pay to avoid pollution is greater the lower the level of pollution. If, on the other hand, the property value function is concave from below as shown in panel b, marginal damages are highest (that is, the implicit price is a large negative number) at high pollution levels.

The second derivative of the property value function gives the slope of the marginal implicit price curve and determines the economic interpretation to be given to that curve. The functional forms that have been used in empirical property value research are listed in table 1, along with their second derivatives, and the signs of the second derivative (assuming that the coefficient b is negative). The most commonly used functional forms have been the log and semi-log. They both have positive second derivatives. This is also true of the inverse semi-log.

The exponential, semi-log exponential, quadratic, and Box-Cox transformation are capable of producing negatively sloped marginal implicit price curves. The first two of these functional forms were discussed by Harrison and Rubinfeld (1978) and the semi-log exponential form was used by them in their empirical work. They used a grid search technique to find the best value for the unknown parameter c. This turned out to be $c = 2$. It is interesting to note that for the mean value of pollution in their sample, and given the estimated value for b, the condition for a negative second derivative is satisfied. This lends some empirical support to the hypothesis that the marginal implicit price function is in fact downward sloping. But this is a question which deserves further investigation.

Market Segmentation

Mahlon Straszheim (1974) was the first to raise the question of market segmentation in the context of estimating hedonic price functions for housing. He argued that the urban housing market really consisted of a series of separate, compartmentalized markets with different hedonic price functions in each. As evidence in support of the segmentation hypothesis, Straszheim showed that estimating separate hedonic price functions for different geographic areas of the San Francisco Bay area reduced the sum of squared errors for the sample as a whole.

For different hedonic price functions to exist in an urban area, two conditions must be met. First purchasers in one market stratum must not participate significantly in other market strata. In other words, there must be some barrier to mobility of buyers among market strata. These barriers could be due to geography, discrimination, lack of information, or a desire for ethnically homogeneous neighborhoods, for example. The second condition is that either the structure of demand, the structure of supply, or both, must be different across regions. Either buyers in separate submarkets must have different structures of demands, or the structure of characteristics of the housing stocks must be different. Even with buyer immobility, if demand and supply structures are the same, they will produce similar structures of hedonic prices. And perfect mobility and information on the part of buyers will eliminate differences in the implicit prices for any characteristic across market strata.

If market segmentation does exist, the hedonic price function estimated for the urban area as a whole will provide faulty estimates of the implicit prices facing subsets of buyers in different market segments. Thus estimates of benefits and estimates of demand functions based on faulty price data will also be faulty. If market segmentation does exist, separate hedonic price functions must be estimated for each segment; and benefit and demand functions must be separately estimated for each segment with a different set of implicit prices.

It is not clear how significant the problem of market segmentation is for air pollution–property value studies. Only two studies of the property value–air pollution relationship have tested their data for market segmentation. Harrison and Rubinfeld (1978) stratified their Boston data on the basis of income, accessibility to employment, and household social status. They did not report the effects of stratification on the implicit price function. But they did report that estimates of benefits calculated from the implicit price function were reduced by up to 41 percent, depending upon the basis for market stratification. Thus there apparently was a significant effect on the implicit price function. On the other hand, Nelson (1978a) stratified his Washington, D.C., sample according to urban versus suburban census tracts. A Chow (F) test could not reject the hypothesis that the hedonic price functions were the same in the two submarkets.[31] One may conclude that market stratification might be a significant problem for empirical property value studies. And as with other topics mentioned here, it is a problem deserving further research.

APPROXIMATING BENEFITS
FROM THE IMPLICIT PRICE FUNCTION

An earlier section described how individuals' inverse demand functions for clean air or avoidance of pollution could be estimated from implicit price data. It is also possible to obtain estimates of margi-

[31] In a study that did not include air pollution, Schnare and Struyk (1976) stratified their sample of individual sales transactions from the Boston SMSA (standard metropolitan statistical area) on the basis of: median income of the census tract in which the housing unit was located; number of rooms in the housing unit; a measure of the accessibility of the housing unit; and by political jurisdiction. Their tests indicated different hedonic price functions for submarkets stratified by these characteristics.

nal benefits and approximations of benefits of nonmarginal changes in air pollution directly from the marginal implicit price function.

Marginal benefits of pollution reduction can be estimated directly from the regression equation and the underlying data set. The following expressions are meant to be illustrative. Assume that a property value equation has been estimated for homeowners in the log specification $(R_i = aP_i{}^b)$. The ith household's marginal benefit is equal to its marginal willingness to pay for a reduction in pollution. And if the household is in equilibrium, marginal willingness to pay is equal to marginal implicit price. Therefore the household's marginal willingness to pay or marginal benefit is

$$w_i = -\partial R_i / \partial P_i (i + t)(1 - g_i)$$
$$= -b(R_i / P_i)(i + t)(1 - g_i)$$

where g_i is the household's marginal income tax rate.

Note that since benefits are defined as a flow (rate per year), the expression includes a conversion into equivalent annual rents (r) by the appropriate discount and tax rate factors. Corresponding expressions can be derived for other specifications of the rent function. For the log specification the aggregate marginal benefit is

$$B' = -b(i + t) \sum_{i=1}^{n} \frac{R_i}{P_i} (1 - g_i)$$

In addition to having estimates of marginal benefits, we would like to be able to obtain at least approximate measures of the benefits of proposed nonmarginal changes in air quality. For example, what are the benefits of achieving a given set of ambient air quality standards? Assume that a property value equation has been estimated and the implicit (capitalized) price function for P has been computed. This is shown in figure 14. Note that this form could not be obtained from the log specification. Also assume that the new pattern of air quality is known so that the changes in air pollution $(\Delta P_i = P_i{}^* - P_i < 0)$ can be calculated for every household. This is also shown in figure 14. One point, B, on each household's capitalized inverse demand function is known. But by assumption, the whole function $w_i(P)$ is not known. If the true demand function were known, capitalized benefits could be measured by the area under that function, *ABFG*.

Lacking full knowledge of each household's inverse demand function, we must fall back on some assumption as to the shape of the curve

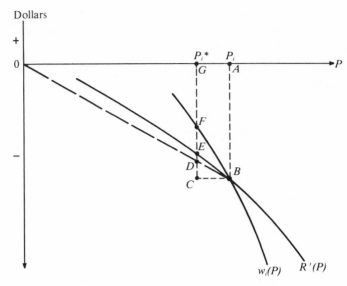

Figure 14. Approximate measures of benefits based on the marginal implicit price function

through the known point in order to approximate benefits. Three alternatives are discussed here. The first is to assume that the marginal willingness to pay for each household is constant, that is, the inverse demand function is a horizontal line through the known point. In this case, the ith household's capitalized benefit for the postulated improvement in air quality is approximated by the area $ABCG$. The aggregate benefit is obtained by summing over all individuals. In annual terms, aggregate benefits would be approximated by

$$B = (i + t) \sum_{i=1}^{n} R'_i(P)\Delta P_i(1 - g_i)$$

in the general case, or in the log form

$$B = b(i + t) \sum_{i=1}^{n} \frac{R_i}{P_i} \Delta P_i(1 - g_i)$$

This assumption leads to an estimate of aggregate benefits that is likely to be biased upward.[32]

[32] The constant marginal willingness-to-pay assumption is implicit in Ridker and Henning's estimate of pollution damages for St. Louis (1967). Their regres-

A plausible and convenient assumption would be that each household's inverse demand curve decreases linearly from its observed point B to the origin. Marginal willingness to pay would be zero where pollution is zero. The total annual benefits of eliminating air pollution can be approximated by areas of triangles as follows

$$B = - \frac{(i + t)}{2} \sum_{i=1}^{n} R'_i(P)P_i(1 - g_i)$$

The benefit for the ith household for reducing pollution to P_i^* is approximated by the area $ABDG$ in figure 14. Aggregate benefits are approximated by

$$B = (i + t) \sum_{i=1}^{n} R'_i(P)\Delta P_i \left(1 + \frac{\Delta P_i}{2P_i}\right)(1 - g_i)$$

It is not clear whether this approximation would lead to an overestimate or underestimate of true benefits.

Finally, as noted above, given the assumption that all households' marginal willingness-to-pay functions are identical, the marginal implicit price curve is identified as the marginal willingness-to-pay curve for the representative household. Under this assumption aggregate benefits are estimated by

$$B = - (i + t) \sum_{i=1}^{n} \int_{P_i^*}^{P_i} R'_i(P)(1 - g_i) \, dP_i$$

To summarize, it has been shown that households' aggregate marginal benefits for air pollution reduction at their residence sites can be

---

sions were estimates in the linear form so that capitalized aggregate benefits were calculated as

$$B = b \sum_{i=1}^{n} \Delta P_i$$

This shows that in the context of this model and given the assumption of constant marginal willingness to pay, the Ridker-Henning calculation was correct even though they gave the wrong justification for it. They argued that B was an estimate of the change in aggregate property values. But as discussed in an earlier section, this would only be true under conditions of perfect mobility in the open city model of Polinsky and Shavell.

measured directly from information contained in the hedonic price function for housing. It has also been shown how plausible assumptions can be used to enable the calculation of approximate aggregate benefits for nonmarginal changes in air quality. These calculations do not require additional information, but can be based on the data files used for the estimation of the hedonic price function.

PROPERTY VALUES AND
WATER QUALITY BENEFITS

Changes in the pollution levels of water bodies are likely to affect the utilities of households owning property on or near the shoreline. These properties could be primary residences or camps and cottages used for recreational purposes. Property values may reflect these utility changes; and under some assumptions, property value studies can provide information on a portion of the benefits caused by changes in water quality. The main limitation is that property value data reflect only benefits to property owners, not to others who make use of the water body. And for some water bodies, nonresident use is substantial.

Applying the Hedonic Technique

To utilize the hedonic technique, it must be possible to assume that the data come from a single market, that is, that there is no market segmentation. For example, assume that there is a region with a number of small lakes that are popular for resort, cottage, and second-home use. If the lakes have different degrees of water quality, comparison among lakes will help to shed light on the property value– water quality relationship. Another possible situation would be a river along which water quality varied from poor to good because of the locational pattern of dischargers.

In such a case, the data set should consist of property values, characteristics of the structure and lot, locational characteristics such as distance from urban centers, and appropriate measures of water quality. The data set could be limited to waterfront properties, or could include neighboring properties along with the measure of distance from the shoreline.[33]

As outlined in a preceding section, the hedonic price equation derived from these data can be used to calculate the implicit price of water quality. And with additional data on income and other socio-economic characteristics of households, it may be possible to identify the demand curve for water quality in a second stage of estimation.

For examples of the application of the hedonic technique to water quality benefit estimation see David (1968) and Brown and Pollakowski (1977). David investigated property values surrounding sixty artificial lakes in Wisconsin. Lakes were classified as having poor, moderate, or good water quality. This judgment was made by officials at state agencies. Water quality was a significant variable in explaining property values around the sixty lakes. David did not interpret her regression equation in terms of benefits or marginal willingness to pay, nor did she attempt to derive the demand function.

Brown and Pollakowski were not concerned with water quality per se, but rather with the value of access to the shoreline and the value of "setback" or open space between the residential area and the shoreline around lakes in Seattle. They regressed residential values on distance from shoreline and distance of setback along with other structural and locational characteristics. They assumed identical utility functions and income so that they could interpret the marginal implicit price function as a marginal willingness-to-pay curve.

Changes in Property Values

Recall that in order to interpret observed or predicted changes in property values as benefits, it is necessary that all surpluses resulting from water quality changes be eliminated by the land market and that there be no induced changes in the prices of other goods to households. Where land is used for residential and private recreational purposes rather than for production for the market, the latter "no price change" assumption seems reasonable. The zero surplus assumption may be reasonable under conditions analogous to the open city model

---

[33] Obtaining a relevant measure of water quality is itself a difficult task involving many questions. Discussion is deferred to chapter 8.

of Polinsky-Shavell (1976). An example would be a small lake or river which is part of a much larger urban housing market.

A model of the general land market is required in order to make ex ante predictions of changes in property values as a consequence of changes in water quality. Even if actual property value changes are observed empirically ex poste, a model can be helpful by providing a framework for controlling for other influences on property values over the time period in question.

Assume all individuals have identical utility functions of the following form

$$U = U(X, H, Q, d)$$

where X = composite consumption good with unitary price

H = housing services consumed

Q = water quality in the lake nearest the residence

d = distance of residence from nearest lake.

The budget constraint is

$$M = X + R(Q, d)H$$

and all individuals have the same income. Water quality can affect the utility of those who reside some distance from the lake as well as lakefront residents. Distance is an argument in the utility function to reflect the accessibility, amenity value, or both, of proximity to the lake.

Assume that there are many small lakes in a large, otherwise homogeneous urban area. If households are perfectly mobile in terms of residential location within the urban area, a pattern of housing prices will emerge that will equate the utilities of all households. Following the reasoning of Polinsky-Shavell (1976), we can derive the indirect utility function as a function of prices, income, and water quality and solve for housing prices as a function of the common utility level, income, water quality of the nearest lake, and distance to the lake

$$R = R(U^*, M, Q, d) \tag{22}$$

where U^* is the common utility level.

This specification of the model reveals an important difference between the air quality and water quality models. In the air quality model, Q is a known function of distance, that is, the Q at each residence is known. And the task is to estimate the willingness to pay for Q. In the water quality model, Q is known only at $d = O$. Not only must we discover the willingness to pay for different levels of Q for households at $d = O$, but also for any given Q, we must discover the willingness to pay to live at different distances from that Q.

Examining housing prices around one lake will reveal the relationship between R and d, given Q. But the implicit price function for distance can be different at other lakes with different Qs, and can change at this lake if water quality changes.[34] Now assume that the housing price function, equation (22), has been estimated empirically. Further assume that water quality increases at one lake. If the properties around this lake are a small part of the total urban housing market, competition from other households should bid up the price of housing here so as to eliminate the surpluses generated by the change in Q. Further, the effect of the change in Q on the common utility level U^* for the region as a whole should be negligible. Given these assumptions, it is possible to predict the new housing prices around the lake from equation (22). The sum of the increases in housing prices is an exact compensating variation measure of benefits of the change in Q.

If the "small lake" assumption does not hold, there will be a change in U^* in equation (22). Thus, unless the utility function is known and solved for the new utility level, equation (22) cannot be used to predict the new level of housing prices. Furthermore, any observed change in housing prices cannot be taken as a measure of benefits, since there are also utility changes not captured by the property value measure.

I am not aware of any efforts to measure water quality benefits using the model outlined here. The study of Dornbusch (1975) for the National Commission on Water Quality used observed changes in property values. But the econometric equations for estimation were not derived from a formal model of property values. And they appear to be seriously mis-specified.[35]

---

[34] In general we expect $\partial R / \partial d < 0$, that is, housing prices decline with distance from the lake. But for some very low levels of Q, we could have $\partial R / \partial d > 0$.

[35] For each of seventeen areas, Dornbusch (1975) estimated

(a) $\% \Delta R = b_0 + b_1 d^{-1} + \ldots$

and

(b) $b_1 = f(\Delta Q, \ldots)$ *(continued)*

NOISE

Noise is another disamenity that varies spatially. For example, exposure to noise from highway traffic, factories, or airports can be viewed as a characteristic of residences. If the appropriate assumptions underlying the hedonic price technique are satisfied, some measure of noise exposure can be used as an argument in the hedonic price function for housing. The possibility of obtaining estimates of individuals' willingness to pay to avoid noise from property value data has been recognized for some time.[36] But most of the noise–property value studies have not been based on an explicit model such as the hedonic price model. One exception is the work by Jon Nelson (1978a). His study of the Washington, D.C., SMSA involved determining the hedonic implicit marginal prices for the avoidance of both air pollution and noise.[37]

CONCLUSIONS

In this chapter I have discussed two approaches to utilizing data on property values to estimate pollution control benefits—property value changes and property value differentials. The two approaches are not contradictory. Although they are based on quite different theoretical models, make different sets of assumptions, and utilize different sets of data, they should in principle yield consistent estimates of benefits and of the underlying demand for air quality. In fact, this would make a good test of the validity of the data and estimation procedures.[38]

In general, property value changes can be interpreted as benefits only when there is some mechanism to assure that there are no economic surpluses accruing to households, and when there are no changes in wages or other factor prices. If goods and factor prices are held constant and equal between cities, for example by intercity trade, then

---

The form for the dependent variable in (a) is difficult to justify. For several plausible forms of property value functions derivable from a Polinsky-Shavell type model, the percentage change in property values due to a change in Q is independent of distance. Also the way d enters (a) imposes a particular relationship between the property value functions observed before and after the change in Q. There does not seem to be any economic rationale for this relationship.

[36] See Walters (1975) for a survey of earlier studies and an application to the question of airport siting in the London area.

[37] See especially chapters 7, 8, and 10 of Nelson's book.

[38] For an example of such a test see footnote 11 above.

property value changes measure benefits. Where trade equalizes goods prices but not factor prices, labor mobility in response to amenity changes can lead to changes in both wages and residential property values. Both must be counted in measuring benefits. Except for these two cases, it was shown that there is no simple straightforward relationship between the benefits of amenity changes and changes in either wages or property values.

In contrast, the hedonic price technique does not require assumptions about interurban mobility or factor price equalization. According to the hedonic theory the implicit prices of characteristics of commodities such as housing can be identified from the pattern of prices within a given housing market, assuming a well-functioning market in equilibrium. Not only can the implicit marginal price of air quality be observed, but given certain apparently reasonable conditions, the inverse demand function for air quality can also be identified.

There are some limitations to the property value approaches to benefit estimation. First, since the property value approaches are based on the consequences of households' choices of residence, they do not capture households' willingness to pay for improvements in air quality at other points in the urban area, for example, the work place, shopping areas, or parks and recreational areas. However, wage changes may reflect general urban amenities in addition to opportunities for choosing high amenity residences.

Second, because the approaches are based on observing behavioral responses to the effects of pollution, they are limited to estimating willingness to pay for perceived effects of improved air quality. It is important to be clear about what is being assumed. If one residential site has better air quality and as a consequence individuals there experience less respiratory disease, what is required is that individuals know that they will feel better if they choose to live at this site. They need not know why they feel better, that is, they need not know the cause of the perceived effects. It is likely that individuals do not perceive subtle long-term effects on health and mortality. So it is unlikely that property value measures pick up these health effects.

If property value measures of benefits are combined with benefit measures from other sources, there is a danger of double counting. For example, soiling damages as measured by cleaning costs, or the residential component of materials damage are probably not additive to property value measures of benefits. This is probably also true of at least a portion of short-term health benefits. However at least a portion of short-term health effects are caused by exposure away from the residence.

In summary, it is clear that property value measures do not capture all of the components of air pollution benefits. But it is not clear to what extent benefit measures from other sources can be added to property value measures without leading to double counting. However one should not conclude from this that property value measures are not useful. For broad policy decisions, order-of-magnitude or lower bound estimates may be quite valuable to decisionmakers.

APPENDIX
A SHORT REVIEW OF
AIR POLLUTION–PROPERTY VALUE STUDIES

I am aware of fifteen different studies covering eleven cities in the United States and Canada which have been based implicitly or explicitly on the hedonic price approach, and one which was based on the Polinsky-Shavell general equilibrium model. All of these studies have used cross-sectional data within a city to test for a relationship between air pollution and property values or monthly rentals. In one case, St. Louis, there are four separate studies examining basically the same set of data. There are three studies for Boston, and two studies each for Chicago and Washington—all using different sets of data.

The purpose of this appendix is to provide a short summary of the key features of each of these studies and to make comparisons of the results where this is possible. The key features and the results for each study are summarized in table 2 at the end of this appendix.

Most of the studies have used data from the U.S. Census of Housing and Population, both for property value and rental measures and for explanatory variables. For each census tract the census reports the median of owner estimates of the value of the property for owner-occupied housing. Two of the studies summarized here use means computed from the census tapes. One uses data further disaggregated by enumeration districts. The main question is the accuracy of owner-reported valuations; that is, do they accurately reflect market conditions? Nelson was able to compare the census estimates with professional assessments of individual parcels aggregated by census tract. He found very high zero order correlation coefficients between professional assessments and owner estimates. Owner estimates were systematically higher by between 3 and 6 percent.[1] As an alternative to the aggregate Census data, Crocker (1970), B. Smith (1978), and Sonstelie and Portney (1977) were able to use data on transactions in individual properties in their studies of Chicago and San Mateo County.

The census also reports rents paid for renter-occupied housing. Goodwin (1976) studied the rental market only. Anderson-Crocker (1971) and Spore (1972) estimated separate relationships for both property values and rentals. In these two studies the effect of air pollution on rentals does not appear to be as strong as on property values.

As for air pollution measures, the earlier studies focused primarily on the major stationary source air pollutants, that is sulfur dioxide and suspended particulates. Particulates were measured either by the standard hi-vol sampler method or in the cases of Zerbe (1969) and Spore (1972), by dustfall. However, except for Steele (1972), the sulfur dioxide variable actually used was sulfation as measured by the lead peroxide candle method. These measures are not comparable to the sulfur dioxide measures on which the ambient air quality standards are based or which are presently reported.

Another problem with the air pollution data is that they are often not contemporary with data on property values and other explanatory variables. For example, all four of the St. Louis studies used 1963 pollution variables to explain 1960 property values. The most extreme case is Peckham's 1970 study of Philadelphia which uses 1969 pollution data to explain 1960 property values. Those studies using property values from the 1970 Census have been able to use essentially contemporary air pollution data.

Four studies, Nelson (1978a), Harrison-MacDonald (1974), Harrison-Rubinfeld (1978), and Sonstelie and Portney (1977), have focused attention on mobile-source pollutants, that is, oxidants and nitrogen oxide. The Harrison-MacDonald and Harrison-Rubinfeld studies were innovative in their reliance on air pollution values calculated from a dispersion model rather than from actual readings. The question here is whether the state of the art in dispersion modeling is adequate to support this use of such models.

Estimates of the hedonic price function must control for other variables that describe characteristics of the property and its neighborhood and location. Table 2 does not attempt to detail the model specifications for the various studies. One major question is the inclusion of

---

[1] For further discussion see Nelson (1978a), pp. 80–81.

income as an explanatory variable. As discussed in chapter 6, the hedonic theory calls for using variables which describe the characteristics of the commodity, rather than characteristics of the purchaser. Several studies include census tract median income, but they make it clear that they regard this income measure as a proxy for characteristics of the neighborhood. However Anderson-Crocker (1971), Crocker (1970), and Spore (1972) attempted to justify the inclusion of income on the basis of a supply–demand model in which income is one determinant of the demand for air quality. And the Polinsky-Rubinfeld (1977) study derived a general model of residential choice and land market equilibrium in which income is an argument in the equilibrium rent function.

The effects of accessibility to the central business district (CBD), that is, distance from the CBD, could be confounded with the effects of air pollution (which is often worse closer to the CBD). It is important to control for accessibility and the value of reduced travel time by including some accessibility variable in the property value equation. All but one of the studies used distance to CBD or some other locational measures to control for accessibility. The exception is the Harrison-MacDonald (1974) study of Los Angeles where it is difficult to identify a single center to use as a point of reference. Instead Harrison and MacDonald used a variable that reflected accessibility to major freeways.

All but one of the studies reported results either for a linear, log-linear, or semi-log functional form.[2] For the linear form, the coefficient on the air pollution variable is interpreted as a difference in property value between two otherwise similar properties for a one-unit difference in air pollution. Of course the coefficient is constant through the range of variation of the air pollution variable.[3] For the log-linear form, the coefficient is an elasticity which relates the percentage difference in property values to the percentage difference in air pollution. For example, an elasticity of .1 means that a 10 percent difference in air pollution is associated with a 1 percent difference in property values. The log-linear form has a constant elasticity throughout the range of actual variation in property values. The reported differences in property

---

[2] The exception is Sonstelie and Portney (1977) who used a Box-Cox transformation of the dependent variable.

[3] For those studies reporting linear estimates for sulfation, I have defined a unit change in sulfation as 0.25 micrograms per 100 square centimeters per day. This has been done to make the results of the various studies comparable.

Table 2. Key features of air pollution–property value studies

City & author	Base year & dependent variables	Pollutants & measures	Other independent variables	Functional form	Results
St. Louis Ridker-Henning (1967)	1960 *Property value* census tract median, owner-occupied	*Sulfation* annual geometric mean by lead candle (1963)	*Property* 3 variables *Neighborhood* 8 variables *Income* as proxy for neighborhood	Linear	In best equations, the linear coefficient indicates that median property values fall by $186.50–245.00 per .25 μm/100 cm²/day increase in sulfation
Wieand (1973)	1960 *Housing expenditures* per acre by census tract (a proxy for land value)	*Sulfation* annual geometric mean by lead candle (1963) *Particulates* annual mean; measures of temporal variation were also tried but did not improve the fit (1963)	*Property* 3 variables *Neighborhood* 7 variables *Income* as proxy for neighborhood	Linear	Neither pollution variable was significant
Anderson-Crocker (1971)	1960 *Property value* census tract median, separate equation for owner and rental	*Sulfation* annual arithmetic mean by lead candle (1963) *Particulates* annual arithmetic mean (1963)	*Property* 3 variables *Neighborhood* 2 variables *Income* on basis that each census tract is a submarket in equilibrium	Log-linear	Sulfation and particulates both included; best results with owner-occupied property value; coefficients on log $S = -.102$ log $P = -.119$; they imply a "composite elasticity" of .1–.2; at the mean an additional 10 μg/m³ of particulates *plus* .1 μg/100 cm²/day of sulfation reduces value of mean property by $300–700

Study	Date	Property value variable	Pollution variables	Property/Neighborhood/Income variables	Functional form	Results
Polinsky-Rubinfeld (1977)	1960	*Property value* census tract median, separate equations for owner and rental	*Sulfation* annual arithmetic mean by lead candle (1963); *Particulates* annual arithmetic mean (1963)	*Property* 2 variables; *Neighborhood* 2 variables; *Income* from derivation of open city model	Log-linear	Sulfation and particulates both included; owner equation coefficients on: $\log S = -.063$[a]; $\log P = -.132$[b]; rental equation coefficients on $\log S = -.006$ $\log P = -.137$[b]; they imply a "composite elasticity" of about .2
Chicago Crocker (1970)	1964–1967	*Property value* individual transactions	*Sulfation* annual arithmetic mean by lead candle (1964–1967); *Particulates* annual arithmetic mean (1964–1967)	*Property* 6 variables; *Neighborhood* 4 variables; *Income* based on interpretation of housing price equation as a bid function	Log-linear	Many equations with different specifications; when S and particulates are both included, coefficient on particulates usually negative and significant in range .2–.5; S often positive and usually not significant; when only one pollution variable included, it was always negative and significant; elasticities imply at the mean an additional 10 $\mu g/m^3$ of particulates plus 1 ppb of SO_2 reduces value of mean property by \$350–600
B. Smith (1978)	1971	*Site value premium* from individual transactions in new houses	*Particulates* computed from dispersion model	*Neighborhood* 9 variables	Linear	Individual site values fall by \$430–510 per 10 $\mu g/m^3$ increase in particulates
Washington, D.C. Anderson-Crocker (1971)	1960	Same as St. Louis study	Same as St. Louis study	Same as St. Louis study	Log-linear	Sulfation and particulates both included; two equations for owner and two for renter;

Table 2. Key features of air pollution–property value studies (continued)

City & author	Base year & dependent variables	Pollutants & measures	Other independent variables	Functional form	Results
Nelson (1978a)	1970 *Property value* census tract median, owner-occupied	*Particulates* monthly geometric mean, Feb.–July 1967 *Oxidants* arithmetic average of daily means, May–Sept. 1968	*Property* 5 variables *Neighborhood* 6 variables	Linear, semi-log, inverse semi-log, and log-linear form were tested; semi-log and log-linear forms gave best results; only the latter were reported	one pollutant variable significant at .01 level in each equation; coefficients range from .07–17 (also see St. Louis study). Particulate coefficient always significant in range .048–.116; oxidant significant in range .007–.019; at the mean an additional 10 $\mu g/m^3$ of particulates reduces value of mean property by $576–693; at the mean an additional .01 ppm of oxidants reduces value of mean property by $141–152
Boston Harrison-Rubinfeld (1978)	1970 *Property value* census tract, median value of owner-occupied housing	Mean concentration of nitrogen oxide and particulates calculated from dispersion model	*Property* 2 variables *Neighborhood* 10 variables	Exponential semi-log: $\log MV = a_0 + a_1 NO_x{}^c \ldots$ where c is an unspecified parameter. Best results obtained with $c = 2$	Separate equations run for each pollutant; each pollutant significant at .01 level; many alternative specifications employed; authors conclude that pollution coefficient is quite sensitive to the specification of the hedonic housing value equation
Goodwin (1977)	1970 *Monthly rent* census tract, median value	Towns and Boston subdivisions classified as "little," "moderate," or "high";	*Property* 3 variables *Neighborhood* 23 socioeconomic variables	Linear	Pollution index variable negative and significant

Study	Year / Property value	Pollution variable	Other variables	Functional form	Results
Schnare (1976)	1970 Property value owner estimate Gross rent	pollutants and averaging times not specified Particulates year and averaging period not stated	Location 21 accessibility and transportation variables Property 7 variables Neighborhood 11 variables Income as proxy for neighborhood	Semi-Log	Particulates negative and significant
Miscellaneous Kansas City Anderson-Crocker (1971)	1960 Same as St. Louis study	Same as St. Louis study	Same as St. Louis study	Log-linear	Sulfation and particulates both included; at least one pollution variable significant at the .05 level in each equation (also see St. Louis and Washington, D.C. studies),
Toronto-Hamilton Zerbe (1969)	1961 Property value census tract median, owner-occupied	Sulfation annual average by lead candle, median of averages 1961–1967 Dustfall (Toronto only) annual average, median of averages 1961–1967	Property 5 variables Neighborhood 8 variables Income as proxy for neighborhood characteristics	Both linear and log-linear	Sulfation, linear form coefficients ranged from $200–$450 per .25 μg/100 cm²/day; log linear coefficients .061–.121 for Toronto; for Hamilton, linear coefficient ranged from $580–882, and the log-linear estimate was .081
Philadelphia Peckham (1970)	1960 Property value census tract median, owner-occupied	Sulfation one-month average by lead candle for Jan. 1969 Particulates arithmetic mean, averaging period not stated, 1969	Property 3 variables Neighborhood 3 variables Income as proxy for neighborhood characteristics	Linear and log-linear	Sulfation, in linear form, the coefficient was $298 per .25 μg/100 cm²/day; the log linear coefficient was .096; particulates significant only in the log form with a coefficient of .116

Table 2. Key features of air pollution–property value studies (continued)

City & author	Base year & dependent variables	Pollutants & measures	Other independent variables	Functional form	Results
Charlestown, S.C. Steele (1972)	1970 *Mean value per room* of owner-occupied housing census enumeration district	*SO₂ and particulates* averaging period not stated	*Neighborhood* 14 variables *Income* as a proxy for other neighborhood characteristics	Linear	Pollution variables had expected signs but were not significant at .05 level
Pittsburgh Spore (1972)	1970 *Property value* census tract mean values of owner-occupied housing and mean values of contract rent for renter-occupied housing	*Sulfation* annual geometric mean and maximum monthly value by lead candle (1967) *Dustfall* annual geometric mean and maximum monthly value (1969)	*Property* 3 variables *Neighborhood* 12 variables *Income* as a determinant of demand	Log-linear	Many alternative specifications with sulfation and dustfall both entering; annual mean or maximum dustfall almost always significant at .05 level; dustfall coefficients (elasticities) generally in .092–.149 range
Los Angeles Harrison-MacDonald (1974)	1970 *Property value* census tract median value of owner-occupied housing	Mean concentration of hydrocarbons, nitrogen oxide, and oxidant index calculated from dispersion model	*Property* 3 variables *Neighborhood* 4 variables	Linear and semilog	Separate equations run for each pollutant; each pollutant significant at .05 level; coefficients substantially different from similar analysis of Boston also reported; a more detailed analysis of the Boston area is presented above
San Mateo County, Calif. Sonstelie and Portney (1977)	1970 *Imputed gross rent* calculated from individual sales data	*Photochemical oxidant* number of days per year reading exceeded .10 ppm.	*Property* 10 variables *Neighborhood* 9 variables	Box-Cox transformation	Pollution variable negative and significant

ᵃ Significant at the 10 percent level.
ᵇ Significant at the 5 percent level.

values in table 2 are computed by taking the mean values for the urban areas for property values and air pollution. They are not representative of the differences to be expected in either low pollution or higher pollution areas.

One of the purposes of the Harrison-Rubinfeld (1978) study was to examine the sensitivity of the air pollution–property value relationship (and benefit estimates derived therefrom) to the specification of the hedonic housing price functions. They experimented with various functional forms, and they re-estimated the relationship after deleting or adding other pollution measures and measures of property and neighborhood characteristics. They concluded that the estimates of the implicit price function for air quality are quite sensitive to the specification of the housing value equation. However given the implicit price function, estimates of the inverse demand function and benefits are relatively stable across alternative specifications.

V. Kerry Smith (1976) took a different approach by regressing median owner-occupied property values in the central city in each of eighty-five SMSAs against annual geometric means for suspended particulates, local property tax rates, local public expenditures, and principal components variables reflecting structural characteristics. A similar regression was run for renter-occupied housing in the central city areas. The underlying model was a variation of the Polinsky-Rubinfeld model with the assumption of perfect mobility among cities. The pollution variable was not significant in the renter equation and negative and almost significant (significant at the 90 percent level) in the owner equation.

It is difficult to summarize the results of the studies reported here, since they cover a number of cities, different time periods, use different data bases, empirical techniques, and model specifications. However, two things stand out. First, the hypothesis that property values are affected by air pollution is generally supported by the evidence. Only three studies, Wieand (1973), Steele (1972), and V. Kerry Smith (1976) report negative results. The first two studies constructed alternatives to the standard property value dependent variable, while Smith investigated differences among SMSAs in central city residential property values. Second, the numerical values reported are generally plausible and broadly consistent both within cities as derived from different studies and between cities. Precise comparisons are not warranted because of differences in the approaches taken. For example, Anderson-Crocker (1971) incorporated both sulfation and particulates in one equation and reported the results of a simultaneous change in both pollution variables, while other authors reported results separately for these two pollutants.

REFERENCES

Anderson, Robert J., and Thomas Crocker. 1971. "Air Pollution and Residential Property Values," *Urban Studies* vol. 8, pp. 171–180.

Berry, Brian, and Robert S. Bednarz. 1975. "A Hedonic Model of Prices and Assessments for Single Family Homes: Does the Assessor Follow the Market or the Market Follow the Assessor?" *Land Economics* vol. 51 (February) pp. 21–40.

Brown, Gardner M., and Henry O. Pollakowski. 1977. "Economic Valuation of Shoreline," *Review of Economics and Statistics* vol. 59 (August) pp. 272–278.

Caves, Richard E., and Ronald W. Jones. 1973. *World Trade and Payments: An Introduction* (Boston, Little Brown).

Crocker, Thomas. 1970. *Urban Air Pollution Damage Functions: Theory and Measurement* (Riverside, Calif., University of California) (NTIS PB 197–668).

David, Elizabeth L. 1968. "Lake Shore Property Values: A Guide to Public Investment in Recreation," *Water Resources Research* vol. 4, no. 4 (August) pp. 697–707.

Dornbusch, David M. 1975. *The Impact of Water Quality Improvements on Residential Property Prices.* Prepared for the National Commission on Water Quality (NTIS, PB 248–805).

Freeman, A. Myrick, III. 1974. "On Estimating Air Pollution Control Benefits from Land Value Studies," *Journal of Environmental Economics and Management* vol. 1, no. 1 (May) pp. 74–83.

————. 1975. "Spatial Equilibrium, the Theory of Rents, and the Measurement of Benefits from Public Programs: A Comment," *Quarterly Journal of Economics* vol. 89, no. 3 (August) pp. 470–473.

Goodwin, Susan A. 1977. "Measuring the Value of Housing Quality—A Note," *Journal of Regional Science* vol. 17, no. 1 (April) pp. 107–115.

Harrison, David, Jr., and Robert MacDonald. 1974. "Willingness to Pay in Boston and Los Angeles for a Reduction in Automobile-Related Pollutants," in National Academy of Sciences, *The Costs and Benefits of Automobile Emission Control,* Volume 4 of *Air Quality and Automobile Emission Control* (Washington, D.C.: NAS).

————, and Daniel L. Rubinfeld. 1978. "Hedonic Housing Prices and the Demand for Clean Air," *Journal of Environmental Economics and Management* vol. 5, no. 2 (March) pp. 81–102.

Heller, H. Robert. 1973. *International Trade: Theory and Empirical Evidence* (Englewood Cliffs, N.J., Prentice-Hall).

Larsen, Ralph I. 1971. *A Mathematical Model for Relating Air Quality Measurements to Air Quality Standards* (Washington, D.C., U.S. Environmental Protection Agency).

Lave, Lester. 1972. "Air Pollution Damage: Some Difficulties in Estimating the Value of Abatement," in Allen V. Kneese and Blair T. Bower, eds., *Environmental Quality Analysis* (Baltimore, Johns Hopkins University Press for Resources for the Future).

Lind, Robert C. 1973. "Spatial Equilibrium, the Theory of Rents, and the Measurement of Benefits from Public Programs," *Quarterly Journal of Economics* vol. 87, no. 2 (May) pp. 188–207.

———. 1975. "Spatial Equilibrium, the Theory of Rents, and the Measurement of Benefits from Public Programs: A Reply," *Quarterly Journal of Economics* vol. 89, no. 3 (August) pp. 474–476.

Meyer, John R., and Robert A. Leone. 1977. "The Urban Disamenity Revisited," in Lowdon Wingo and Alan Evans, eds., *Public Economics and the Quality of Life* (Baltimore, Johns Hopkins University Press for Resources for the Future and the Centre for Environmental Studies).

Nelson, Jon P. 1978a. *Economic Analysis of Transportation Noise Abatement* (Cambridge, Mass., Ballinger).

———. 1978b. "Residential Choice, Hedonic Prices, and the Demand for Urban Air Quality," *Journal of Urban Economics,* vol. 5 (July) pp. 357–369.

Niskanen, William A., and Steve H. Hanke. 1977. "Land Prices Substantially Underestimate the Value of Environmental Quality," *Review of Economics and Statistics* vol. 59 (August) pp. 375–377.

Peckham, Brian. 1970. "Air Pollution and Residential Property Values in Philadelphia." (mimeo).

Polinsky, A. Mitchell, and Daniel L. Rubinfeld. 1977. "Property Values and the Benefits of Environmental Improvements: Theory and Measurement," in Lowdon Wingo and Alan Evans, eds., *Public Economics and the Quality of Life* (Baltimore, Johns Hopkins University Press for Resources for the Future and the Centre for Environmental Studies).

———, and Steven Shavell. 1975. "The Air Pollution and Property Value Debate," *Review of Economics and Statistics* vol. 57, no. 1 (February) pp. 100–104.

———, and ———. 1976. "Amenities and Property Values in a Model of an Urban Area," *Journal of Public Economics* vol. 5, no. 1-2 (January-February) pp. 119–129.

Ridker, Ronald G. 1967. *Economic Costs of Air Pollution: Studies in Measurement* (New York, Praeger).

———, and John A. Henning. 1967. "The Determinants of Residential Property Values with Special Reference to Air Pollution," *Review of Economics and Statistics* vol. 49, no. 2 (May) pp. 246–257.

Rubinfeld, Daniel. 1978. "Market Approaches to the Measurement of the Benefits of Air Pollution Abatement," in Ann F. Friedlaender, ed., *Approaches to Controlling Air Pollution* (Cambridge, Mass., MIT Press).

Schnare, Ann B. 1976. "Racial and Ethnic Price Differentials in an Urban Housing Market," *Urban Studies* vol. 13, pp. 107–120.

———, and Raymond J. Struyk. 1976. "Segmentation in Urban Housing Markets," *Journal of Urban Economics* vol. 3, no. 2 (April) pp. 146–166.

Smith, Barton A. 1978. "Measuring the Value of Urban Amenities," *Journal of Urban Economics* vol. 5 (July) pp. 370–387.

Smith, V. Kerry. 1976. *The Economic Consequences of Air Pollution* (Cambridge, Mass., Ballinger).

Sonstelie, Jon C., and Paul R. Portney. 1977. "Gross Rent and a Reinterpretation of the Tiebout Hypothesis" (mimeo).

Spore, Robert, 1972. *Property Value Differentials as a Measure of the Economic Costs of Air Pollution* (University Park, Pa., Pennsylvania State University, Center for Air Environment Studies).

Steele, William. 1972. "The Effect of Air Pollution on the Value of Single-Family Owner-Occupied Residential Property in Charleston, South Carolina" (Masters thesis Clemson University).

Straszheim, Mahlon. 1974. "Hedonic Estimation of Housing Market Prices: A Further Comment," *Review of Economics and Statistics* vol. 56, no. 3 (August) pp. 404–406.

Strotz, Robert H. 1968. "The Use of Land Value Changes to Measure the Welfare Benefits of Land Improvements," in Joseph E. Haring, ed., *The New Economics of Regulated Industries* (Los Angeles, Occidental College).

Walters, A. A. 1975. *Noise and Prices* (Oxford, Clarendon Press).

Wieand, Kenneth F. 1973. "Air Pollution and Property Values: A Study of the St. Louis Area," *Journal of Regional Science* vol. 13, no. 2 (April) pp. 91–95.

Zeckhauser, Richard, and Anthony Fisher. 1976. "Averting Behavior and External Diseconomics" (mimeo).

Zerbe, Robert, Jr. 1969. *The Economics of Air Pollution: A Cost Benefit Approach* (Toronto, Ontario Department of Public Health).

CHAPTER 7

The Value of Longevity

A major category of potential air pollution control benefits is the improved health and reduced mortality that will result from a decrease in the pollution-related diseases such as bronchitis, emphysema, and cancer. The National Academy of Sciences (1974) has estimated that the potential health benefits of controlling automotive air pollution lie between $0.36 billion and $3.0 billion per year. Another study undertaken for the Environmental Protection Agency estimates the total damages to human health related to air pollution at $5.7 billion per year. This is over one quarter of the total damages in all categories due to air pollution (Heintz, Hershaft, and Horak, 1976). There may also be significant water pollution control benefits associated with the reduced incidence of waterborne bacterial and viral diseases and cancer.[1] Heintz, Hershaft, and Horak (1976) estimate that waterborne diseases cause damages of $0.6 billion per year. This is about 6 percent of their estimate of total water pollution damages.

The estimates of monetary benefits such as those cited here require both the quantification or measurement of the relationship between pollution and health and the valuation of health effects. Although economists using the tools of regression analysis have made major contributions toward the quantification of the health effects of pollution, this task is normally outside the boundaries of the discipline of economics as it is usually defined.[2] A complete discussion of the measurement problem is beyond the scope of this book.[3] My principal concern is

---

[1] For evidence linking cancer mortality to drinking water supplies, see Page, Harris, and Epstein (1976).

[2] See Lave and Seskin (1977) and Page, Harris, and Epstein (1976).

[3] However, for the reader interested in pursuing this aspect of the problem, the following references should prove useful. The most comprehensive research effort is Lave and Seskin (1977). This book contains a discussion of methodological and empirical problems as well as the results of extensive quantitative research. For a discussion of some difficulties in using conventional statistical techniques to identify the effects of environmental insults on mortality, see Neyman (1977), Amdur (1976), and Dinman (1976) who discuss problems in quantifying

with the economic concept of value as applied to improved health and longevity, or as it has sometimes been dramatically and misleadingly termed, "the value of life."

Some people might say that putting a price or monetary value on human life is insensitive, crass, or even inhuman. But this point of view does not give sufficient weight to the fact that individuals in their day-to-day actions and governments in their decisions about social policy do in fact make tradeoffs between changes in the probability of death and other goods which have monetary values. These tradeoffs imply money price tags being attached to human life. The subject of this chapter is the economic theory of value as it is applied to these decisions about tradeoffs by individuals and governments. In the next section we review several approaches to defining and measuring these economic values, and settle upon individuals' willingness to pay for increased longevity or reduced probability of death as the approach most consistent with the economic theory of benefits. Subsequent sections elaborate the theory of individual choice and both theoretical and empirical aspects of the measurement of willingness to pay.

APPROACHES TO VALUING LONGEVITY

A number of approaches to assigning monetary values to the loss of life have been proposed in the literature on the economics of health and safety.[4] These approaches can be broadly categorized as determining values by political processes, according to resource or opportunity costs, or according to individual preferences (willingness to pay). The latter is the only approach which is consistent with the welfare theory framework for benefit estimation. However, the individual preference approach has proven difficult to implement empirically. The other approaches can perhaps be seen as the result of a search for an easily

---

the relationship between some specific air pollutants and health effects. For reports of other efforts to quantify the pollution–health effects relationship or reviews of existing knowledge of health effects due to air pollution, see Liu and Yu (1976), U.S. Environmental Protection Agency (1974), Heintz, Hershaft, and Horak (1976), National Academy of Sciences (1974), National Academy of Sciences (1975), Grad and coauthors (1975), and U.S. House of Representatives (1976). Heintz, Hershaft, and Horak (1976) also contains a review of the literature on the effects of water pollution on bacterial and viral disease rates.

[4] For reviews of the empirical literature see Jones-Lee (1976), chapter 2, and Joksch (1975).

measurable surrogate for the conceptually appropriate measure. Some of the other approaches have been widely used in a variety of settings and are the bases for the benefit estimates cited in the introduction to this chapter. Because of the frequency with which such estimates are encountered, it is important to understand the strengths and limitations of all of these approaches. The purpose of this section is to provide a brief review and evaluation of these approaches.[5]

Willingness to Pay

In keeping with the assumption that individuals' preferences provide a valid basis for making judgments concerning changes in their economic welfare, I propose that increases in longevity or reductions in the probability of death due to accident or illness be valued according to what an individual is willing to pay to achieve them. This presupposes that individuals treat longevity more or less like any other good rather than as a hierarchical value. That is, they do not view longevity as a higher goal to be achieved at any cost. But this seems to be a reasonable assumption. Individuals in a variety of actions act as if their preference functions included probability of death or life expectancy as arguments. They make decisions which involve reductions in life expectancy or increased probability of death in return for increases in income or other goods and services, revealing thereby that they perceive themselves to be better off having made these choices. Individuals who continue to smoke despite the surgeon general's warnings could be viewed as trading off the consumer surplus attached to smoking against the now widely publicized reduction in life expectancy. Some people accept risky or hazardous jobs because they have higher wages. Some people make their trips between cities by airplane rather than by bus because it is quicker and more convenient, even though the chance of accidental death is greater.

As these examples make clear, the question is not how much a specific individual would be willing to pay to avoid his certain death tomorrow. Rather, for the relevant policy questions (for example, health

---

[5] For more extensive discussions of alternative concepts of the value of life or safety, see Schelling (1968), Mishan (1971), Usher (1973), Acton (1975), and Jones-Lee (1976). Raiffa, Schwartz, and Weinstein (1977) present an excellent discussion of concepts and applications in the context of public sector decision-making.

effects of pollution control or safety and accident prevention), it is the fact that the precise identity of the people affected is not known. And the changes in probabilities are small. For this kind of situation, the theory of individual choice under uncertainty provides a useful analytical framework. Individuals do not know which of several alternative states of the world will exist at some specified date in the future. But they must make certain choices affecting their future utility before the future is revealed. Individuals are assumed to assign probabilities to alternative states of the world and to make their choices so as to maximize their expected utility—that is, the weighted average of the utilities associated with alternative states, where the weights are the probabilities assigned to each alternative. One aspect of uncertainty about the future is the date of one's death, or to put it differently, whether one will survive or succumb to some hazard during some time interval. Individuals can affect the probabilities of accidental death during present and future periods by the choices they make. The value of a reduction in risk to an individual is the amount of money he would be willing to pay to achieve it, other things being equal.

Individuals' willingnesses to pay for changes in the probability of death can be translated into a more convenient figure for purposes of policy evaluation, the value of *statistical life* or the value of a *statistical death avoided*. Suppose a group of n similar individuals each has a willingness to pay of w_i $(i = 1, \ldots, n)$ for a policy which would reduce the probability of death by some cause by $-dm_j$ (where m_j is the probability of death by cause j). Since the policy would affect all members of the group equally, it is a form of collective good for the individuals involved. The benefit to the group is found by adding across all individuals. The aggregate willingness to pay is $\sum_i w_i$, and the expected number of deaths avoided is $n\ dm_j$. The aggregate willingness to pay on the part of the group as a whole to avoid the future death of one unidentified member of the group is simply $\sum w_i / n\ dm_j$. This is the statistical value per life. For example, if the average individual willingness to pay for a policy that reduced the mortality of a given group from seven per 100,000 to six per 100,000 were \$5, the value of statistical life would be \$500,000.

As discussed thus far the willingness-to-pay approach focuses on the individualistic or self-centered dimensions of human behavior, that is, an individual's willingness to pay to increase his *own* safety or longevity. But there is nothing in the logic of the willingness-to-pay approach to prevent consideration of the effects of kinship and friendship, that is, an individual's willingness to pay to reduce the probability of death of close relatives and friends.[6] Again, we should make it clear that the question is not the willingness to pay to prevent an imminent or highly probable death (that is, the ransom for the kidnapped child or the search for the lost hiker or boater) but the willingness to pay for a small reduction in the probability of death for the group of which the friend or relative is a part. Needleman (1976) has suggested an ingenious way of examining the relationship between the willingness to pay for one's own safety and the willingness to pay for the safety of friends and relatives. His analysis suggests that the addition of others' willingnesses to pay may add between 25 percent and 100 percent to the person's own value of statistical life depending upon the age, sex, and kinship relationships for the individuals under consideration.[7]

Productivity or Human Capital

The most common approach to valuation of life in the literature is the so-called productivity or human capital technique. It values each life lost at the present value of the expected stream of future earnings for that individual, had that individual's death been avoided. The benefit of preventing the death of individual i (B_i) in any one year can be expressed as

$$B_i = \sum_{t=1}^{T} q_t^* E_t / (1 + i)^t \tag{1}$$

where q_t^* = probability of individual surviving through year t

E_t = earnings of individual in year t

i = discount rate

This is a form of resource or opportunity cost approach to assigning values. It is based on the assumption that earnings reflect the indi-

---

[6] See Mishan (1971) for a further discussion of the external effects of the risk of death.

[7] Needleman (1976) observed that individuals do sometimes increase their own risk of death in order to decrease the risk of that of a close relative or family member. One manifestation of this is the willingness to donate organs such as kidneys for transplant operations. Needleman analyzed data on kidney donors to derive a ratio of concern for relatives' risk to own risk. This gave the results cited in the text.

Table 3. Present value of lifetime earnings, discounted at 6 percent, by age, sex, and race, 1972
(dollars)

Years of age	Men			Women		
	Total	White	Other	Total	White	Other
Under 1	48,720	51,011	31,232	30,976	31,557	27,069
1–4	55,433	57,962	35,768	35,148	35,765	30,890
5–9	74,418	77,785	48,082	47,141	47,960	41,459
10–14	99,742	104,263	64,458	63,172	64,267	55,573
15–19	129,394	135,142	83,955	80,588	82,016	70,692
20–24	156,640	163,469	101,006	91,114	92,834	79,123
25–29	170,988	178,483	107,823	90,439	92,237	77,800
30–34	170,788	178,519	104,179	84,513	86,378	71,237
35–39	161,072	168,609	94,492	77,513	79,444	63,204
40–44	144,209	150,904	82,760	69,215	71,135	54,158
45–49	121,856	127,250	69,586	59,187	61,074	43,578
50–54	96,158	100,033	55,968	47,115	48,873	31,897
55–59	67,763	70,128	41,785	33,825	35,317	20,349
60–64	38,588	39,830	24,964	21,406	22,436	11,702
65–69	18,107	18,631	12,656	11,890	12,436	6,467
70–74	9,886	10,184	6,911	6,598	6,861	3,685
75–79	5,434	5,675	3,168	3,396	3,526	1,956
80–84	3,209	3,354	1,839	1,507	1,562	912
85 & over	519	543	291	194	200	128

Source: Cooper and Rice (1976), p. 28.

vidual's marginal productivity, that is, the individual's contribution to total economic output. With the death of the individual, that output is lost.

The benefits of saving a life as calculated by (1) depend upon the age, sex, race, and other characteristics of the individuals involved. Some typical figures are presented in table 3. Women have lower discounted lifetime earnings than men on average. People in the 25–29 year age bracket are "worth more" than children; while individuals over 65 have much lower values as measured by discounted earnings.

The first point to make is that the productivity measure of benefits has no necessary relationship to individual willingness to pay. The productivity approach allows no role for the probabilistic nature of death and death avoidance in the health and safety areas or for differing individual attitudes or preferences toward risk and risk avoidance. While by definition an individual could pay no more than the present value of his earnings stream to avoid certain death, his statistical value of life based on willingness to pay for small probability changes could be several times his discounted expected earnings stream.[8] Thus the productivity or human capital approach cannot be accepted for benefit measurement on the grounds that it is a useful approximation to willingness to pay. Rather it is derived from an alternative value judgment, namely that an individual is worth what he or she does, that is, that output is a measure of worth. Putting the matter in this way helps to bring out some of the important unresolved issues about both the application of and validity of this approach. First, should an individual's productivity be measured *net* or inclusive of his own consumption? Netting out own consumption leaves a measure of the individual's worth as a producing asset to the rest of society. This measure is the antithesis of the individualistic premise of conventional welfare economics. Some might argue that productivity should be measured inclusive of own consumption on the grounds that an individual's consumption is at least an approximate measure of the utility he derives from his own life. But we have argued that there is no necessary relationship between an individual's own statistical value of life and his earnings or consumption. And if one wishes to take into account the individual's utility, it seems conceptually superior to begin with a measure which is based explicitly on that value judgment.

The second question concerns the role of nonmarket production in the measure of productivity and therefore value. The omission of nonmarket productivity is particularly serious and troublesome in the case of housewives and nonworking parents. Some studies have attempted to correct for this omission by imputing earnings equal to the wages of domestic servants. Others have argued that the average earnings of employed females provides a measure of the opportunity cost of working at home for women. If women are rational, the value of home production must be equal to or greater than this opportunity cost. But even these adjustments do not capture the nonmarket productivity of other members of the household.[9]

Another question concerns the functioning of the markets for labor and for human capital formation. These markets are characterized by

---

[8] Conley (1976) has developed a model of individual choice for lifetime bundles of consumption and risk. One of the major theoretical findings is that the statistical value of life is greater than discounted expected earnings. This theoretical result tends to be confirmed by available empirical estimates of the value of statistical life. See below.

[9] For further discussion and some efforts to remedy these shortcomings, see Acton (1975, pp. 25–28).

barriers to mobility, imperfect information, discrimination, imperfections due to monopsony and monopoly (union) market power, and the like, and, of course, involuntary unemployment. These problems become more serious as one deals with smaller subsets of the total population, since these forces may have very serious impacts on *relative* earnings of narrowly defined segments of the labor force.

Finally, the approach has the ethically troublesome implication of assigning no value to the truly nonproductive members of the population who are totally disabled by illness or handicap.

Medical and Burial Costs

If a death is preceded by illness, the medical care provided imposes costs on society as a whole. And premature death results in the premature imposition of burial costs (Ridker, 1967).[10] The role of medical costs in the assessment of the value of longevity depends among other things on the underlying value judgment on which these measures are based. If a productivity measure is being used, then it is conceptually consistent to add medical costs to measure the total loss to society from illness and death. On the other hand, if the individualistic value judgment is accepted, and all individuals must themselves bear the medical costs of illness, individuals' willingness to pay to reduce the probability of illness and death will already include the expected medical costs as well as the disutility of illness. In this case whether medical costs should be estimated separately and added to measures of individual willingness to pay depends on the social organization of the provision of medical care.

Revealed Political Preference

Governments also regularly make decisions that involve tradeoffs between the health and safety of their citizens and other goods and services with economic value. If it could be assumed that governments

---

[10] Mishan (1971) dismisses the premature burial cost component with the wry observation that "if the unfortunate person died at a very early age, some useful savings might be effected from the lower cost of a smaller coffin" (p. 688). In any event, by Ridker's calculations, these represent a miniscule component of the total cost of air pollution-induced illness.

act purposefully, rationally, and consistently, then the observed willingness to pay for increased longevity could be interpreted as a politically determined value of statistical life. The main problems with using data derived from the political process as the basis for assigning values are the strong assumption concerning the rationality and consistency of the political process, and the difficulty that even rational decisionmakers would have making consistent decisions in the face of substantial information gaps concerning the effects of various public policies on mortality. One effort to determine the implicit values of life from observations on political decisions revealed values ranging from a few thousand dollars for highway safety to over a million dollars for the protection of military pilots.[11]

Explicit Political Values

Occasionally government agencies are willing to make explicit statements of the value of life for purposes of regulatory decisionmaking or policy evaluation. Can these be taken as expressions of political will to be used in future policy analysis and decisions? I will not attempt to provide an answer to this question. But there are two relevant observations. First, there has not yet been any centralized effort to coordinate decisions about values assigned to life by different agencies. Thus the possibility of inconsistency in values used by different agencies remains. Second, it would be useful to examine the information used and the justifications offered by decisionmakers for the particular values chosen. One's willingness to accept a politically determined value probably depends in part on one's understanding of the data base used and the process by which the figure was arrived at.

Summary of the Approaches

In evaluating the various approaches to assigning values to statistical lives, I conclude that a measure based on individuals' willingness to pay for changes in the probability of death is consistent with the basic theory of measuring changes in welfare. But it must be recalled that

---

[11] See the discussions of Carlson's work in Acton (1975, p. 14) and Conley (1976, p. 54). See also Usher (1973, table 1, p. 210).

acceptance of a willingness-to-pay measure of value implies acceptance of the existing distribution of income (see chapter 3). Granted this assumption, willingness to pay is conceptually superior to the other approaches reviewed here. But in utilizing willingness-to-pay measures it would be appropriate to include external effects, that is the willingness to pay of friends and relatives, and that component of medical costs not borne by the individual at risk. Political measures of value are unreliable because they seem to lack consistency. And they are typically based on acceptance of or adaptations of estimates generated by one of the other approaches. The productivity or human capital approach has serious limitations either as an approximation of willingness to pay or as a conceptually distinct alternative basis for deriving values.

We are left with the question of how to proceed with the task of estimating willingness to pay for decreased mortality. We turn now to some models of individual choice that will provide some insight into empirical applications. These models will also provide a basis for interpreting and evaluating existing empirical estimates of the value of statistical life.

CHOICE AND WILLINGNESS TO PAY

There are two aspects of the choice problem that are of interest in this analysis: uncertainty and time. The uncertainty concerns the unknown timing of one's death and the effects of occupational and consumption activity choices on the probabilities of surviving to any given date. The time aspect concerns the effects of choices made at any given time on the probabilities and utilities associated with future periods. This is of particular relevance for environmental problems since many of the most important environmental policy issues are characterized by a substantial interval between exposure and the perceived effects on health. Most models of intertemporal choice have focused on identifying the optimal consumption stream given an income stream and opportunities for borrowing and lending. Our concern here is with choices made in the present that affect the probabilities of survival at future dates. The problem is to identify the marginal willingness to pay now for increases in the probabilities of survival at some future period.

I begin with a simple one-period choice model to avoid the complications of intertemporal choice, identify the marginal willingness to pay for increases in survival probability, and then extend the model to the intertemporal case to see whether estimates of the value of statistical life based on intratemporal models can be applied to the intertemporal case. I also examine the question of consistent choice over time.

Assume that an individual derives utility from the consumption of a composite or numeraire good, X. The initial endowment of X and the probability of surviving to enjoy its consumption, q, are both given to the individual. Let X^0 and q^0 represent the initial endowment. The element of choice arises if the individual has the opportunity to rearrange his consumption and survival position through exchange, for example by giving up some X in order to improve his chances of surviving to enjoy the remainder. Let P_q represent the price at which consumption can be exchanged for enhanced survival probability, or vice versa. The basic behavioral assumption is that individuals make choices so as to maximize their *expected* utility. In other words

maximize $EU = qU(X)$

subject to $P_x X^0 + P_q q^0 - P_x X - P_q q = 0$

where EU is expected utility, and the utility associated with nonsurvival is assumed to be zero.[12] First order conditions for a maximum of expected utility are

$$\frac{U(X)}{q \, \partial U / \partial X} = \frac{P_q}{P_x} \tag{2}$$

or

$$P_q = P_x \frac{U(X)}{q \, \partial U / \partial X} \tag{3}$$

The latter expression requires that the individual equate his marginal willingness to pay for enhanced survival (the right-hand side of the expression) with the given price of enhanced survival.

The utility-maximizing individual may choose either to forego consumption in order to enhance his survival probability or to take on increasing risk (lower q) in order to enhance consumption opportunities. The actual choices depend on the initial endowment, X^0 and q^0,

---

[12] Comprehensive models encompassing bequest motivation (utility derived from unconsumed X remaining at death) and insurance behavior can be developed. For examples, see Jones-Lee (1976), Conley (1976), Weinstein, Shepard, and Pliskin (1976), and Thaler and Rosen (1976).

the price of q relative to the price of X, and the individual's preferences. Whatever the final outcome, equation (3) allows us to infer the individual's marginal willingness to pay for enhanced survival.

The expenditure function can be written as

$$E = E(P_x, P_q, U^0)$$

The function

$$\frac{\partial E(P_x, P_q, U^0)}{\partial P_q}$$

gives the compensated demand curve for q.

If there are no opportunities for trading in q, that is, the individual must accept q^0, the expenditure function becomes

$$E = E(P_x, q^0, U^0)$$

and its derivative

$$\frac{\partial E(P_x, q^0, U^0)}{\partial q} = -P_x MRS_{qx} = -P_x \frac{U(X)}{q\, \partial U/\partial X} \tag{4}$$

defines the marginal willingness to pay and the inverse demand function for changes in q. In the absence of an explicit market for q, estimates of the benefits of enhanced survival probabilities require some way of inferring (4) indirectly from market data or more directly from questionnaires and bidding games.

One implication of equation (4) is that if individuals are not free to adjust their survival probabilities in the market, their marginal willingness to pay for enhanced survival will not be independent of their initial survival situation. Other things equal, the marginal willingness to pay will be higher, the lower the initial survival probability.[13] In addition, diminishing marginal utility of X implies a higher marginal willingness to pay for q with higher initial endowments of X, other things equal. Extension of the basic model to include bequest motivations, insurance, and the existence of both wage and property income leads to more interesting results.[14]

The next step in our analysis is to generalize the single-period model to encompass three types of causes of death. The first type is

---

[13] For more rigorous proofs of this proposition, see Jones-Lee (1976), Weinstein, Shepard, and Pliskin (1976), and Thaler and Rosen (1976).

[14] See, for example, Jones-Lee (1976) and Thaler and Rosen (1976).

exogenous to the individual. This includes purely random accidents, diseases related to aging, and those related to exposure to environmental pollutants. The probabilities of death by these causes are beyond the control of any individual. However some of these probabilities can be influenced by public policy, hence our interest in identifying and measuring individuals' willingness to pay to reduce these probabilities. The second type is death related to consumption activities, for example, skydiving, amateur sports car racing, or vacation travel by airplane or automobile. Some consumption activities are more risky than others. I assume that individuals are not risk preferers, but rather view the risk as part of the cost associated with undertaking that consumption activity. Individuals can reduce the probabilities of death by these causes by reducing their consumption of these activities. The third type of cause of death might be called occupational. Assume that all types of jobs are alike in every respect except the risk of accidental death. The wage premiums offered for more risky jobs provide individuals with an opportunity for trading-off income or consumption with safety.

Specifically, I assume that individuals maximize their expected utility by choosing a level of job risk, level of consumption of a composite good, and level of consumption of risky goods subject to the constraints provided by exogenous risks, the schedule of risk premiums on wages, and prices of all consumption activities. Specifically

maximize $EU = q\, U(X, Y)$

subject to $S(m_h) - P_x X - \sum_j P_{y_j} Y_j = 0$

where

$Y_j \equiv$ risky consumption activity $j\,(j = k + 1, \ldots, n)$[15]

$m_i \equiv$ probability of death during period from the ith exogenous cause $(i = 1, \ldots, k)$

$m_j \equiv$ probability of death during period from consumption activity $Y_j(j = k + 1, \ldots, n)$

$= m_j(Y_j)$, with $m_j(0) = 0$; $\partial m_j / \partial Y_j > 0$

$m_h \equiv$ probability of job-related death during period

$S(m_h) \equiv$ wage premiums schedule, $\partial S / \partial m_h > 0$

$$q = 1 - \sum_{i=1}^{k} m_i - \sum_{j=k+1}^{n} m_j - m_h$$

$P_{y_j} \equiv$ price of the jth risky consumption activity

[15] The model could easily be extended to include consumption activities that reduced risk of death, for example health foods and jogging.

The most interesting way of expressing the relevant first order conditions for a maximum is in terms of marginal rates of substitution[16]

$$\partial S/\partial m_h = -P_x MRS_{m_h x}$$
$$= P_x \frac{U(X,Y)}{q\ \partial U/\partial X} \tag{5}$$

and

$$P_{yj} = P_x \frac{q\ \partial U/\partial Y_j - \partial m_j/\partial Y_j\ U(X,Y)}{q\ \partial U/\partial X}$$
$$= P_x \frac{\partial U/\partial Y_j - \frac{1}{q}\ \partial m_j/\partial Y_j\ U(X,Y)}{\partial U/\partial Y} \tag{6}$$

The right-hand side of equation (5) is an expression for the marginal willingness to pay to reduce the risk associated with employment m_h. The rational individual chooses that level of job risk which equates his marginal willingness to pay for reduced risk with the marginal wage premiums, or, with the appropriate sign changes, the marginal implicit price of safety. If the wage function is known, $\partial S/\partial m_h$ for each individual can be calculated and taken as an observation of that individual's marginal willingness to pay for safety. This is a straightforward application of the hedonic price technique. This is the basis of the empirical work by Thaler and Rosen (1976), to be discussed in a later section.

One interesting implication of equation (5) is that the marginal willingness to pay for job safety increases, *ceteris paribus,* with an increase in *any* of the components of risk. For example, as individuals grow older, the exogeneous probabilities of dying, m_i, increase, decreasing the survival probability q. Thus one would expect older people to be more conservative about controllable risk such as occupational risk.

Another conclusion is that once the marginal willingness to pay for increased job safety has been measured, the marginal willingness to pay for reductions in the exogenous probabilities of death is also known.

---

[16] The minus sign in (5) follows from the convention of defining the marginal rate of substitution between two *goods* as a positive number, that is

$$MRS_{yx} = \frac{-dx}{dy}.$$ Thus $MRS_{m_h x}$ is negative.

This is because dm_i and dm_h are perfect substitutes in the expected utility function.[17] At least this is true assuming the individual has no preferences about the manner of his death. Thus if an individual's willingness to pay to reduce controllable risks can be observed, it can be used as the basis for measuring the marginal benefits for controlling exogenous risks.

Turning to equation (6), the marginal rate of substitution between Y_j and X is like the conventional ratio of marginal utilities, except that the marginal utility of Y_j is reduced by a term reflecting the proportional reduction in survival probabilities which is associated with the consumption of the marginal unit of Y_j. Since the prices of X and Y_j are known, the equilibrium marginal rate of substitution can be inferred from market data. However, since the utility of consuming Y_j and the disutility of the associated risk are jointly produced, it is not possible to estimate the marginal willingness to pay for risk reduction from these data. However, if Y_j represented a class of differentiated products, and if m_j were not correlated with the other attributes of Y_j, it would be possible to employ the hedonic price technique to measure the marginal implicit price of risk avoidance.

We turn now to the development of a simple multi-period model which allows us to investigate how the willingness to pay now for a reduction in the probability of death is influenced by the time period to which the probability applies. The preceding model was relevant to questions such as transportation and occupational safety in which one's actions today affect the probabilities of dying today. Many of the important environmental and occupational health questions involve actions taken today whose effects on the probability of dying are realized only at some time, perhaps fifty years, in the future. How much would an individual be willing to pay now to control current pollution when the effects of improved health may be realized only twenty to fifty years in the future? To focus on the intertemporal aspect of the problem, we assume only one cause of death, and one consumption activity.

We assume that individuals maximize the present value of expected utility, or

$$EU = \sum_{t=1}^{T} q_t^* D^t U(X_t) \tag{7}$$

---

[17] This can be seen by taking the total differential of the expected utility function, setting it equal to zero, and rearranging terms.

where $D = 1/(1 + d)$

$d \equiv$ subjective rate of discount or own time preference

$q_t^* \equiv$ probability of surviving from period one through period t, or the probability of living for at least t years from now (year one)

$$q_t^* = \prod_{i=1}^{t} q_i$$

$$= \prod_{i=1}^{t} (1 - m_i^*)$$

The term m_i^* is a *conditional* probability of dying during year i, that is, the probability of dying in year i, given that the individual has survived to the beginning of year i. Similarly, q_i is the probability of surviving the year given being alive at the beginning of the year.

The form of the intertemporal utility function deserves a brief comment. The assumption of maximizing *discounted* utilities does not necessarily impose any restrictions on the nature of individuals' preferences regarding present versus future consumption. The subjective rate of discount d could be positive, negative, or zero. A variety of types of preferences and behavior can be encompassed in this model, depending on the value of d.[18]

We now ask the following question. Suppose that the marginal rate of substitution between present mortality reduction and present consumption is known, for example, from a study of the demand for occupational safety. Can this marginal rate of substitution be used to estimate the demand for reductions in future mortality which might be obtained through an environmental or occupational health program? From equation (7) the marginal rate of substitution between present consumption and present mortality reduction is as follows

$$MRS_{q_1 x_1} = \frac{U(X_1) + \sum_{t=2}^{T} \frac{q_t^*}{q_1} D^{t-1} U(X_t)}{q_1 \, \partial U / \partial X_1} \tag{8}$$

[18] The marginal rate of substitution between present and future consumption is

$$MRS_{X_j X_i} = D^{(j-i)} \frac{\partial U / \partial X_j}{\partial U / \partial X_i}$$

Since in equilibrium the *MRS* is equated with the market discount factor, $1/(1+r)^{j-i}$, borrowing and lending behavior depends on market interest rates, present and future income levels, and the rate at which the marginal utility of income is diminishing, as well as time preference.

The marginal rate of substitution between a mortality reduction in future period t' and present consumption is

$$MRS_{q_{t'}x_1} = \frac{\sum_{t=t'}^{T} \frac{q_t^*}{q_{t'}} D^{t-1}U(X_t)}{q_1\, \partial U/\partial X_1} \tag{9}$$

The two marginal rates of substitution may differ for three reasons. One reason for (8) to be greater is that it includes a term for first period utility, $U(X_1)$. Also the more distant period t' is from the present, the smaller is the stream of future periods being summed in (9). However (9) could be greater than (8) if q_t' is sufficiently smaller than q_1.

In conclusion, marginal rates of substitution estimated from one type of probability choice problem, for example, the single period problem, cannot be used as predictors of the marginal rates of substitution for other types of probability choice problems with different intertemporal dimensions. The implications of this conclusion will become clearer when we turn to the discussion of empirical efforts to estimate the value of a statistical life.

The models outlined in this section assume rational behavior and stability of preferences. These may be reasonable assumptions for the single-period choice model, provided that individuals are given adequate information on risks and that they have had some training in the interpretation and analysis of probability information. But the assumptions are more troublesome in the multi-period case.

In these models individuals can be viewed as playing games with nature. In the single-period game, individuals are asked how much compensation is required in order to induce them to place themselves immediately at risk where the outcome will be known after a short interval of time. Choices are made, the game is carried out, and the outcomes are made known in fairly short order. One crude test of consistency and stability of preferences is whether individuals who have won the game, that is who have survived, choose to play it again in the next period. If a substantial proportion of the players choose to play the game again (always assuming adequate information), this implies that they did not regret their earlier decision, the preferences which led them to make that earlier choice have not changed significantly in the intervening time period, or both. The extent of repetitive behavior is a test of the assumptions of rationality and stability of preferences.

In the multi-period environmental health game, this test of rationality is not available. In this game, individuals are asked how much compensation they require to induce them to swallow a "time bomb." They are told the probability that the bomb will go off. The probability is small. They know also that if the bomb does go off, the date is itself a random variable. But they know that the bomb will not go off until some time interval, say twenty years, has elapsed. Finally, they know that they might die before the bomb goes off from any number of other causes that are quite independent of the game.

It is reasonable to expect that some people would agree to play this game at some positive compensation. But there is a sense in which the choice might be considered not rational, that is, one which he or she later regrets having made. In fact it is possible that some people, having survived the twenty-year waiting period, would be willing to pay more than the original compensation plus interest in order to cancel the game, that is to have the time bomb removed.

Consider a simple three-period extension of the above model in which an individual is paid a bribe to accept a marginal decrease in q_3. By solving the utility maximization problem as of the beginning of period one, we can find the minimum necessary bribe

$$P_x MRS_{q_3 x_1} = P_x \frac{q_2 D^2 \, U(X_3)}{\partial U / \partial X_1} \tag{10}$$

The marginal rate of substitution between period-two consumption and period-three probability of death can also be determined in the same way. The marginal willingness to pay in period two to reduce the period-three probability of death is

$$P_x MRS_{q_3 x_2} = P_x \frac{D \, U(X_3)}{\partial U / \partial X_2} \tag{11}$$

Is (10), plus interest at the market rate, greater or less than (11)?

If (11) is greater than (10) plus interest at the rate r, then the individual could be interpreted as experiencing a reversal in his preference ordering. In other words he would now wish to reverse a transaction previously entered into, even though there has been no change in the parameters governing choice except the passage of time.

Combining (10) with the appropriate interest term and (11) and cancelling terms gives

$$\frac{1+r}{1+d} q_2 \overset{?}{\underset{<}{>}} \frac{\partial U / \partial X_1}{\partial U / \partial X_2} \tag{12}$$

If the left-hand side of (13) is less, the reversal exists. This possibility cannot be ruled out on a priori grounds. The reversal would be more likely, the higher the own rate of time preference, the higher period-two consumption relative to period one, and the lower the probability of surviving from period two through period three.[19]

This potential for inconsistent valuation of reduced risk of death raises at least two troublesome questions concerning the use of the willingness-to-pay approach to measure the benefits of life-enhancing public policies. The first question is which value should be used, that given by (10), or the present value of (11)?[20] If resources must be committed today to control the emissions of carcinogens with long latency periods, should the benefits be calculated according to today's willingness to pay to reduce future risk—or the future willingness to pay properly discounted? Using today's values leaves the possibility of future regret regarding the resource commitments made. Using future values means that policies will appear optimal as their outcomes are realized even though they give the appearance of being nonoptimal today.

The second question concerns the scope for decentralized decision-making, or consumer sovereignty in the realm of long-run safety and health. Smith (1976) and Thaler and Rosen (1976), for example, have made the argument that with much improved information on occupational risks, labor market mobility, and employer liability, a properly functioning market system could provide the optimal amount of occupational safety without detailed regulation by the government. Workers would only accept jobs with higher risks of accident if wage premiums equalled or exceeded their marginal rate of substitution between present consumption and present survival probability. Employers would increase job safety as long as the marginal benefits in the form of reduced risk premiums in wages were greater than the marginal costs of safety programs.

One can criticize this argument on grounds that lack of information, difficulties that untrained people have in interpreting probability

---

[19] Of course the right-hand side of (12) could be less, meaning the individual would purchase more future risk reduction than he or she would later deem optimal. Strotz (1956) identified a similar kind of potential inconsistency or myopia with respect to optimal consumption plans over time.

[20] Actually, for policies affecting the conditional probability of surviving year t, there are t possible values, one from the perspective of each year from 1 to t.

data (especially low probabilities), and limits on labor mobility all impede the functioning of the market, even for current risks. But the criticism of the proposed market solution offered here is more fundamental. Many of the most serious occupational health problems involve long latency periods between the employment-related exposures and the possible consequences. As (12) shows, even with perfect information, workers might make choices which appeared optimal today but which would be regretted in the future. Is this their right? Or should there be some form of intervention to correct for market failue due to myopia?

PROBABILITY VECTORS VERSUS LIFE EXPECTANCY

In the preceding model of choice, the individual's state has been described by a vector of probabilities. A change in state involves a change in one or more of the elements of this vector. In the simplest cases analyzed here, only one element of the probability vector was changed. This simple description of change is probably realistic for questions of occupational safety and risks associated with certain kinds of consumption activities. But environmental and occupational health questions are likely to involve simultaneous changes in a number of probabilities over future years. A full analysis of such policy questions in terms of the probability model would be cumbersome at best. There may be useful economies made in the analysis by focusing on changes in some summary statistic.

The obvious candidate is life expectancy. The probability vector can be viewed as being derived from the probability density function. The demographic concept of life expectancy is the mean of that function.[21] If the changes in the vector of probabilities are known, the change in life expectancy can be computed. Life expectancy has the further advantage that it is a fairly simple concept, and one can envisage utilizing life expectancy information when confronted with the necessity to make choices about the risk of death.

---

[21] Probabilities of death (mortality rates) and life expectancy are elements of the "life table," a description of the mortality experience of population often utilized by demographers. For further discussion, see one of the standard references on technical demography, for example Barclay (1958). See also Jones-Lee (1976, pp. 121–124).

The major disadvantage of life expectancy as a measure of risk is that it loses information on the shape of the probability vector. Specifically, it would be possible to have two probability vectors with the same mean or life expectancy but with different expected utilities because of differences in the variance or higher order moments of the probability density function. If the probability density function is known, life expectancy can be computed. But the converse is not true. Knowledge of life expectancy is not sufficient to generate the probability density function. The question of which measure is to be preferred for empirical work appears to be one of convenience and analytical tractability. Most of the empirical work to date has focused on changes in single-period probabilities. As more research effort is focused on longer term problems, it would be useful to explore the possibility of using life expectancy as a summary measure.

EMPIRICAL ESTIMATES OF WILLINGNESS TO PAY

Conceptually there are two approaches to the empirical measurement of willingness to pay. One is to observe market transactions where people actually purchase or sell changes in their own risk level. For example, if wage differentials among occupations are related to differences in occupational risk levels, these differences may be interpreted as reflecting at the margin individuals' tradeoffs between risk or safety and money. The other approach is to ask individuals a series of questions about hypothetical situations involving tradeoffs between risk and money. If the questions are carefully designed, and if individuals are truly capable of predicting how they would act if placed in these hypothetical situations, then their answers might reveal the money values they attach to reductions in risk. The purpose of this section is to provide a critical review and evaluation of studies that have used these approaches and to compare their results with other values sometimes used in policy evaluation, for example those based on productivity, or explicit value judgments.

The hedonic price approach is potentially very fruitful not only in providing estimates of the marginal willingness to pay for individuals but also, if the identification problems associated with the supply of safety can be resolved, providing estimates of the underlying inverse demand functions for safety.[22] The hedonic price approach could be applied not only to wage rate data but also price data for differentiated consumer goods where riskiness in use is one of the differentiated characteristics. Empirical applications to date have been limited to the wage rate data.

There are two significant empirical problems that must be overcome in applying the technique. The first is to obtain accident or safety data in sufficient detail to be able accurately to measure the risk associated with specific jobs. The U.S. Bureau of Labor Statistics (BLS) reports accident data only by industry. Within any industry, there is likely to be substantial variation in accident rates for different occupational categories within the industry, and even within broadly defined occupations. Thus the reported data will tend to obscure the actual differences among jobs which tend to generate wage differentials. The second problem is to control adequately for other job and worker characteristics that can influence wage rate differentials.

There are several pitfalls in the interpretation of the results of applying the hedonic approach to wage rate data. First, the value of statistical life derived from the data is strictly speaking only applicable to *marginal* changes in the probability of death. Second, willingness-to-pay estimates are only applicable over the range of mortality probabilities which generated the data. In other words, it is risky to extrapolate the results beyond the range of the data. If the approach is applied to wage data from a fairly risky group of occupations, the willingness-to-pay estimates must be interpreted as applying only to marginal reductions in the probability of death within that range and *for only those workers who chose these risky occupations.* They can be generalized to the population as a whole only if all individuals have identical utility functions. But in general, the behavior of this group toward risk is likely to be different from the behavior or preferences of the population as a whole. In fact this group, by its choice of the risky jobs, *ceteris paribus,* has revealed itself to be less risk averse than the population as a whole.

Third, if the wage function is nonlinear in the probability of death, the marginal willingnesses to pay of different individuals will be different. And they must be separately measured and added to get an accurate measure of aggregate willingness to pay for a statistical life.

---

[22] For a theoretical elaboration of the supply side of the market for safety, see Thaler and Rosen (1976).

These problems are similar to those discussed in the chapter on property values.[23]

Fourth, wage premiums are likely to reflect both the higher risk of death, and the higher risk of nonfatal accidents. If the wage rate equation is not controlled for the risk of a nonfatal accident, and if nonfatal and fatal accidents are correlated, the estimate of the willingness to pay for a statistical life would be biased.[24]

Finally, the wage rate differential model is probably more consistent with the single-period model of choice outlined above than the long-term, multi-period model. Extrapolation of these results to long-term environmental and occupational health problems may not be valid. This is particularly true where the risk data measure fatal job-related accidents. This is the case with Smith's study described below. Thaler and Rosen's (1976) data measured excess mortality from all causes. Thus the Thaler-Rosen estimates may have picked up some of the effect of long-term job-related health problems.

Thaler and Rosen used data from the Survey of Economic Opportunity for 1967 to identify industry and occupation of a sample of workers, along with their earnings and other socioeconomic characteristics. They used data provided by an insurance industry organization as measures of the occupational risk associated with certain of the industry-occupation categories. As indicated above, occupational risk was measured by excess mortality from all causes. A number of other variables were used to control for the effect of age, education, race, and the like, on wage rates within the sample. Regressions were run in both linear and semi-log linear form. There was no statistical basis for choosing one functional form as superior to the other.

Each functional form was estimated in two alternative specifications with different sets of socioeconomic control variables. The linear functional form imposes a constant marginal willingness to pay on all members of the sample. When this estimate is used to calculate the aggregate value of a statistical life, the results are $176,000 and $260,000 for the two alternative specifications. With the semi-log form, the marginal willingness to pay varies across the sample. Thaler and Rosen evaluated the marginal willingness to pay at the sample mean.

---

[23] See chapter 6.

[24] In a study to be discussed in more detail below, Smith (1976) did control for temporary and permanent disabilities associated with nonfatal accidents. These variables were not significant in his regressions. However he did not discuss possible problems of multicollinearity among risk variables.

The results were an aggregate value of statistical life of $136,000, or $189,000 for the two specifications. They conclude that their best estimate of statistical life is $200,000 plus or minus $60,000.

These figures are in sharp contrast to results obtained by Smith (1976) with the same empirical technique, the same wages and earnings data, but different risk data. Smith also used the 1967 Survey of Economic Opportunity as a source for earnings and worker characteristics. He used the Bureau of Labor Statistics accident data as recorded by industry. But the estimated value of statistical life, $2.6 million, was an order of magnitude higher than Thaler and Rosen's estimate. Replications of the regression with 1973 earnings and wage data and 1970 accident data from the same sources yielded an estimated value of statistical life of $1.5 million. Smith takes note of the limitations in using accident data classified only by industry. He argues that this would result in an "errors-in-variables" problem which would normally bias the least squares estimator downward (1976, p. 91).

In sum, the disparity in the estimates suggests that the results of applying the hedonic technique are sensitive to the specification of the empirical model, the other variables included to explain wage rates, and the source of data for occupational risk. Until research produces estimates that are more robust with respect to model specification and data source, these estimates should not be given great weight in policy evaluation.

There are similar striking differences in the results of two efforts to carry out the willingness-to-pay approach to estimating the values of statistical life. Acton (1973) obtained thirty-six responses from a stratified random sample of residents in the Boston area. The questionnaire contained a number of questions about attitudes and value judgments about efforts to save lives in emergency situations. The questions of greatest interest concerned the individual's own willingness to pay for a program of emergency coronary care which would reduce his probability of death by heart attack. Two different forms of the question implied values for statistical life of $28,000 and $43,000.[25] Jones-Lee (1976) asked a similarly small sample of individuals several questions about their willingness to accept higher (or lower) airplane fares to travel on lines with lower (or higher) probabilities of experi-

_____

[25] In a later study Acton (1975) compared these values with those derived from the productivity or human capital approach. The willingness-to-pay measures were from 25–50 percent higher than the productivity measures, depending on the particular assumptions used. See Acton (1975, pp. 50–51).

encing a fatal crash. The value of statistical life implied by respondents was about £3 million or $5 million at then prevailing exchange rates.

Given our reservations about the questionnaire approach to estimating willingness to pay, it is perhaps not surprising that the range of estimates is even higher (two orders of magnitude) for this approach than for the hedonic approach based on observations of actual behavior.

It is interesting to compare the empirical willingness-to-pay measures with figures derived from applications of the productivity approach and explicit statements of values used by government agencies. The earliest official use of an explicit value of life for purposes of policy analysis of which I am aware appeared in the so-called RECAT report (Office of Science and Technology, 1972). In this report, a value of life of $140,000 was used to estimate the costs of fatalities associated with automobile accidents. The figure was justified as representing "the average foregone participation in the personal income of the nation." Per capita personal income in 1970 was computed. The average automobile fatality was estimated to have reduced the expected life span of its victim by about 37 years. The product of per capita income and lost years was $140,000. Thus although the figure is rooted in the income and productivity experience of the population, this value is imputed to individuals whether or not they were in the labor market or active producers. Also in contrast to the human capital approach, per capita income was not discounted.

A second official use of a value of life was in a report by the National Academy of Sciences (1974). The value of improved health to be expected from controlling automotive air pollution was valued at $200,000 per death avoided. There is virtually no discussion of the basis for choosing this figure, except for references to the RECAT report and Thaler and Rosen (1976).

The Nuclear Regulatory Commission has officially established a value of $1,000 per man-rem of total body exposure to radiation for use in cost–benefit analyses of radiation control regulations.[26] In the official rulemaking in which the figure was established, the commission made the following statement:

> The record, in our view, does not provide an adequate basis to choose a specific dollar value for the worth of decreasing the population dose by a man-rem or a man-thyroid-rem. Published values for the worth of a man-rem were shown in the record to range from about $10 to

[26] See *Federal Register* (May 5, 1975), pp. 19439–19443.

$980. . . . One of the hearing participants chose $1000 per man-rem. . . . This choice for worth of a man-rem simply reflected a value slightly more conservative than the highest previously published value (*Federal Register*, 1975, pp. 19440–19441).

I have not been able to review all of the studies referred to at the hearing. But it appears that the basis for at least some of the figures cited within that range was a combination of rather crude estimates of medical costs incurred because of radiation-induced illness and crude applications of lost earnings or productivity measures of the value of life.[27]

Finally, in a study prepared for the Environmental Protection Agency (EPA), Heintz, Hershaft, and Horak (1976) estimated the total costs of air pollution. Although no value of life was stated as part of the analysis, it is possible to calculate the value of life inferred by their total benefits and estimates of reduced mortality. The Heintz computation involved two steps. The first was to estimate the total cost of illness in the United States for 1973. This step involved an updating of earlier estimates for 1963 by Dorothy Rice (1966). The total costs of illness are the sum of direct costs of health care, indirect costs of morbidity, and indirect costs of mortality, the latter both measured by lost earnings.[28] The second step was to use Lave and Seskin's (1970) estimate that 2.3 percent of the total cost of illness is attributable to air pollution.[29] The estimate of indirect costs of mortality for 1973 divided by actual number of deaths in that year, yields the implied value of statistical life. This turns out to be $33,182 per life. When the data are disaggregated by sex, male deaths are valued at $39,000, while female deaths are valued at $25,500.[30]

---

[27] See for example, Lederberg (1971) and Sagan (1972). Sagan estimates lost earnings at $300,000 per death. The basis is $50 per day and 6,000 days lost per death. When this is combined with assumptions and data on medical costs and dose-effect relationships, the value per man-rem is about $30, well toward the lower end of the range cited by the National Regulatory Commission.

[28] Both estimates involve adjustments and imputations for individuals not in the labor force.

[29] On the basis of their more recent work, Lave and Seskin estimate that meeting the air pollution standards of the Clean Air Act Amendments of 1970 would reduce total mortality and morbidity by 7 percent each. See Lave and Seskin (1977, pp. 224–225).

[30] The figures would be raised perhaps by as much as 50 percent if that portion of the total direct costs of health care attributable to care of the dying were added to lost earnings.

MORBIDITY

The principal concern of this chapter has been valuing longevity or reductions in mortality. But any environmental program which increases longevity is also likely to reduce morbidity. This has value; and the value should be measured and incorporated in the estimate of total benefits.

As with reductions in mortality, there are questions both of the appropriate units for measuring morbidity changes and the conceptual and empirical bases for determining values. Morbidity could be measured by cases of different types of illness, or episodes, for example, cases of asthma, hepatitis, and so forth. But this means that reductions of different types of morbidity are not directly comparable, and that differences in severity within categories are ignored. The latter difficulty can be corrected by measuring number of days of involvement or days of restricted activity. But because of differences in pain, suffering, and anxiety, there may be differences in the values attached to avoiding days of morbidity across categories.

There has been relatively little empirical work done on the value of reducing morbidity. The most common approach taken is to utilize some measure of lost earnings or medical costs or both.[31] While the latter is an appropriate component of the benefits of reduced morbidity, the former suffers all the weaknesses and disadvantages (and advantages) of the human capital approach to valuing life. The willingness-to-pay concept is preferable on theoretical grounds. However I am not aware of any empirical estimate of willingness to pay to avoid any category of morbidity.

CONCLUSIONS

Since health benefits appear to be a major component of overall benefits from environmental protection programs, it is important to improve our ability to provide monetary measures of these benefits. This requires knowledge of both the relationships between environmental pollution levels and health effects and individuals' willingness to pay for improved longevity and decreased morbidity. I have shown that

---

[31] See for example Heintz, Hershaft, and Horak (1976, p. III-45–III-46).

there are models which can be used to analyze individual choice regarding changes in the risk of death. These models suggest that there is no single value of life applicable to all individuals. Individual valuations are likely to vary across individuals according to income levels, age, and basic preferences toward risk taking. Empirical estimates of the values of life must attempt to take these differences into account.

The models are based on the assumptions that individuals act to maximize expected utility, that they possess good information on the risks associated with various activities—for example, for different occupations—and that they can reason using probability and other statistical concepts. If these assumptions are valid, then we would expect not only that research would reveal that the qualitative aspects of individual behavior are consistent with the model, but also that consistent quantitative estimates of marginal values and demand functions could be obtained. On the latter point, results have not been encouraging to date. Estimates based on wage rate studies and willingness-to-pay surveys span two orders of magnitude. Thus whether the model represents a useful way of analyzing and explaining individual behavior in these circumstances must still be considered an open question.

Thus it appears appropriate not only to recommend additional efforts aimed at estimating the values of life for different groups using different data sources, but also to call for other empirical tests of hypotheses derived from the underlying model of choice in an effort to determine its appropriateness as a framework for benefit estimation and valuation.

REFERENCES

Acton, Jan P. 1973. *Evaluating Public Programs to Save Lives: The Case of Heart Attacks* (Santa Monica, Calif., Rand Corp.).

———. 1975. *Measuring the Social Impact of Heart and Circulatory Disease Programs: Preliminary Framework and Estimates* (Santa Monica, Calif., Rand Corp.).

Amdur, Mary O. 1976. "Toxicological Guidelines for Research on Sulfur Oxides and Particulates," in American Statistical Association, *Statistics and the Environment,* Proceedings of the 4th Symposium, Washington, D.C.

Barclay, G. W. 1958. *Techniques of Population Analysis* (New York, Wiley).

Conley, B. C. 1976. "The Value of Human Life in the Demand for Safety," *American Economic Review* vol. 66, no. 1, pp. 45–55.

Cooper, B. S., and D. P. Rice. 1976. "The Economic Cost of Illness Revisited," *Social Security Bulletin* vol. 39, no. 2, pp. 21–36.

Dinman, Bertram D. 1976. "The SO_2 Ambient Air Quality Standard, with Special Reference to the 24-hour Standard—An Inquiry into the Health Bases," in American Statistical Association, *Statistics and the Environment,* Proceedings of the 4th Symposium, Washington, D.C.

Federal Register. 1975. vol. 40, no. 87 (May 5).

Grad, Frank P., A. J. Rosenthal, L. R. Rockett, J. A. Fay, J. Heywood, J. F. Kain, G. K. Ingram, D. Harrison, Jr., and T. Tietenberg. 1975. *The Automobile and the Regulation of Its Impact on the Environment* (Norman, Okla., University of Oklahoma Press).

Heintz, H. T., Jr., A. Hershaft, and G. C. Horak. 1976. *National Damages of Air and Water Pollution,* a report to the U.S. Environmental Protection Agency (Rockville, Md., Enviro Control, Inc.).

Joksch, H. C. 1975. "A Critical Appraisal of the Applicability of Benefit–Cost Analysis to Highway Traffic Safety," *Accident Analysis and Prevention* vol. 7, pp. 133–153.

Jones-Lee, Michael W. 1976. *The Value of Life: An Economic Analysis* (Chicago, University of Chicago Press).

Lave, Lester B., and Eugene P. Seskin. 1970. "Air Pollution and Human Health," *Science* vol. 169 (August 21) pp. 723–731.

———. 1977. *Air Pollution and Human Health* (Baltimore, Johns Hopkins University Press for Resources for the Future).

Lederberg, J. 1971. "Squaring an Infinite Circle: Radiobiology and the Value of Life," *Bulletin of Atomic Scientists* vol. 43.

Liu, B., and E. S. Yu. 1976. *Physical and Economic Damage Functions for Air Pollutants by Receptor* (Corvallis, Ore., Environmental Protection Agency).

Mishan, Ezra J. 1971. "Evaluation of Life and Limb: A Theoretical Approach," *Journal of Political Economy* vol. 79, no. 4 (July/August) pp. 687–705.

National Academy of Sciences, Commission on Natural Resources. 1975. *Air Quality and Stationary Source Emission Control.* Committee Print, Senate Committee on Public Works, 94 Cong. 1 sess. (March).

———, Coordinating Committee on Air Quality Studies. 1974. *The Costs and Benefits of Automobile Emission Control,* volume 4 of *Air Quality and Automobile Emission Control* (Washington, D.C., NAS).

Needleman, L. 1976. "Valuing Other People's Lives," *Manchester School of Economic and Social Studies* vol. 44, no. 4 (December) pp. 309–342.

Neyman, J. 1977. "Public Health Hazards from Electricity-Producing Plants," *Science* vol. 195 (February 25) pp. 754–758.

Office of Science and Technology. 1972. *Cumulative Regulatory Effects on* the Cost of Automotive Transportation. Report of the Ad Hoc Committee, (Washington, D.C., GPO.).

Page, R. T., R. H. Harris, and S. S. Epstein. 1976. "Drinking Water and Cancer Mortality in Louisiana," Science vol. 193, no. 4247 (July 2) pp. 55–57.

Raiffa, Howard, William B. Schwartz, and Milton C. Weinstein. 1977. "Evaluating Health Effects of Societal Decisions and Programs," in National Academy of Sciences, Decision Making in the Environmental Protection Agency, vol. IIb, Selected Working Papers (Washington, D.C.).

Rice, Dorothy. 1966. Estimating the Cost of Illness (Washington, D.C., U.S. Department of Health, Education and Welfare, Public Health Service) Publication 947-6.

Ridker, R. G. 1967. Economic Costs of Air Pollution: Studies and Measurement (New York, Praeger).

Sagan, L. A. 1972. "Human Costs of Nuclear Power," Science vol. 177 (August 1972) pp. 487–493.

Schelling, Thomas C. 1968. "The Life You Save May Be Your Own," in Samuel B. Chase, Jr., ed., Problems in Public Expenditure Analysis (Washington, D.C., The Brookings Institution).

Smith, Robert S. 1976. The Occupational Safety and Health Act: Its Goals and Its Achievements (Washington, D.C., American Enterprise Institute for Public Policy Research).

Strotz, Robert. 1956. "Myopia and Inconsistency in Dynamic Utility Maximization," Review of Economic Studies vol. 23, pp. 165–180.

Thaler, R. H., and S. Rosen. 1976. "The Value of Saving a Life: Evidence from the Labor Market," in N. E. Terleckyj, ed., Household Production and Consumption (New York, Columbia University Press).

U.S. Environmental Protection Agency. 1974. Health Consequences of Sulfur Oxides: A Report from CHESS, 1970–1971 (Research Triangle Park, N.C.).

U.S. House of Representatives, Committee on Interstate and Foreign Commerce. 1976. Report: Clean Air Act Amendments of 1976. House Report 94–1175, 93 Cong. 2 sess.

Usher, Dan. 1973. "An Imputation to the Measure of Economic Growth for Changes in Life Expectancy," in Milton Moss, ed., The Measurement of Economic and Social Performance (New York, Columbia University Press).

Weinstein, M., D. Shepard, and J. Pliskin. 1976. The Economic Value of Changing Mortality Probabilities: A Decision-Theoretic Approach. Discussion Paper 46D (Cambridge, Mass., John Fitzgerald Kennedy School of Government, Harvard University).

CHAPTER 8

Recreation Benefits

It is generally believed that an increase in water-based recreation activity will be the major source of the benefits to be derived from controlling water pollution. A recent report prepared for EPA estimated that about 60 percent of the $10.1 billion in damages attributable to all water pollution in the United States was associated with the loss of water-based recreation opportunities (Heintz, Hershaft, and Horak, 1976). Similarly the staff of the National Commission on Water Quality estimated that the benefits in 1980 of achieving the best practical treatment effluent standards would be between $3.2 and $4.2 billion per year; and the bulk of these benefits would be due to increased recreational fishing, boating, and swimming (National Commission on Water Quality, 1976).[1]

There is a substantial body of literature on the theoretical and empirical aspects of estimating the demand for recreation but relatively little work has been done on the role of the attributes of recreation sites, for example water quality, in influencing the demand for recreation or the benefits of improved recreation opportunities. Integrating water quality into the analysis of recreation demand is the major research task that must be confronted before sound estimates of the recreation benefits due to water pollution control can be provided.

In this chapter I shall first review the definition of benefits in terms of willingness to pay for water quality and discuss an approach to the measurement of willingness to pay through the analysis of the demand for recreation activities at a specific site. Given certain assumptions, the demand curve for a specific recreation site can be derived from an analysis of the travel costs incurred by users. After outlining the travel cost technique, I shall discuss some problems that arise with the incorporation of water quality variables into recreation demand analysis.

---

[1] For a skeptical view of the magnitude and importance of recreation benefits, see Ackerman and coauthors (1974), especially chapters 7 and 8.

An alternative approach to the analysis of recreation demand is to examine the recreation behavior of a national or large regional population and to relate levels of recreation activity to measures of accessibility and quality of available recreation sites. For example, a sample could be surveyed to determine the level of participation in various forms of recreation activity. If participation rates can be related to the availability and quality of recreation resources, then it may be possible to predict the changes in overall recreation activity to be expected from changes in water quality. This kind of analysis could be the basis for developing estimates of national water pollution control recreation benefits. This approach will be discussed in the final two sections of this chapter.

BENEFITS DEFINED

Assume that individual utility depends on the consumption of a vector of private goods X, the number of days of recreation at various sites V_j ($j = 1, \ldots, n$), and water quality at these sites Q_j. The way in which water quality influences the utility of recreationists is itself a difficult question which will be discussed in a later section.

Generalizing from the discussion in chapters 3 and 4, there is an expenditure function for the ith individual which is a function of private goods prices, gate fees, unit travel costs, and the distances and water qualities of the various sites. The marginal demand price for Q_j is the partial derivative of the expenditure function with respect to Q_j. And the benefit to the ith individual of a change in water quality at the jth site is

$$B_j = - \int_{Q_j}^{Q_j'} \partial E_i / \partial Q_j dQ_j \tag{1}$$

Since recreation activity is a divisible good which can be—and in some cases is—provided through private markets, we can specify a set of individual ordinary demand functions for each potential recreation site where quantity (visits) is a function of prices, incomes, travel costs, and qualitative characteristics such as water quality. For each individual there are separate demand functions for each site

$$V_{ij} = V_{ij}(P_v, P_x, D_i, c, t_i, h_i, Q, M_i) \tag{2}$$

where V_{ij} = number of visits by individual i to site j

P_v = vector of money prices of entry (possibly zero) to the various sites

P_x = vector of private goods prices

D_i = vector of distances from residence of individual i to the various sites and return

c = unit travel cost

t_i = vector of travel times to the various sites[2]

h_i = cost of travel time

Q = vector of water quality measures of the various sites

M_i = money income of individual i

This general representation of the demand relationship shows that the number of visits to a particular site depends not only on its own price, distance, travel time, and quality, but also on the attributes of competing or substitute sites.

The question is whether it is possible to determine (1) from knowledge of (2). If the assumptions underlying "weak complementarity" can be satisfied, the answer is yes.[3] Recall that a public good and a private good are weakly complementary if, when the private good consumption is zero, the marginal value or marginal willingness to pay for the public good is also zero. We assume that weak complementarity holds for water-based recreation. In other words, we assume that individuals' utilities are unaffected by changes in water quality in areas which the individual does not visit for recreation. This may be a somewhat unrealistic assumption. It is possible that individuals might have option value demands for water quality improvements at sites that they do not presently plan to use for recreation.[4] Or individuals may

---

[2] Time and distance are of course highly correlated. But they are entered separately because of their different roles in the individual's constraint set and maximization problem. Distance affects out-of-pocket monetary travel costs—an element in the budget constraint—while the time cost of travel to the site is an opportunity cost whose monetary value may not be directly observable. Time spent on the site also has an opportunity cost. The separate roles of time and money costs, and their importance in the estimation of demand and benefits will be discussed below.

[3] See chapter 4 of this book.

[4] See Cicchetti and Freeman (1971) for discussion of the option value concept.

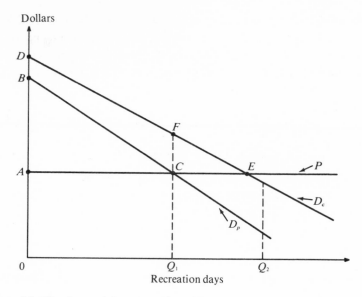

Figure 15. The demand for recreation visits and the benefit of water quality improvement

be willing to pay for water quality improvements everywhere because of some form of "preservation demand" or an environmental ethic.[5] These possibilities do not invalidate the weak complementarity approach. But they do mean that benefits as estimated by the weak complementarity approach will understate true benefits to the extent that these forms of nonuser benefits are present.

An improvement in water quality shifts the demand curve for visits to the site out and to the right. According to the analysis of weak complementarity, the area between the two demand curves for the site is an exact measure of equation (1), that is, of the benefits of a water quality improvement. A graphical analysis is developed in figure 15. The demand curves are aggregate demand curves, that is, the horizontal summation of equations of (2) across individuals. The demand curves are drawn holding all private goods prices, distances and travel times to other sites, quality levels at other sites, and incomes constant. When the price of entry to this site is known, as indicated by the line P, actual recreation use or quantity demanded can be predicted. Of course price could be zero. When the facility has pollution, the demand curve is D_p

[5] See Krutilla (1967).

and the quantity of recreation days is $0-Q_1$. Now assume that water quality is improved and that the new demand curve reflecting the quality improvement is D_c. Individuals could be taxed an amount equal to the area between the two demand curves to maintain the original utility level. The area *BCEFD* is the benefit attributable to the improvement of water quality.

The net benefit can be divided into two categories. The first is the increase in utility or consumer surplus associated with the original $0-Q_1$ level of use when the facility was polluted. This is the area *BCFD*. This area represents the increase in willingness to pay to maintain present use rates at this recreation site rather than do without. In addition, the greater attractiveness of this site relative to alternative sites and alternative consumption activities (other than recreation) results in an increase in recreation days at this site equal to Q_1-Q_2. This increase could be in part a diversion of activity from other sites where, by assumption, quality has not changed, and in part an increase in aggregate recreation activity. The benefit associated with this increase in use is the area *CEF*.

In utilizing this measure of benefits, there is no need to take into account changes in recreation use at other sites or savings in travel cost (Knetsch, 1977). These are captured by the *BCED* benefit measure. For example, if recreation is switched from an alternative site, the demand curve for that site shifts in to the left. But it would be incorrect to measure the area between those demand curves to adjust the measure of benefits. There has been no change in water quality at the alternative site, so the integral equation (1) for that site is zero.

If there are simultaneous changes in water quality at several recreation sites, the theory of welfare change under multiple price or quantity changes applies.[6] Consider for example two sites with a simultaneous improvement in water quality. In principle, benefits are measured by evaluating the integral equation (1) for site *A* holding, by assumption, the quality at site *B* at its original level, then evaluating the integral equation (1) for site *B* given the improved level of quality at site *A*. The welfare measure is independent of the order in which the quality changes are evaluated.

A graphical representation of these benefit measures will show a pitfall which is to be avoided in the empirical application of this technique through measurement of areas under demand curves. In figure 16 the heavy lines represent the demand curves for the two sites at the

[6] See chapter 3.

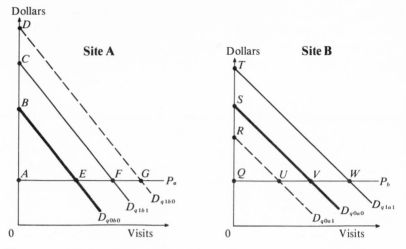

Figure 16. Benefits when quality changes at two sites simultaneously

original level of quality. The fine lines represent the demand curves after the quality has changed at both sites. Assume first that only site A experiences an improvement in quality. The demand curve for A will shift out to the dashed line, D_{q1b0}. Because sites A and B are substitutes for recreationists, the demand curve for B shifts to the left to D_{q0a1}. The benefit of the improved quality at A, *ceteris paribus,* is the area *BEGD*. Now assume an improvement at site B, holding quality at A constant at the improved level. The demand curve for B shifts from D_{q0a1} to D_{q1a1} while the substitution effect causes the demand curve for A to shift back to D_{q1b1}. The benefit of the improvement at B is the area *RUWT*. The total benefit is the sum of these two components.[7] Note that the correct measure of benefits is substantially larger than the estimate that would be obtained by observing the areas between the initial and final equilibrium demand curves, that is, *BEFC* + *SVWT*. In order to obtain the correct estimates, we require full knowledge of the demand functions including the substitution effects of quality changes.

In order to use demand curves for recreation visits to a site to measure benefits, we need to have not only knowledge of the function

---

[7] If the integrability conditions for the system of demand equations are satisfied, following the same procedure but starting with an improvement at site B first will yield the same answer. This case is not shown in figure 16.

relating the quantity of visits to a site to the price of entry, that is, the price–quantity relationship, but also knowledge of how this demand function shifts with changes in quality, that is the quality–quantity relationship. The next two sections deal with each of these questions in turn.

ESTIMATING THE DEMAND FOR A SITE

In this section I focus attention on the problem of estimating demand as a function of price, leaving for a later section the problem of estimating the influence of water quality (or perhaps other attributes of the site) on quantity demanded. Of course, the problem of demand estimation would be quite straightforward if the normal practice were to charge an entry fee, and if fees varied substantially. But the typical practice for publicly provided recreation sites is to charge a zero price or only a nominal entry fee. Without variation in the entry fee, it is not possible to estimate demand functions through normal procedures. However it may be possible to infer how a given group of people would respond to changes in the entry price by examining data on how different people respond to differences in money travel cost. This is the basic hypothesis of the so-called Clawson-Knetsch (CK) travel cost method of demand estimation. This section will briefly review the basic CK technique and then discuss some problems in its application that are particularly relevant to the task of benefit estimation.[8]

It must be emphasized that the CK method is site specific. That is, it estimates the demand function for a specific recreation site rather than for recreation activities in general. The site demand is a derived demand and depends on the ability of the site to "produce" the desired activities.[9] While this may reduce the usefulness of the CK method for some purposes—for example, predicting the trends in total recreation

[8] The basic references are Clawson and Knetsch (1966); and Knetsch (1964). For a clear exposition and numerical example of its application see Mäler and Wyzga (1976). Other useful references include Sindon (1974); Beardsley (1971); Reiling, Gibbs, and Stoevener (1973); and Knetsch (1974). Also Smith (1975) presents a useful discussion of alternative techniques for modeling and estimating recreation demand. Additional references will be provided below on specific points to be discussed.

[9] The household production framework can be used to formalize this point. See for example Cicchetti and Smith (1976), Cicchetti, Fisher, and Smith (1976), and Deyak and Smith (1977).

activity over time—it is precisely this feature which makes the approach attractive for estimating the economic value of water quality improvements at specific recreation sites.

The initial exposition is based on the assumption that there is only one recreation site available to individuals in a given region. For the moment, the role of time is ignored in order to simplify the exposition. The CK technique has been generalized and applied to the task of estimating systems of demand functions for several sites, taking into account the interrelated natures of their demands. This generalization will be discussed below.

In implementing the CK technique, it must be assumed that the primary purpose of the recreation trip is to visit that site. When trips involve purposes other than visiting the site, at least some portion of the total travel cost is a joint cost which cannot be allocated meaningfully to the visit.

The simplest version of the procedure is as follows

1. For a given recreation site, the surrounding area is divided into concentric circular zones for the purpose of measuring the travel cost from each zone to the site and return.
2. Visitors at the site are sampled to determine their zones of origin.
3. Visitation rates defined as visitor days per capita are calculated for each zone of origin.
4. A travel cost measure is constructed to indicate the cost of travel from the origin zone to the recreation site and return.[10]
5. Visitation rates are regressed on travel costs and socioeconomic variables such as average income, median educational attainment, and the like. The regression tests the hypothesis that visitation rates depend in part on travel cost.
6. The observed total visitation for the site from all travel cost zones represents one point on the demand curve for that site, that is, the intersection of the present horizontal price line (either at zero price or the typical nominal entry fee) with the true economic demand curve.[11]
7. Other points on the demand curve are found by assuming that

---

[10] Early studies used money travel cost, calculated in cents per mile. In general, time costs must also be included in some manner. The role of time in the analysis of demand will be discussed below.

[11] If the site is characterized by congestion among users, the CK approach is not valid. The observed point on the demand curve represents an intersection of the unknown demand curve with a supply or congestion cost curve of

visitors will respond to a $1 increase in admission price in the same way that they would to a $1 increase in computed travel cost. To find the point on the demand curve for the site when the admission price rises by $1, the estimated visitation-rate equation is used to compute visitation rates and total visits for all travel cost zones with the existing travel cost plus $1. Visits are summed across travel cost zones to determine the predicted total visitation at the higher price. These calculations are repeated for higher and higher hypothetical admission prices and the full demand curve is traced out.[12]

The CK technique as explained here and as carried out by, for example, Knetsch (1964), is based on the pooling of data by travel cost zones. It is also possible to base the regression analysis on individual observations. However, this form of disaggregation may not be appropriate in all cases. For example, with individual observations, the dependent variable in the regression is number of visits per individual, rather than visits per capita. If the nature and location of the recreation site is such that the typical pattern of behavior involves no more than one visit per year, then the effect of distance on the probability of

---

unknown shape. The absence of congestion is required for the establishment of the necessary a priori restrictions on the parameters of the model for proper identification of the demand function. For discussion of the identification problem in connection with estimating the demand for recreation sites, see Cicchetti and coauthors (1972). Other aspects of the congestion problem will be discussed below.

[12] Algebraically, the steps involved are

1. Estimate for each distance or travel cost zone d

$$V_d = V(M_d, S_d, C_d)$$

where $d = (= 1, \ldots, n)$ is the index of the travel cost zone

M_d is average income in the zone

S_d represents other socioeconomic variables, and

C_d is a measure of travel cost.

2. Assuming no admission fee, find total visits

$$V = \sum_{d=1}^{n} V_d$$

3. Let increments of tracel cost ΔC stand as proxies for posited admission fees. Compute

$$V^i = \sum_{d=1}^{n} V[M_d, S_d, (C_d + j\Delta C)]$$

for successive j. V^j as a function of $j\Delta C$ is the demand function for visits.

making such a visit would be more difficult to measure by simple linear regression techniques.

The procedure described above involves sampling only users at the site. This sampling procedure would be adequate if the objective were simply to determine the existing demand curve. However if the objective of the analysis is to predict how a population would respond to changes in quality or to take into account the effect of alternative recreation sites on site-specific demand, then samples should be drawn from the whole regional population. This would permit the inclusion in the sample of present nonusers who might shift from other sites or begin to be involved in recreation activity after an improvement in water quality.[13]

The Role of Time

This description of the basic CK technique has ignored time as an element in recreation behavior. The basic model is based on a simplified but distorted and fundamentally incorrect view of the choice problem facing individuals. When the time dimension of choice is included in the model, two sets of issues emerge. The first concerns what elements of time are to be interpreted as costs of recreation activity and how they affect estimates of demand and benefits. The second concerns the monetary values to be assigned to time costs in demand and benefit estimation.

We first use a simple example to show that treating travel time as a cost can have a substantial effect on benefit estimates derived from the simple CK model. We then develop a general model to investigate more thoroughly the different possible components of time cost and the reason why different monetary values might be attached to different components of time cost.

In the basic CK technique, time is not considered as a component of travel cost separate from the money cost of travel, for example, gasoline, tolls, and the like. Cesario and Knetsch (1970) were the first to point out the bias that this introduces into the demand and benefit estimates. A simple numerical example will suffice to make the nature and direction of the bias clear. Consider just two travel cost zones with the following data.

[13] For examples of empirical studies based on samples of the regional population see Burt and Brewer (1971), Brown and Nawas (1973), and Gum and Martin (1975).

Zone	Distance	Travel Cost	Time for Trip
1	10 mi.	$1	15 min.
2	20 mi.	$2	30 min.

Suppose that the visitation rate has been estimated as a function of only money travel cost. One step in the computation of the demand curve is to assume the imposition of an entry fee, of, for example, $1, and to examine its effects on visitation from each zone. The hypothetical entry fee raises the money cost of a visit from zone 1 to $2. The conventional assumption is that individuals in zone 1 would have the same visitation rate as was originally observed with zone 2 (when its money travel cost was $2). For individuals in zone 1, the full cost of the visit is $2 plus 15 minutes; but for individuals in zone 2, the original full cost of travel was $2 plus 30 minutes. If the difference in time cost between zone 1 with the fee and zone 2 without the fee is ignored, the model tends to overestimate the reduction in use associated with the hypothetical admission fee. As a consequence the computed demand curve is more elastic than the true demand curve. And the benefits of the recreation site (the area under the demand curve)are underestimated.

The problem could be resolved if there were a way of estimating the separate effects of time cost and money cost on visitation rates. But if the only money costs that vary across individuals are those associated with travel, then money cost and time cost are likely to be too highly correlated statistically to permit the separate estimation of their effects. An alternative solution to the problem is to convert the observed time cost to a monetary value by the use of an appropriate shadow price of time. Let us assume that time spent in travel is valued at $2 per hour by recreationists. Then the full cost of travel for a visit in zone 1 is $1.50 while in zone 2 it is $3. A hypothetical $1 entry fee raises the money cost for zone 1 to $2.50. Since the new money cost for zone 1 is less than the original money cost of zone 2, predicted visits from zone 1 with the fee will be higher than the prediction obtained by ignoring time as a separate element in cost.

The choice of the shadow price of time is critical to the estimation of the elasticity of demand for the site and calculation of the benefits of the site. The choice of a high shadow price of time raises the importance of time cost in explaining visits as a function of distance. This leads to lower predicted changes in visitation rates with the imposition of the hypothetical entry fee and makes the computed demand curve less elastic. Ignoring time cost has the effect of biasing the elasticity estimate upward and the benefit estimate downward. But clearly, using too high a shadow price of time can have the opposite effect on estimates of elasticity and benefits.

I shall return to the question of the appropriate shadow price of time. But first I turn to another issue concerning the components of time cost, that is, whether the opportunity cost of time at the site is part of the cost of the visit. McConnell (1975) has shown that in the context of a model of individual choice and utility maximization, time spent at the site involved in the recreation activity is a relevant component of the total cost of the visit.[14] McConnell does not analyze travel time. But I shall now show that both components of time cost may be relevant; but they need not have the same shadow price.

Assume that an individual's utility is a function of the consumption of a composite good X, the numbers of visits V_j ($j = 1, \ldots, n$) to various recreation sites, and the total distances traveled to the various sites, Z_j. The marginal utility of Z_j could be positive, implying pleasure from travel along a scenic route to the site. Or it could be zero or negative. The individual maximizes his utility subject to the constraints of his money income and time budgets.

$$\text{Maximize } U = U(X, V_j, Z_j) \tag{3}$$

subject to

$$M - P_x X - \sum_j P_{v_j} V_j - \sum_j c Z_j = 0$$

and

$$T - \sum_j a_j V_j - \sum_j t_j Z_j = 0$$

where $Z_j \equiv$ total distance travelled to site j

$\qquad = V_j D_j$

$\quad c \equiv$ unit travel cost per mile

$\quad T \equiv$ total time available for recreation (assumed to be fixed for simplification)

$\quad a_j \equiv$ time on site per visit (also assumed to be fixed for each site)

$\quad t_j \equiv$ travel time per mile

---

[14] See also the exchange between Knetsch and Cesario (1976) and McConnell (1976), and a recent paper by Wilman (1977). The following model is based on Wilman.

Note that the choice of the number of recreation visits also determines the time spent in travel—another argument in the utility function. In deriving the first order conditions, the partial derivative $\partial U/\partial V_j$ includes two components: the marginal utility of the on-site visit, and the marginal utility (positive or negative) of the travel time. The implications of this can most easily be seen by specifying a functional form for (3) as an illustration.

For example consider the additive form[15]

$$U = U_1(X) + U_2(V_j) + U_3(Z_j)$$

The first order conditions for a maximum include

$$\frac{\partial U_2}{\partial V_j} = \lambda P_{v_j} + \lambda c D_j + \mu a_j + \mu t_j D_j - D_j \frac{\partial U_3}{\partial Z_j}$$

where λ and μ are the Lagrangian multipliers for the money and time constraints, or the marginal utilities of income and time respectively.

The individual chooses V_j so as to equate the marginal utility of the on-site experience with its total cost in money and time. These total costs consist of:

—the opportunity cost of money spent on the admission price λP_{vj}
—the opportunity cost of money travel costs $\lambda c D_j$
—the opportunity cost of time on the site μa_j, and
—the net opportunity cost of time spent in travel.

This last component is the opportunity cost of time in travel reduced (augmented) by any positive (negative) utility associated with the travel experience itself. If the marginal utility of travel time is zero, travel time and on-site time can simply be added and a single shadow price of time applied in assessing the time costs of recreation. However if the marginal utility of travel is not zero, then the effective shadow prices of on-site and travel time are different.

How do these components of cost influence empirical estimates of demand and benefits? If time on the site is independent of distance and travel cost, then including on-site cost has no effect on the variables being measured. Adding on-site time cost to the travel cost measure displaces the relationship between cost and visits by a constant factor but does not affect the marginal relationship between changes in the

---

[15] Other functional forms yield qualitatively similar results.

full costs of visits and changes in the number of visits. On the other hand, if time on site varies inversely with distance, then including on-site costs increases the measure of full cost more, both absolutely and relatively, for individuals living closer to the site. For a given pattern of visits, the computed demand curve will be more elastic if on-site costs are included in the measure of full costs. Thus measurements which fail to include on-site time costs will result in underestimates of the true demand elasticity and overestimates of site benefits. It remains to be seen how important a question this is in practice. There has been very little empirical work on the relationship between travel time and on-site time.

As the earlier example showed, the treatment of net cost of travel time does influence demand and benefit estimates. Failure to account for these costs properly can lead to biased estimates. Yet the model gives very little guidance as to how to assign a value of travel time for empirical purposes. One possible choice for the shadow price of time is the marginal wage rate. The argument is that the wage rate reflects the opportunity cost of time at the margin between the choice of work and leisure. But institutional constraints such as the 8-hour work day distort the work–leisure tradeoff. And there is little empirical support for the wage rate as the actual shadow price. On the other hand there is a body of empirical evidence showing that the shadow price of travel time is substantially less than the wage rate. Commuters reveal something about their valuation of travel time in their choices among modes of commuter transportation. Commuters may choose more costly modes of transportation which reduce travel time, or they may conserve money by choosing slower modes of travel. Cesario has reviewed a number of travel time and transportation cost studies in an effort to determine a reasonable shadow price of time for use in recreation travel studies. He concluded, ". . . that on the basis of evidence collected to date, the value of time with respect of nonwork travel is between one quarter and one half of the wage rate." (1976, p. 37)[16] In his empirical estimates of recreation benefits, Cesario used a time value from within this range, that is, one third of the average wage rate. This suggests that the marginal utility of commuter travel time is positive. But since the routes and perhaps the mode of travel are different, there is no reason

---

[16] Nelson estimated of the marginal implicit price of proximity to the central business district from housing market data from Washington, D.C. (Nelson, 1977). He used this to derive a value of computing time. His estimates fall in the same range as that mentioned by Cesario.

to believe that the marginal utility of travel to work is the same as the marginal utility of recreation-related travel. This is an area which needs substantially more investigation.

Demand Functions With Many Sites

If within a region there are several recreation sites that are less than perfect substitutes for one another, then following the above procedures to estimate the demand for any one site would lead to biased results. To prevent bias, the prices and distances of competing sites must enter as variables in the demand functions for each site. The procedure involves the estimation of a set of visitation functions where the number of visits per individual to each site (or the visitation rate) is a function of the distances to that site, distances of competing sites, and socioeconomic variables.[17] Once the visitation equations have been estimated, the demand function for any one site can be computed following the procedures outlined above on the assumption that the prices of all other sites are fixed at the level prevailing when the visitation data were gathered. These equations can be used to predict changes in visitation rates at a site for changes in its entry price, *ceteris paribus*. It is also possible to estimate visitation at a new site in a region on the assumption that it is a perfect substitute for a nearby site.[18]

INCORPORATING WATER QUALITY EFFECTS

There are two questions which must be resolved if measures of water quality are to be successfully incorporated into CK estimates of recreation site demand and benefits. The first question concerns the structure of the model and the form of the equations to be estimated econometrically. The second is how to define and measure water quality in quantitative terms. We take up the specification question first on the

[17] The introduction of water quality into a system of visitation functions is discussed in the next section.

[18] See Burt and Brewer (1971); Cicchetti, Fisher, and Smith (1976); Cesario and Knetsch (1976); and Cesario (1976) for examples of the empirical estimation of multi-site models. It is interesting to compare the benefit estimates reported in the last two papers. Although both studies utilized essentially the same data set, the benefit estimates differ substantially. Apparently the benefit estimates are quite sensitive to model specification.

assumption that there exists a single parameter Q which is an argument in individuals' utility functions, and that the Q of any water body can be measured objectively.

Specification

In order to estimate the benefits of water quality improvement, we need to know the demand curve relating the number of visits to price and Q. The demand curve can be computed from an equation explaining number of visits as a function of distance, travel cost, and Q. In estimating visitation functions econometrically, we confront two kinds of problems. One is in obtaining data with sufficient variation in Q so that the separate effects of Q on visitation can be identified. The second problem concerns how to take into account alternative or competing recreation sites and especially their water quality levels.

Consider first a region with a single recreation site. If there are no alternative or substitute sites, the individual demand functions can be specified as follows

$$V_i = V_i(P_x, P_v, D_i, c, t_i, h_i, Q, M_i)$$
for individuals $i = 1, \ldots, i, \ldots, n$ \hfill (4)

where the variables are as defined above.

For a given population and its individual demand functions, the aggregate demand function for the site is

$$V = V(P_x, P_v, Q, \ldots) \hfill (5)$$

where $V = \sum_{i=1}^{n} V_i$

This site demand function is specified for a given distribution of population and socioeconomic characteristics within the region it serves. It can be computed by the travel cost method after first estimating (4).

If (4) and (5) are estimated from data collected at a point in time, there would be no variation in Q across the sample. If the data are collected over a longer period of time during which Q changes, it may be very difficult to separate the effects of quality change from other factors which also are changing over time. For example, if Q and income are both increasing over the time period, it may not be possible to separate statistically their effects on demand. Also, if the site is so polluted that recreational activity is precluded, then the travel cost approach to estimating demand and benefits simply cannot be applied directly.

An alternative approach to investigating the effects of Q on recreation demand is to examine recreation behavior with respect to a group of sites with various levels of Q. Suppose there are several sites within a region, each with different levels of water quality. The individual demand functions are

$$V_{ij} = V_j(P_x, P_{v_j}, D_{ij}, D_{ik}, c, t_{ij}, t_{ik}, h_i, Q_j, Q_k, M_i) \tag{6}$$

for individuals $i = 1, \ldots, i, \ldots, n$, and sites $j, k = 1, \ldots, j$, $k, \ldots, m, (j \neq k)$. Again for a given population and its characteristics, the site demand function can be computed. It is

$$V_j = V(P_x, P_{v_j}, Q_j, Q_k, \ldots) \tag{7}$$

If (6) is estimated from data gathered at a point in time simply by entering the vector of Qs, the vectors will be the same for all households. Thus the effect of quality on visitation cannot be identified. Rather, what is required is a set of quality-related variables defined so that they vary across the sample of individuals.

Cesario and Knetsch (1976) have used a specification derived from a gravity model of the interactions among sites to account for the effects of site characteristics on demand. In the gravity model the quality variables for competing sites are weighted in inverse proportion to their distances from the recreationist. One form of weighting function is the exponential where the visitation equation is specified as follows

$$V_{ij} = aP_{v_j}{}^\alpha Q_j{}^\beta D_{ij}{}^\gamma Q_k{}^\delta D_{ik}{}^\eta \ldots$$

The exponents are parameters to be estimated. It is hypothesized that they have the following signs

$$\alpha, \gamma, \delta \leq 0$$

$$\beta, \eta \geq 0$$

Cesario and Knetsch (1976) estimated a slightly different specification[19]

$$V_{ij} = aP_v{}^\alpha Q_j{}^\beta e^{\gamma D_{ij}}[\sum Q_k{}^\delta e^{\gamma D_{ik}}]^\eta$$

[19] Cesario and Knetsch did not use water quality explicitly. Their model utilized an "attractiveness" variable which was a weighted average of subjective evaluations of the quality of the site for specified activities.

Both of these specifications have an *ad hoc* flavor, since they are not derived from an underlying model of behavior. But if the estimated parameters have the hypothesized signs, these equations will permit the effects of quality at various sites to work in the expected directions.

An alternative approach to introducing quality effects is to estimate demand functions for each site separately without quality variables, and then to attempt to explain differences in the coefficients on price terms by regressing them on the quality variables. To take a simple example, the demand function

$$V_j = a + b_j P_{v_j} \tag{8}$$

would be estimated by the CK technique. This equation could include prices of substitute sites. Then the price coefficients would be regressed against the quality variables

$$b_j = c + dQ_j \tag{9}$$

By substitution, this is equivalent to including interaction terms[20]

$$V_j = a + cP_{v_j} + dQ_j P_{v_j}$$

Equation (9) could be specified to include only quality variables for site *j*, or it could include quality variables for other sites as well to test for substitution effects. If this is done, the discussion of the ways in which the quality of substitute sites is entered is relevant.

Suppose there is one site in the region which is so polluted that it has no recreation activity. Controlling pollution at this site so as to permit recreation is equivalent to creating a new recreation site in the regional recreational system. If the only improvement in water quality is at those sites where the initial $V_j = 0$, then the methodology developed and utilized by Burt and Brewer (1971) and Cicchetti, Fisher, and Smith (1976) can be used.

There have been two studies of recreation demand and water quality in regions with multiple sites.[21] In both cases, the investigators

---

[20] For further discussion of this approach and the econometric issues involved, see Saxonhouse (1977).

[21] Binkley and Hanemann (1975) and Reiling, Gibbs, and Stoevener (1973).

pooled all of the data on visits to all of the sites to estimate a single visitation equation of the following form[22]

$$V_{ij} = V(D_{ij}, t_{ij}, Q_j, M_i) \tag{10}$$

The independent variables include only distance and time costs to the site visited and quality at that site. In other words, substitution effects and the quality and distance of competing sites are ignored. To use equation (10) for predictive purposes or to estimate benefits, it is necessary to assume that the estimated coefficients apply uniformly to all sites, in other words, that except for distance and quality all sites are essentially identical and are perfect substitutes for one another.

The coefficient on Q in (10) can be used to predict the change in visits to site j given a change in Q_j. But because the model does not take into account substitution effects, the predicted change in visits is likely to be an overestimate. To see this, suppose that there are two sites, j and k, which are identical in all respects except for their Q. Let Q_j be less than Q_k. Assume that equation (10) has been estimated for the region. Then postulate an improvement in Q at Q_j such that $Q_j = Q_k$. The model of equation (10) would predict an increase in V_j such that $V_j = V_k$, with no changes in visitation at k or any other site at the region. However the more likely outcome is a diversion of activity from k to j, with only a small increase in the total activity at the two sites. Sites j and k would have the same activity levels, but they would be equalized at a level somewhat below the original level for k. Thus equation (10) would tend to overestimate the actual increase in visits to j and total visits to the two sites combined.

The discussion up to this point has been concerned primarily with the problem of estimating recreation visits as a function of both travel cost and water quality, using a single data set. One study dealing with benefits of changes in water quality has approached the problem somewhat differently. Stevens (1966) estimated a demand curve for a site using the CK methodology and estimated a relationship between activity and a proxy for water quality from a separate data set. He then assumed that this relationship would apply to the recreation site in ques-

---

[22] Reiling, Gibbs, and Stoevener (1973) developed a somewhat different model to take into account the fixed cost per trip and the variable cost per day for a multiple day visit to a site. Thus their estimating equations were somewhat different from (10). But their treatment of substitution effects is essentially the same as that described in the text.

tion. Stevens was analyzing a sports fishery resource (Yaquina Bay, Oregon). He defined Q as the number of fish caught per angler trip, or the success/effort ratio. Stevens estimated the relationship between total angling effort and the success/effort ratio (Q) from time series data from other sports fishing areas along the Oregon coast. Regression analysis was used to estimate the coefficients and the elasticities of angling effort with respect to Q for daily, weekly, and annual time periods. Since one might expect the daily and weekly data to be dominated by such factors as weather and fish movement, Stevens argued that the annual data might best indicate the possible long-term relationship between pollution-caused changes in the success/effort ratio and the resulting changes in total angler effort. Therefore, Stevens assumed that the elasticity of effort with respect to pollution-caused changes in the success/effort ratio at Yaquina Bay would be the same as the elasticity estimated from annual data for another fishing area where pollution was not a factor affecting angler success. There are two critical questions with respect to Stevens' method. The first is whether other influences on fishing effort at the alternative sites can be adequately controlled. In other words can a relationship derived from one data base be applied in a different context? The second is whether the behavioral response to changes in angler success is invariant to the cause of changes in success.

The Quality Variable

The word "quality" is a proxy for a variety of parameters that are affected by the presence of man-made pollutants as well as natural insults. There are several questions concerning what measures of quality are appropriate and how they should be used.

—Should analysis be based on objective measures of water quality such as dissolved oxygen and pH? Or should some measure of perceived water quality be derived by questioning recreationists?

—Given the heterogeneity of water quality measures, should analysis disaggregate the quality concept into several distinct measures?

—If an index approach is chosen to consolidate measures, how are the weights to be chosen?

The measures actually chosen for empirical work should satisfy three criteria. The first is logical consistency. In other words, the measures should be in accord with our a priori notions of what matters to recreationists. Second, they should be objective in the sense that they can be replicated by different observers. For example, if two observers were asked to rate the quality of several water bodies, the recorded evaluations should be substantially identical across observers. The third criterion is empirical validity. Does the measure actually help to predict recreation demand? In other words, is there a significant correlation between the quality measures used and the dependent variable to be explained.

Three studies dealing with water quality have examined various measures of perceived water quality and how they relate to objective water quality measures and to individuals' behavior. These studies are briefly reviewed here, not because they are definitive, but because they illustrate the difficulties and complexities of the problem.

The first is a survey study by Elizabeth David (1971) of individuals' perceptions of water quality. David asked a sample of individuals in Wisconsin to name the descriptive characteristics of water quality which indicated polluted water to them. Those most frequently mentioned reflected visual characteristics of water bodies. These were algae and green scum (40 percent of respondents), murky-dark (35 percent), and odor and floating debris (20 percent). Few respondents mentioned hidden pollutants such as toxic chemicals or fecal coliform bacteria.

David then asked her sample to indicate bodies of water in Wisconsin which they perceived to be polluted. The water bodies named by respondents were also regarded as polluted by experts in the field according to such conventional measures of water quality as low dissolved oxygen, high suspended solids, or high fecal coliform bacteria. David concluded that although individuals seemed to react to different characteristics of polluted water, their classification of water bodies as polluted or not made a good match with the conventional objective classifications.

A major limitation of the David study is that it did not treat pollution or water quality as continuous variables. Also, her study did not go on to the second stage of evaluating water quality measures, that is, testing the hypothesis that the given measures of water quality do affect recreation choices.

A second study, by Dornbusch (1975), had the objective of developing an index of the perceived changes in water quality for use as an explanatory variable in the analysis of property value changes. In the analysis seven categories or characteristics of water quality were defined. The numbers in parentheses after each indicate the weight to be attached to each in the computation of an index.

—Presence of industrial wastes (0.10)
—Debris and obstructions, for example, weeds, bottles, and cans (0.05)
—Clearness of water (that is, depth of visibility) (0.07)
—Algae (0.04)
—Odor (0.05)
—Wildlife support capacity (0.43)
—Recreation opportunities (0.26)

The weights were determined from a survey in which respondents were asked to allocate a hypothetical 100 points among the seven categories according to their own perception of their relative importance. Wildlife and recreation were quite important to the sample respondents. In contrast to the David study, algae, clarity, odor, and debris were deemed relatively unimportant. But this is probably the result of the mingling of objective characteristics (odor, and the like) and uses which are affected by these characteristics.

For each category, the Dornbusch research team wrote descriptions of five states of water quality from excellent (A) to poor (E). For example for recreation, the A condition was described as follows: "The water quality is good enough to permit swimming, fishing and boating, as well as picnicking, walking, relaxing, or sunbathing along the water's banks." For odor, the E condition was described as, "strong unpleasant odor all of the time."

Then, for each characteristic, a sample of households was asked to scale the five conditions from 0 to 100 percent in terms of acceptability. "Totally unacceptable was 0 percent; totally acceptable was 100 percent." For any body of water, an individual's acceptability ratings for the seven characteristics at two points in time can be used to compute a "perceived water quality change index"

$$PWQCI = \sum_{i=1}^{7} b_i \Delta A_i$$

where ΔA_i = change in acceptability rating for ith characteristic

b_i = weight for ith characteristic

$\sum b_i = 1$

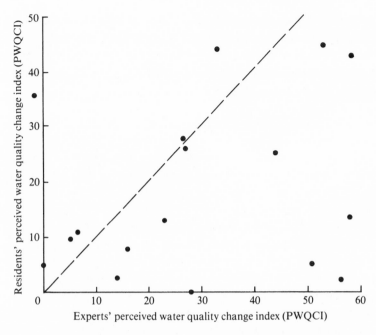

Figure 17. Comparison of residents' and experts' perceptions of changes in water quality

In the empirical application, residents living near seventeen different water bodies were asked to record their impressions of present levels of acceptability for each of the seven categories and also to indicate their recollection of perceived acceptability at a specified earlier date before a pollution control program had begun. These responses were used to compute indexes of changes in perceived water quality. Of course a major limitation of this approach is the retrospective nature of the index of perceived water quality before pollution control began. Recollections can be unreliable.

Dornbusch carried out two kinds of tests of these indexes. The first was a comparison of the average index value provided by residents for each locality with index values gathered from polling water quality experts. For many of the water bodies there were substantial differences in the evaluations given by the experts and the residents. The indexes as calculated by experts and residents are plotted in figure 17. Dornbusch did not perform a statistical analysis of the degree of association between experts' and residents' evaluations. From figure 17, it appears that there may be a small positive association. But what is remarkable is the number of differences of opinion—particularly those where the experts saw substantial quality improvements while the residents saw little or none. In one instance, the residents and experts even disagreed as to the direction of the change in water quality.

The second test was to use the average of residents' perceptions of water quality change as an independent variable in a regression model explaining property value changes over the same time interval. However, while Dornbusch reports good statistical results with the residents' water quality variable, the importance of this finding is difficult to assess because of the misspecification of the property value change model.[23]

The third study, by Binkley and Hanemann (1975), involved an attempt to explain day trips for recreation at a number of beaches in the Boston metropolitan area. The analysis dealt with several questions pertinent to the present discussion. For one, the water quality ratings by recreationists for twenty-nine beach sites were compared to the objective measures of water quality as determined by experts on the research team. Correlation coefficients were determined for recreationists' ratings for each of sixteen objective measures of water quality. Only one of the correlation coefficients was significantly different from zero at the 5 percent level. Regression analysis of recreationists' ratings as a function of objective water quality measures showed significant coefficients for many of the objective measures but relatively low explanatory power. The authors concluded that, "while there is a significant connection between objective water quality conditions and the subjective water quality ratings, the degree of association between them does not appear to be very great." (Binkley and Hanemann, 1975, p. 110)

Respondents to the survey were also asked to choose from a list of those reasons that were most important to them in choosing the recreation site they actually visited. Water quality was relatively unimportant in most responses. The most important factors were proximity of the beach to their residence and beach characteristics such as nature of the facilities, cleanliness, and setting.

Finally the authors regressed the probability of resident i visiting site j and, for those actually visiting a site, the number of visits, on explanatory variables such as distance, socioeconomic factors, and al-

---

[23] See footnote 35 in chapter 6 of the present book.

ternatively, subjective and objective measures of quality. They summarized their results as follows: "Subjective water quality rating always has a significant positive coefficient—respondents make more visits to a site which they considered to be of higher quality. This is not a surprising conclusion, although the direction of causation is ambiguous. . . . However, there is very little relationship between objective measures of site quality and the frequency with which a site is visited." (Binkley and Hanemann, 1975, pp. 167–170)

To summarize, this discussion of measures of water quality suggests two principal conclusions. First, individuals' perceptions of water quality may sometimes be difficult to reconcile with objective water quality indicators or experts' perceptions of water quality. Where differences between experts' and individuals' judgments exist, this must reduce our faith in individuals' ability to analyze information and to respond objectively and rationally to their observations. At best, this makes the predictions of changes in recreation behavior associated with changes in water quality difficult. If recreation behavior is governed by perceptions, but if we are unable to link perceptions with objective water quality indicators, the predictive link between policy-induced changes in water quality and a resulting change in the recreation behavior is broken. At worst, the use of water quality perceptions to explain recreation behavior could introduce a degree of circularity into the analysis. It is difficult to tell whether people choose to recreate at a given site because they perceive that it has high water quality or whether they tell questioners that they think the water quality is high to justify their choice of that site ("come on in; the water is fine").[24]

The second conclusion is that the ability of perceptions of water quality to explain recreation choices among alternative sites has not been proven as yet. Of course, this could be either because of weaknesses in our techniques of measuring perceived water quality, or because perceived water quality does not in fact matter to individuals. Since the latter clashes with a priori expectations, the recommendation is for further research on perceptions of water quality and their relationship to recreation activities.

[24] In fact in a survey of recreationists in the Toronto area, Barker (1971) found that "there was a tendency among beach users, especially those who used the same beach frequently, to deny or discount the pollution levels at the place with which they were most familiar and to express the view that pollution was worse or more widespread elsewhere." (p. 41)

CONGESTION AND RECREATION DEMAND

Congestion of a recreation site occurs when the number of users is so large that it diminishes the utility and therefore the willingness to pay of users.[25] The presence of congestion at a recreation site has implications for the estimation of recreation demand and the measurement of the benefits of water quality change.[26] Congestion, like water pollution, is a negative externality. It affects all users of the site. However, users may have different marginal willingnesses to pay to avoid congestion. Also, like water quality, the congestion case satisfies the conditions of weak complementarity. Thus the benefits of avoiding congestion can be evaluated by measuring areas between demand curves.

In this section, a simple model of congestion is developed to show the effects of congestion on demand and on the prediction of recreation use.[27] The model is then used to show how the benefits of improving water quality at a site are reduced if congestion is present and how improving water quality at one site can lead to additional benefits by reducing congestion at other sites. Suppose we have recorded the level of recreation use at a particular site which we know to be congested. Let this level of use be $0-V_1$ in figure 18. Assume that we have surveyed users and recorded distance, travel cost, and the like; and that by application of the CK technique, we have computed the demand curve D_1-V_1. This will be called a *constant-congestion demand curve* because it reflects the behavior of a set of users, all of whom are experiencing the same level of congestion when they visit this site. The triangular area, $0-D_1-V_1$ is the benefit or consumer surplus associated with having this recreation site available, given its present level of use, congestion, and water quality.

---

[25] I ignore the possibility that numbers might increase the utility of users because of enhanced opportunities for social interaction.

[26] A number of recent studies have dealt with aspects of the effects of congestion on various types of recreation behavior. For analyses of the effects of congestion on wilderness recreation use and benefits, see Fisher and Krutilla (1972) and Cicchetti and Smith (1976). McConnell (1977) and Deyak and Smith (1978) have estimated the effects of congestion on recreation behavior. And McConnell and Duff (1976) have shown how one manifestation of congestion (the probability of exclusion if the facility is filled to capacity) affects estimates of the benefits or consumer surplus derived from the travel cost model.

[27] This model of congestion is developed more fully in Freeman and Haveman (1977). The main purpose of that paper was to develop rules for optimal pricing and show how these are affected by assumptions about the incidence of congestion costs.

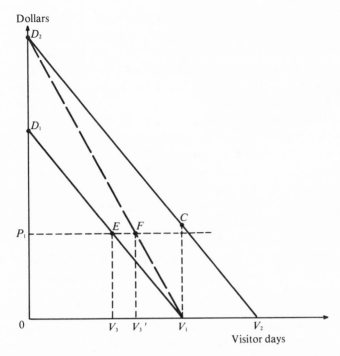

Figure 18. The effect of congestion on the demand for a recreation site

Suppose it is known what each individual would be willing to pay to use this site, if it were uncongested. Aggregating the individual willingnesses to pay for an uncongested site gives an *uncongested demand curve*, $D_2 - V_2$. According to figure 18, congestion deters some users $(V_2 - V_1)$ from using the site. Their loss is the area $C - V_1 - V_2$. We can identify the costs of congestion to existing users. At use level $0 - V_1$, those users incur congestion costs of $D_1 - D_2 - C - V_1$. This is their total willingness to pay to avoid the present level of congestion at the site.

Now suppose a gate fee of $0 - P_1$ is imposed. Can the new level of use be predicted from the information at hand? The answer is no. The constant-congestion demand curve, $D_1 - V_1$ would predict a reduction in recreation use to $0 - V_3$. But with lower use, congestion is reduced. With less congestion, willingness to pay is higher, and more people are willing to use the site at a given price. Thus we would expect use to be greater than that predicted by the constant-congestion demand curve. Suppose actual use is $0 - V'_3$. There is another constant-congestion demand curve through point F. In fact there is a whole family of constant-congestion demand curves. Each one represents the aggregation of individual willingnesses to pay conditional on a level of total use and its associated congestion. Only one point on a particular constant-congestion demand curve can ever be observed. That is the point that corresponds to the level of use on which the curve is conditioned. However any one of these constant-congestion demand curves could be estimated by the CK technique if that level of use were actually observed, since the CK technique predicts individuals' responses to price changes conditioned on a given observed level of total use.

The locus of these observable points traces out another kind of demand curve, a *congestion-adjusted demand curve*. This is represented as $D_2 - V_1$ in figure 18. The congestion-adjusted demand curve can be used for predicting the effect of changes in entry fees on use levels. But the area under this curve has no significance for benefit evaluation. This curve could not be derived from a Clawson-Knetsch travel cost study, since for the latter, all recreationists experience the same congestion level.

Now let us examine the benefits of improving water quality at a site when congestion exists. (See figure 19.) The constant-congestion demand curve $D_1 - V_1$ has been computed from travel cost data based on a level of use of $0 - V_1$. Now let there be a water quality improvement at the site. Suppose the constant-congestion demand curve were shifted out to the right to $D_1' - V_1'$. This would indicate the potential increase in use and potential benefits (the area $D_1 - D_1' - V_1' - V_1$) if increases in congestion could be avoided. But of course the additional users impose additional congestion costs on one another. This partially offsets the effects of improved quality on use and benefits.

Suppose the actual increase in use is to $0 - V_1''$. There is a new constant-congestion demand curve through this point, $D_1'' - V_1''$. The net benefit of improving water quality, taking into account the increased congestion, is the area $D_1 - D_1'' - V_1'' - V_1$. The increase in congestion has dissipated some of the potential benefits from improving water quality.

In order to take into account the separate effect of congestion empirically, it is necessary to include terms reflecting congestion as a site characteristic in the system of the visitation equations for a set of sites in a given region. The estimation of the coefficients on the congestion term poses the same set of problems that was discussed above regarding the estimation of the effects of water quality on visitation.

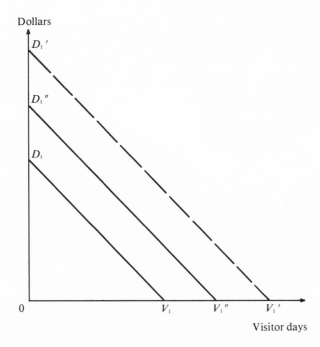

Figure 19. The benefits of water quality improvement with congestion

Now consider two sites, A and B, where A presently has polluted water and B, which is cleaner, has congestion. The constant-congestion demand curve for site B is $D_1 - V_1$ as in figure 20. Now let there be an improvement in water quality at site A. We expect visits to A to increase while visits to B will decrease. Assume that the constant-congestion demand curve for site B shifted down to $D_1' - V_1'$. If B were uncongested, the shift in the demand curve for B would be ignored in the benefit calculation for water quality improvement at site A (see above). But given that B is congested, the shift in recreation use from B toward A reduces that congestion. Assume that the new level of use of site B is $0 - V_1''$. The area between this constant-congestion demand curve $(D_1'' - V_1'')$ and the other constant-congestion demand curve conditioned on a higher level of use $(D_1' - V_1')$ is the benefit to the remaining users of site B for reducing congestion. Since this is a consequence of the water quality improvement at A, this benefit measure should be added to benefits for site A in computing the impact of the water quality change.

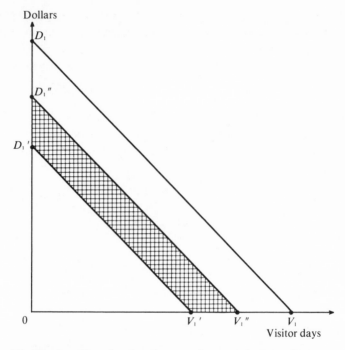

Figure 20. The benefits of reduced congestion at substitute sites

ESTIMATING PARTICIPATION

Up to this point the discussion has been about site-specific analyses which have as their objective the measurement of economic demand and value. Another approach to the analysis of recreation and water quality involves less stringent data requirements, assumptions, and estimation techniques. These less stringent requirements can be considered advantages, but they entail the loss of ability to infer values from the empirical analysis (Cicchetti, and coauthors, 1972). This approach is to estimate reduced-form equations relating the participation in specified recreation activities by a given population to the socioeconomic characteristics of that population and to the supply and quality of recreation opportunities available to that population.[28] If such reduced-form, population-specific participation equations can be

---

[28] For examples of efforts to predict future recreation activity, see Cicchetti, Seneca, and Davidson (1969), and Cicchetti (1973). These studies did not incorporate water quality variables.

estimated, it would be possible to predict the increase in participation to be expected with an increase in the supply of recreation opportunities or with an improvement in water quality. If the value of additional recreation days of a particular type could be inferred from other sources, then one component of recreation benefits can be estimated by multiplying the increase in recreation days and the value per day.[29]

A participation model of this type was used by Davidson, Adams, and Seneca (1966) as part of their study of the economic benefits of improving water quality in the Delaware Estuary. These authors used data from the 1959 Nationwide Outdoor Recreation Survey to estimate equations for participation in boating, swimming, and fishing. One set of explanatory variables in these equations reflected the availability of water area for water-based recreation. Actual socioeconomic data for 1960 and projected values for these variables for 1975 and 1990 were combined with the estimated reduced-form equations to predict recreation activity in the eleven-county area around the Delaware Estuary for those years. The variables for availability of water area were those actually observed at the time of the study, excluding the Delaware Estuary itself. This gave an estimate of recreational use assuming no improvement in water quality in the estuary.

Then it was assumed that the water quality of the Delaware would be improved sufficiently to allow water-based recreation. In other words, an improvement in water quality was assumed to be equivalent to an increase in the supply of recreation water of a given quality in order to make use of the information contained in the reduced-form equations. The projected increase in the availability of water area was used to predict new levels of recreational activity. The difference in the "with" and "without" predictions was attributed to the water quality improvement. Water quality parameters entered the analysis only through a judgment as to whether or not river waters were suitable for recreation. The model did not distinguish possible differences in water quality and the quality of recreation among those water bodies included in the available supply.

This approach could be used either to predict the changes in recreation at a point in time, or as in the case of the Davidson, Adams, Seneca study, to make projections of changes in recreation over a long span of time. Of course in the latter case, estimates are subject to all

[29] This estimate would not capture the increase in utility of the existing users.

of the kinds of limitations inherent in long-term economic projections. And in particular, these projections ignore the possible effects of changing tastes and the impact of improved opportunities on recreation participation through the "learning by doing" phenomenon.[30]

The population-specific approach to relating water quality to recreation behavior is only as good as the data contained in the survey instrument. The survey must include information on availability, including types of water bodies, measures of water quality, other site characteristics such as facilities and improvements, and accessibility. Ideally the survey should record not only levels of participation but some measure of the costs of travel from the residence to the recreation site actually chosen.

V. Kerry Smith has proposed a new approach to recreation analysis which synthesizes certain elements of the population-specific and site-specific models.

> We need to think of predicting not only the participation levels, but also those components of price that are under individual control. That is, assuming an individual can control (over a large but discrete set of alternatives) the distance he or she travels to participate, we might consider a second reduced form equation that predicts distance traveled for individual activities in addition to predicting the level of participation. Such predictions would allow the definition of a set of sites for each cohort group that would be likely candidates for the predicted participation. In order to go beyond this at a national level, we need to solicit more information from users on the nature of the site's characteristics and other inputs important to the production of the recreation service flows. This information, together with the forecasts of participation and distance, should enable a planner to translate from levels of activities to levels of use of a set of sites in regions throughout the nation. (1975, p. 118)

This would be an ambitious undertaking and would require a far more comprehensive recreation survey than those that have been undertaken by the Bureau of Outdoor Recreation in recent years.

IMPUTED VALUES FOR RECREATION

If changes in the quantity of recreation can be predicted through sound analytical techniques, one can gain some feel for the order of

---

[30] See for example, Davidson, Adams, and Seneca (1966), pp. 186–197, and Munley and Smith (1976).

magnitude of benefits by applying an imputed unit value or price to the change in quantity. For example, Davidson, Adams, and Seneca (1966) in the study described above made a series of "illustrative" calculations of monetary benefits by applying arbitrary but "reasonable" dollar values per recreation-day to their estimated recreation outputs. The benefits were then compared with the costs of achieving those outputs. They concluded that at a value of $2.55 per user-day, calculated recreation benefits equalled the cost of the pollution control program.

In many instances the disparity between benefits and costs may be so great that illustrative calculations like these will point fairly clearly and unambiguously toward one conclusion or the other. In such cases further efforts to obtain refined estimates of values may not be warranted.

Deciding unit values could be an acceptable technique if there were sound bases for determining the value to be used. Some feel for a range of plausible unit values can be gained from a review of Clawson-Knetsch travel cost studies. Dwyer, Kelly, and Bowes (1977) have conducted such a review. However there are several reasons why unit values derived for one site may not be valid for application to recreation benefits for another study. First, most of the Clawson-Knetsch studies referred to by Dwyer, Kelly, and Bowes do not control for site characteristics such as water quality. Therefore they do not throw much light on the crucial question of the relationship between quality and value. Second, the demand for a given recreation site depends in part on the range of recreation alternatives in the region. The availability of alternatives differs from site to site. Finally, demand and value depend in part on the socioeconomic characteristics of the regional population. And, of course, these vary across regions.

Another approach to determining unit values is to survey users to determine their willingness to pay to use this specific site. The conceptual difficulties in determining willingness to pay by survey methods were discussed in chapter 5. In spite of the limitations on this technique, there have been several applications. For example, Davis utilized a questionnaire to determine the willingness to pay of recreationists using several public and private recreational areas in northern Maine.[31] He questioned recreationists while they were engaged in the activity, thus making the question less hypothetical, and, perhaps making it possible for the person to envisage the possibility of being excluded from the

[31] See Knetsch and Davis (1966).

recreation site because of nonpayment. It could be argued that this latter factor, the real possibility of exclusion, would minimize the incentives created by the free rider problem in the classical public goods case. It would be possible to use interview methods such as described by Davis as a cross-check on estimates of economic value, or willingness to pay, derived by other methods such as the CK approach. However the simple approach used by Davis appears to be less applicable to the case of evaluating potential improvements in water quality since it poses hypothetical—and perhaps difficult to visualize—alternatives to the individuals being questioned.[32]

The Water Resources Council in its guidelines for evaluating water resource development suggests the assignment of unit values per user-day as a technique for determining recreation benefits (Water Resources Council, 1973). The council suggests valuing "general" recreation days between $0.75 and $2.25 and "specialized" recreation days ("those activities for which opportunities, in general, are limited, intensity of use is low, and often they involve a large personal expense by the user") at $3 to $9 per day. As indicated above, in some circumstances useful information can be gained by trial calculations with such tentative or arbitrary unit prices. However, the danger in the council recommendation is that the suggested prices may be misconstrued by some to be valid and accurate measures of value. In addition, the specification of a fairly narrow range of possible values does not give adequate consideration to the wide range of possible different circumstances. For example, the marginal willingness to pay could be quite high where supply is restricted relative to demand, or where congestion exists, or where there are no close substitutes for the recreation resource in question.

In sum, arbitrary values can be useful in some circumstances, but they should be seen as the last resort and should be used only in the most tentative way. Furthermore, every effort should be made to allow for specialized recreation resources, the availability of substitutes, and supply and demand considerations in selecting the arbitrary values to be used.

---

[32] There have been several applications of the survey technique to environmental questions. However they have not been specifically related to water quality. See Brookshire, Ives, and Schulze (1976), Hammack and Brown (1974), and Randall, Ives, and Eastman (1974).

CONCLUSIONS

Improving recreational opportunities may be the single most important source of benefits of controlling water pollution. It would be useful to have estimates of the willingness to pay for water quality improvements. Benefit information would be helpful in policymaking both at the site or regional level and at the national level.

The Clawson-Knetsch travel cost approach has the most potential for estimating benefits of water quality improvement at particular sites or water bodies. However, the analyst using the technique must make some strong assumptions about the behavior of recreationists, especially concerning the nature and purpose of the trip and the relationship between time cost and money cost. To the extent that these assumptions are not valid, the usefulness of the technique is diminished. Moreover, there are some difficulties in extending the technique to the analysis of demand with changing quality. One concerns the difficulty in measuring the appropriate dimensions of water quality itself. I have also identified some problems in the specification and estimation of demand functions, especially where present levels of pollution preclude any recreation use of the water body in question.

The most fruitful approach for estimating the benefits of achieving national pollution control objectives, for example achieving best practical treatment, is likely to be through national recreation participation surveys and the application of unit values. Earlier surveys have not adequately dealt with the quantity and quality of the available water-based recreation sites and the availability and quality of alternative forms of recreation opportunities as determinants of water-based participation rates. But if such a data base were gathered, it might be possible to discover the relationship between participation rates and the quantity and quality of recreation opportunities. If so, the prediction of changes in the participation rates associated with specific water pollution control programs would be relatively straightforward. Of course, this approach would not reveal values or shadow prices; nor would it capture the change in utility of existing recreationists. But it would be a major addition to what is now a very limited body of information about recreation benefits.

REFERENCES

Ackerman, Bruce A., Susan Rose-Ackerman, James W. Sawyer, Jr., and Dale W. Henderson. 1974. *The Uncertain Search for Water Quality* (New York, The Free Press).

Barker, Mary L. 1971. "Beach Pollution in the Toronto Region," in W. R. D. Sewell, and I. Burton, eds., *Perceptions and Attitudes in Resources Management* (Ottawa, Department of Energy, Mines, and Resources).

Beardsley, Wendell. 1971. "Bias and Non-Comparability in Recreation Evaluation Models," *Land Economics* vol. 47, no. 2 (May) pp. 175–180.

Binkley, Clark S., and W. Michael Hanemann. 1975. "The Recreation Benefits of Water Quality Improvement: Analysis of Day Trips in an Urban Setting." Prepared for the Environmental Protection Agency by Urban Systems Research and Engineering, Inc., Cambridge, Mass. (December).

Brookshire, David, Berry Ives, and William Schulze. 1976. "The Valuation of Aesthetic Preferences," *Journal of Environmental Economics and Management* vol. 3, no. 4 (December) pp. 325–346.

Brown, William G., and Farid Nawas. 1973. "Impact of Aggregation on the Estimation of Outdoor Recreation Demand Functions," *American Journal of Agricultural Economics* vol. 55, no. 2 (May) pp. 246–249.

Burt, Oscar R., and Durwood Brewer. 1971. "Estimation of Net Social Benefits from Outdoor Recreation," *Econometrica* vol. 39, no. 5 (September) pp. 813–827.

Cesario, Frank J. 1976. "Value of Time in Recreation Benefit Studies," *Land Economics* vol. 55, no. 1 (February) pp. 32–41.

———, and Jack L. Knetsch. 1970. "Time Bias in Recreation Benefit Estimates," *Water Resources Research* vol. 6, no. 3 (June) pp. 700–704.

———, ———. 1976. "A Recreation Site Demand and Benefit Estimation Model," *Regional Studies* vol. 10, pp. 97–104.

Cicchetti, Charles J. 1973. *Forecasting Recreation in the United States* (Lexington, Mass., Lexington Books).

———, Anthony C. Fisher, and V. Kerry Smith. 1976. "An Econometric Evaluation of a Generalized Consumer Surplus Measure: The Mineral King Controversy," *Econometrica* vol. 44, no. 6 (November) pp. 1259–1276.

———, and A. Myrick Freeman III. 1971. "Option Demand and Consumer's Surplus: Further Comment," *Quarterly Journal of Economics* vol. 85, no. 3 (August) pp. 528–539.

———, J. J. Seneca, and P. Davidson. 1969. *The Demand and Supply of Outdoor Recreation* (Washington, D.C., U.S. Department of the Interior, Bureau of Outdoor Recreation).

———, and V. Kerry Smith. 1976. *The Costs of Congestion* (Cambridge, Mass., Ballinger).

———, ———, Jack Knetsch, and R. A. Patton. 1972. "Recreation Benefit Estimation and Forecasting: Implications for the Identification Problem," *Water Resources Research* vol. 8, no. 4 (August) pp. 840–850.

Clawson, Marion, and Jack Knetsch. 1966. *Economics of Outdoor Recreation* (Baltimore, Johns Hopkins University Press for Resources for the Future).

David, Elizabeth L. 1971. "Public Perceptions of Water Quality," *Water Resources Research* vol. 7, no. 3 (June) pp. 453–457.

Davidson, Paul, F. G. Adams, and J. Seneca. 1966. "The Social Value of Water Recreational Facilities Resulting from an Improvement in Water Quality: The Delaware Estuary," in Allen V. Kneese and Stephen Smith, eds., *Water Research* (Baltimore, Johns Hopkins University Press for Resources for the Future).

Deyak, Timothy A., and V. Kerry Smith. 1978. "Congestion and Participation in Outdoor Recreation: A Household Production Function Approach," *Journal of Environmental Economics and Management* vol. 5, no. 1 (March) pp. 63–80.

Dornbusch, David M. 1975. *The Impact of Water Quality Improvements on Residential Property Prices*. Prepared for the National Commission on Water Quality (NTIS, PB 248–805).

Dwyer, John F., John R. Kelly, and Michael D. Bowes. 1977. *Improved Procedures for Valuation of the Contribution of Recreation to National Economic Development* (Water Resources Center, University of Illinois, Urbana-Champaign, September).

Fisher, Anthony C., and John V. Krutilla. 1972. "Determination of Optimal Capacity of Resource-Based Recreation Facilities," in John V. Krutilla, ed., *Natural Environments: Studies in Theoretical and Applied Analysis* (Baltimore, Johns Hopkins University Press for Resources for the Future).

Freeman, A. Myrick, III, and Robert H. Haveman. 1977. "Congestion, Quality Deterioration, and Heterogeneous Tastes," *Journal of Public Economics* vol. 8, no. 2 (October) pp. 225–232.

Gum, Russell L., and William E. Martin. 1975. "Problems and Solutions in Estimating the Demand for and Value of Rural Outdoor Recreation," *American Journal of Agricultural Economics* vol. 57 (November) pp. 558–566.

Hammack, Judd, and Gardner M. Brown, Jr. 1974. *Waterfowl and Wetlands: Toward Bioeconomic Analysis* (Baltimore, Johns Hopkins University Press for Resources for the Future).

Heintz, H. T., Jr., A. Hershaft, and G. C. Horak. 1976. *National Damages of Air and Water Pollution*. A report to the U.S. Environmental Protection Agency (Rockville, Md., Enviro Control, Inc.).

Knetsch, Jack L. 1964. "Economics of Including Recreation as a Purpose of Eastern Water Projects," *Journal of Farm Economics* vol. 46, no. 5 (December) pp. 1148–1157.

———. 1974. *Outdoor Recreation and Water Planning,* Water Research

Monograph No. 3 (Washington, D.C., American Geophysical Union).
————. 1977. "Displaced Facilities and Benefit Calculations," *Land Economics* vol. 53, no. 1 (February) pp. 123–129.
————, and Frank Cesario. 1976. "Some Problems in Estimating the Demand for Outdoor Recreation: Comment," *American Journal of Agricultural Economics* vol. 58, no. 3 (August) pp. 596–597.
————, and Robert Davis. 1966. "Comparisons of Methods for Recreation Evaluation," in Allen V. Kneese and Stephen Smith, eds., *Water Research* (Baltimore, Johns Hopkins University Press for Resources for the Future).
Krutilla, John V. 1967. "Conservation Reconsidered," *American Economic Review* vol. 57, no. 4 (September) pp. 777–786.
Mäler, Karl-Göran, and Ronald Wyzga. 1976. *Economic Measurement of Environmental Damage* (Paris, Organisation for Economic Co-operation and Development).
McConnell, Kenneth. 1975. "Some Problems in Estimating the Demand for Outdoor Recreation," *American Journal of Agricultural Economics* vol. 57, no. 2 (May) pp. 330–334.
————. 1976. "Some Problems in Estimating the Demand for Outdoor Recreation: Reply," *American Journal of Agricultural Economics* vol. 58, no. 3 (August) pp. 598–599.
————. 1977. "Congestion and Willingness to Pay: A Study of Beach Use," *Land Economics* vol. 33, no. 2, pp. 185–194.
————, and Virginia A. Duff. 1976. "Estimating Net Benefits of Recreation Under Circumstances of Excess Demand," *Journal of Environmental Economics and Management* vol. 2, no. 3, pp. 224–230.
Munley, Vincent G., and V. Kerry Smith. 1976. "Learning by Doing and Experience: The Case of Whitewater Recreation," *Land Economics* vol. 52, no. 4, pp. 545–553.
National Commission on Water Quality. 1976. *Staff Report* (Washington, D.C. NCWQ).
Nelson, Jon P. 1977. "Accessibility and the Value of Time in Commuting," *Southern Economic Journal* vol. 43, no. 3 (January) pp. 1321–1329.
Randall, Alan, Berry Ives, and Clyde Eastman. 1974. "Bidding Games for Evaluation of Aesthetic Environmental Improvement," *Journal of Environmental Economics and Management* vol. 1, no. 2 (August) pp. 132–149.
Reiling, S. D., K. C. Gibbs, and H. H. Stoevener. 1973. *Economic Benefits from an Improvement in Water Quality* (Washington, D.C., U.S. Environmental Protection Agency).
Saxonhouse, Gary R. 1977. "Regressions from Samples Having Different Characteristics," *Review of Economics and Statistics* vol. 59, no. 2 (May) pp. 234–237.
Sindon, J. A. 1974. "A Utility Approach to the Evaluation of Recreational and Aesthetic Experience," *American Journal of Agricultural Economics* vol. 56, no. 1 (February) pp. 61–72.

Smith, V. Kerry. 1975. "The Estimation and Use of Models of the Demand for Outdoor Recreation," in National Academy of Sciences, *Assessing Demand for Outdoor Recreation* (Washington, D.C., NAS).

Stevens, Joe B. 1966. "Recreation Benefits from Water Pollution Control," *Water Resources Research* vol. 2, no. 2, pp. 167–182.

Water Resources Council. 1973. "Principles and Standards for Planning Water and Related Land Resources," *Federal Register* vol. 38, no. 174 (September 10).

Wilman, Elizabeth A. 1977. "A Note on the Value of Time in Recreation Benefit Studies" (mimeo).

CHAPTER 9

Productivity Benefits

The term "productivity" is used broadly in this chapter. It applies to the economic effects of pollutants on ecological systems the products of which enter into market transactions, for example, fisheries, forests, and agriculture. It applies to the effects of pollutants on nonliving systems in the production sector of the economy, for example, materials and production processes. And it applies to the similar effects on vegetation and materials owned by the household sector, for example, effects on home gardens and ornamental plantings, cleaning costs, and painting.

Although the primary focus is on effects on producers, most of the techniques described in this chapter could also be applied to estimating effects on households. However, estimates of household effects based on the techniques described here may sometimes fail to capture the more subtle effects in the form of utility losses that cannot be prevented by consumer actions such as painting or more frequent cleaning. For households, there is another approach to benefit estimation which in principle will fully capture subtle effects and utility losses. This is the property value approach. However, where property value benefits have been estimated, adding some measure of household vegetation or materials damage is likely to involve some degree of double counting.

THE THEORY

The basic theory of the estimation of productivity effects has been outlined in chapter 4. Briefly, productivity effects may be reflected in changes in returns to factor inputs (including profit) or changes in consumer surpluses if product prices are affected or both. Measuring these effects involves three conceptually distinct steps.

Estimating physical effects entails the identification of a dose-damage function relating the presence of pollutants to some measurable effect. Examples include reduction in physical yield of agricultural crops, reduced service life, and more frequent maintenance and repairs of materials. In more formal terms, this step involves the identification of the way in which environmental quality Q enters into the production function

$$X = X(K, L, Q)$$

where K is capital and L is labor.

Producers may respond to physical effects in a variety of ways to mitigate the economic impact of the physical damage due to pollution. For example, producers might use substitute materials which are not susceptible to pollution damage but are more expensive. They might change production processes. Farmers can shift to less vulnerable crops. Formally, producers' responses can be analyzed in the context of their profit maximization problem.

This maximization is subject to the constraints of the multiple output production function. Product demand functions, factor prices, and Q are taken as given by producers who then choose input and output vectors to maximize the profit function. Producers' responses to a change in Q may involve either changes in inputs or changes in outputs. There may be shifts of marginal cost curves, and depending on market structure, changes in output prices. These producers' responses, that is, changes in inputs, outputs, and costs, must be understood in order to translate physical effects into economic effects.

Finally, an analysis of market structure and supply and demand conditions is required to determine how the economic impact is divided among consumers (in the form of price changes and resulting changes in consumer surpluses), producers (in the form of profits), and variable factors (in the form of quasi-rents).

In chapter 4 it was suggested that in some cases short-cut approaches to benefit estimation may be available. One possibility was to use technical data to identify substitution relationships among inputs. This involves a simplification of the second step above. Another approach is to observe directly changes in factor incomes, especially land rent. This could be especially useful in assessing the effects of air pollution on agricultural productivity. But as explained in chapter 6, land rent changes fully capture benefits only when there are no changes in other surpluses, that is, no changes in prices of outputs, prices of other inputs, or profits. Thus, the land rent approach greatly simplifies the first and second steps; but it is appropriate only if the analysis of the third step shows that there are no price effects.[1]

EMPIRICAL APPLICATION

In developing empirical estimates of productivity effects, the analyst faces problems at each of the three stages described above, that is, physical effects, producers' responses, and market effects. In addition, there are problems in determining the quantity of materials or crops actually exposed to a given level of damage. I shall briefly describe each of these sets of problems, and then discuss them in the context of measuring particular classes of productivity effects.

Physical Effects

Technical dose-damage functions may describe readily identifiable and quantifiable impacts. But they may neglect more subtle but significant forms of damage. For example, in vegetation studies dose-damage functions typically relate pollution levels to physical signs of deterioration such as leaf drop or discoloration. But other forms of impact such as reduced plant vigor, increased susceptibility to pests, or lower growth rates may be neglected. Also materials dose-damage functions may be derived from test procedures that do not accurately correspond to actual conditions of use.

Another problem with measurement of physical effects is determining the marginal impact of man-made pollution when both man-made and natural sources contribute to ambient levels of the pollutant. For example, more accurate and detailed monitoring of photochemical oxidant levels in rural areas indicates many areas that exceed the national primary air quality standards. It is not clear at present to what extent these high levels are due to man-made sources. To attribute all of the agricultural crop damages caused by oxidants to man-made

---

[1] See Crocker (1971) for an application of the land rent technique to estimating damages due to fluoride pollution in Florida.

sources could result in an overestimate of the benefits to be realized by controlling these sources. Even if the proportion of total emissions that are man made is known, estimation of man-caused damages is difficult if the dose-damage function or economic cost function is nonlinear.[2]

Producers' Responses

It is difficult to model fully the economics of production so that producers' responses can be analyzed. For many forms of physical damage, there is a variety of potential responses; and producers may undertake several types of adjustments simultaneously. Corrosion of materials can be countered by painting the material, switching to a substitute material which is corrosion resistant, or simply replacing the material more frequently. On the other hand if the economic life of the material is shorter than its physical life, for example, because of obsolescence, the economic impact of physical deterioration may be negligible.

If materials deterioration increases the probability of the failure of a component in a system, at least part of the economic cost must be measured in terms of the cost of systems failure. Producers can reduce the impact of component failure on the functioning of the system by system design. In this case the analysis must identify the extra cost of system redundancy.

Exposure

Dose-damage and producers' response functions are typically defined in per-unit terms, for example, corrosion rates per square foot of steel. The estimation of economic effects then requires some knowledge of the quantities of materials actually exposed to various levels of air pollution. Where materials such as steel are used in many kinds of production activities, the empirical problem is compounded by the likelihood that producers' responses to a given level of air pollution and potential physical damage may be quite different for different production activities.

[2] See Council on Environmental Quality (1975), pp. 322–324.

Market Effects

For a given class of production activity, physical damages, producers' responses, and their impacts on cost must be aggregated across producers in order to determine the effect, if any, on product price. If supply is less than perfectly elastic, the effect on product price will be less than the effect on marginal cost. Thus, predicting price effects requires analysis of both supply and demand conditions.

Ignoring price effects where they are present could lead to substantial biases in estimates of damages caused by pollution. The analysis should also attempt to assess the impact of changing price on quantity demanded. A short-cut approximation of the effect on consumers could be obtained by multiplying the change in price by the quantity demanded. But this would be an overestimate or underestimate depending on whether the initial quantity or final quantity were used in the calculation. An accurate measure of consumer effects would include the small consumer surplus triangle related to the quantity change.[3]

Agricultural Productivity

Early dose-damage functions for vegetation focused primarily on visible measures of damage such as leaf injury. But it has been found that yields can be affected adversely at pollution levels substantially below those at which visible leaf damage occurs, at least for some species. More recent research has focused on measuring impacts on such variables as growth rates, total plant weight, and yield.[4] These studies will contribute to more accurate estimates of damages at ambient pollution levels.

In estimating economic damages, it is important that producers' responses be accurately identified and accounted for. Measuring land rent or net return per acre may be a more feasible alternative to model-

---

[3] Predicting the quantity change requires a knowledge of the price elasticity of demand for the product. The consumer surplus triangle is equal to $\frac{1}{2}\Delta P \cdot \Delta X$. The percentage error involved in ignoring this term is an increasing function of the price elasticity of demand E and the magnitude of the price change. Specifically,

$$\% \text{ error } = \frac{1}{2}E\Delta P/P$$

[4] For a survey of recent studies, see Heintz, Hershaft, and Horak (1976).

ing the farmer's production decision. Suppose a farmer is growing spinach and in the absence of pollution, the net return per acre is $100. (Net return per acre is the value of the crop produced less production expenses—seed, fertilizer, labor, and the use of capital equipment.) Suppose the pollution reduces yield so that net return per acre is only $55. But further assume that there are countermeasures available to the farmer which partially compensate for the effect of the air pollution. For example, he may change cultivation practices, increase fertilizer applications, and so forth. With countermeasures, suppose the net return per acre is $65.

Damages are $35, that is, the difference in net return between the no pollution situation and the situation with pollution after producers' adjustment. In the absence of data on land rent or net return, the analysis would have to identify first the effect on crop value, second the changes in production cost (including those for countermeasures), and third the effect of the countermeasures on crop value. But with land rent data available, a simple comparison of land rents before pollution and after pollution and producers' adjustments is sufficient to measure damages.

This example has implicitly assumed that there would be no change in cropping pattern. Let us consider an extension of this example to take into account possible changes in land use. Suppose that net returns per acre for spinach and for wheat with clean air and with pollution are as follows

Crop	Clean air	Pollution
Spinach	$100/acre	$65/acre
Wheat	$ 80/acre	$70/acre

With clean air the farmer maximizes his profits by growing spinach since return per acre is higher with that crop. Pollution reduces net returns in spinach to $65. But now wheat is a more profitable use for the land. Taking account of the change in crop, the true measure of damage is $30 ($100 − $70).[5]

Of course, in this example it has been assumed that there are no changes in the prices of agricultural output or other inputs. This may

---

[5] There may be accommodating changes in crops outside of the area affected by pollution. But as Lind's analysis has shown, these may be ignored in estimating damages or benefits (Lind, 1973). See also chapter 6.

be appropriate if the objective is to determine damages or benefits for changes in air quality in one small region, assuming everything else constant. But if the objective is to estimate the benefits from a nation-wide pollution control policy, then price effects would probably have to be taken into account. Other things equal, price effects would be more significant in the benefit measure, the more inelastic the demand curve for output. And, agricultural benefits are believed to have inelastic demands.

The results of this discussion of agricultural effects can be summarized with three statements concerning likely biases in estimates of damages and estimates. First, using available dose-damage functions is likely to lead to an underestimate of damages since they may not accurately reflect more subtle impacts on vigor, growth rates, and ultimately, economic yield. Second, if producers' responses such as counter-measures and crop damages are not taken into account, damage measures are likely to be overestimated. (However the converse is true if damage measures are based on cropping patterns that are observed after a full adjustment to existing pollution levels.) And third, ignoring possible price effects is likely also to lead to an underestimate, and perhaps a substantial underestimate, of damages.

Materials Damages

This discussion applies to materials damages due to air pollution and some types of damages associated with water pollution, for example, sediment deposits in irrigation and drainage structures and in navigation channels, and damages to domestic appliances (Heintz, Hershaft, and Horak, 1976). First, suppose that pollution simply reduces the useful life of a material, that is, it causes it to be replaced more frequently. Assume that producers' responses and price effects can be safely ignored. Damages as an annual flow (dollars per year) can be calculated in two steps. The first step is the computation of the present value of the difference in the stream of replacement cost with and without pollution. For example, assume that the component being replaced is part of a basic structure that has a useful life of twenty years. Further assume that with no pollution, the component must be replaced every ten years; but with pollution it must be replaced every five years. Then the present value calculation over the twenty-year time horizon proceeds as follows[6]

$$PV_c = R + \frac{R}{(1 + i)^{10}}$$

$$PV_{pol} = R + \frac{R}{(1 + i)^5} + \frac{R}{(1 + i)^{10}} + \frac{R}{(1 + i)^{15}}$$

$$PV_{dam} = PV_{pol} - PV_c$$

where R is the replacement cost and i is the interest rate. The annual equivalent flow of damages is

$$\text{Dam} = PV_{dam} \left[\frac{i(1 + i)^n}{(1 + i)^n - 1} \right]$$

where n is the useful life of the system in years.

If the damage is in the form of increased painting, maintenance, or repair cost, or in the form of higher initial cost for damage resistant materials, the calculations are similar. In general, the appropriate measure of damages is the annual equivalent of the difference in life cycle cost.

Of course these calculations ignore other forms of producers' responses and other dimensions of damage such as the cost of materials failure. For detailed studies of specific forms of damage, it might be possible to take these factors into account in a systematic way. But if the objective is to estimate damages for a broad category of users of a class of materials, a detailed analysis is not feasible. And the calculation of damages by the above approach is a second best approximation.

Perhaps the most difficult problem for the empirical estimation of materials damages is determining the size of the inventory of materials being exposed to pollution. Even well-defined categories such as nonferrous metals or painted surfaces embody a heterogeneous mix of specific materials in a wide variety of uses exposed to a range of pollution levels from clean to very dirty. Dose-damage functions derived for a particular set of circumstances will reflect only imperfectly at best the actual damages of a class of materials in a variety of uses. And a good

---

[6] For more detailed discussion and examples, see Mäler and Wyzga (1976).

deal of ingenuity must be used in deriving an estimate of the inventory of materials actually exposed to pollution.

The same factors also make it difficult to analyze price effects. A given category of materials may be used in the production of a variety of different products under different cost and demand conditions. The universal practice in existing empirical damage studies has been to ignore price effects on the assumption that the increase in production cost is small enough to have no effect on market price.

Commercial Fisheries Damages

Ecological production functions for fisheries are not well understood. Thus for this class of pollution problems, there is very little scientific basis for deriving dose-damage functions. The problem of relating pollution to physical damages may be alleviated if the source of the damage is administrative rather than biological. If pollution levels result in the closing of a fishery, for example because of high DDT content of fish or bacteriological pollution of a shellfish bed, then the relationship between pollution levels and the rate of harvest is easier to establish.

But there is a variety of producers' responses for even such relatively straightforward cases as the closing of a shell fishery. Fishermen may shift their efforts to other fishing grounds with relatively small economic impact (perhaps only somewhat higher transportation costs). Or they may focus their efforts on different species with slightly lower market value, higher cost per unit catch, or both. If pollution reduces the stock of a particular species, the fishermen's response may be to increase fishing effort.

Empirically the problem of unraveling these different effects is compounded by the fact that the fishing industry has not been in equilibrium. Rather it is in a state of dynamic adjustment to changing relative prices and costs, declining stocks of some species due to overexploitation, and changing regulatory regimes (for example, the 200-mile limit). Finally, as in the case of agricultural productivity, it seems likely that price effects would be significant and cannot be ignored. And although this is not an intractable analytical problem, it means that simple "back-of-the-envelope" approximations of fisheries damages could be quite wide of the mark.

Water Supply

Where water is withdrawn from lakes and rivers for use in manufacturing or for domestic water supply, there may be economic damages from the pollution. In this case the typical producers' response is to treat the water to raise it to a quality level appropriate to its planned use. Then treatment cost may be an appropriate first approximation of damages. The principal assumptions are that other forms of producers' responses, substitution effects, and price effects are negligible.

Since for many uses of water some form of treatment is necessary even when the water comes from an unpolluted source, the main empirical problem is to determine the increment to treatment cost that results because of pollution.

Household Cleaning and Soiling

One approach to estimating the benefits of reduced soiling is to determine the reduction in cleaning costs or expenditure on cleaning by households.[7] This approach assumes, in effect, that households will always alter cleaning activity and expenditure so as to maintain a constant level of cleanliness no matter what the level of pollution. An alternative approach is to assume that the level of cleanliness and the expenditure necessary to attain it are variables which are determined by supply and demand.

Assume that cleanliness is an argument in households' utility functions. Then a demand for cleanliness can be derived as a function of its price or cost and other variables such as income. Suppose that from an initial equilibrium, pollution levels and therefore the supply price of cleanliness are reduced. Total expenditure on cleaning will increase, remain the same, or decrease depending on whether the elasticity of demand for cleanliness is greater than, equal to, or less than, one. The observed change in expenditure bears no relationship to the benefits of lower pollution—the latter being measured by the appropriate area under the demand curve.

[7] Watson and Jaksch (1978) refer to a number of studies based on this approach. The discussion below is based on the model developed in their paper.

Changes in cleaning expenditure would precisely measure benefits only if the elasticity of demand for cleanliness were zero. Watson and Jaksch (1978) have estimated that this elasticity is close to unity, implying that changes in expenditure would be close to zero as pollution changes, and that expenditure changes would substantially underestimate true benefits.

CONCLUSIONS

The theory of estimating productivity damages or benefits is relatively straightforward. There are no intractable analytical or conceptual problems. But at the practical level it appears to be very difficult to implement conceptually satisfactory techniques. This is because of the variety of materials, the variety of uses, the difficulty of establishing dose-damage relationships, especially with multiple pollutants and synergistic relationships, the complexity of identifying and modeling the variety of producers' responses, and the necessity, at least in some instances, of taking into account price effects for a variety of products in different market structures. Crude approximations of damage measures are possible.[8] But by ignoring or assuming away complications like producers' responses and price effects, these approximations are likely to be biased. In some cases it may even be difficult to know the direction of bias because of countervailing tendencies.

APPENDIX
A GUIDE TO THE LITERATURE ON EMPIRICAL
ESTIMATES OF PRODUCTIVITY BENEFITS

Since there have been several surveys of the literature on empirical estimates of productivity benefits, little would be accomplished by attempting another survey here. Rather my purpose is simply to bring to the reader's attention those sources which would be most useful for becoming acquainted with the field.

---

[8] See the appendix to this chapter for references to the literature on empirical estimates.

A major source of data on the physical effects of air pollution is the set of five Criteria Documents compiled as part of the process of setting ambient air quality standards. These are listed in the references under the issuing agencies: the U.S. Department of Health, Education and Welfare, and the U.S. Environmental Protection Agency.

Grad and coauthors (1975) contains an extensive discussion of the physical effects of automotive air pollutants on materials and vegetation. Waddell (1974) includes a comprehensive survey of those studies which attempted to measure economic rather than physical effects on materials and vegetation. Waddell reviewed eight studies of specific categories of materials damages and a similar number of studies of damages to vegetation. Each of these studies resulted in specific dollar estimates of damages. Waddell then used these studies as a basis for projecting estimates of nationwide damages. He estimated national damages to vegetation in 1970 at $0.2 billion, and damages to materials at $2.2 billion.[1]

National Academy of Sciences (1974) contains a review of most of the same estimates of monetary damages used by Waddell. The academy survey is useful in that it includes some critical discussion of the conceptual bases for the damage estimates.

Heintz, Hershaft, and Horak (1976) include a number of references to studies of physical effects appearing since 1970, the cut-off date for the criteria documents. This report also includes national estimates for materials and vegetation damages caused by air pollution for 1973. For materials, Heintz, Hershaft, and Horak simply adjusted the Waddell figure for inflation. Vegetation damages were calculated primarily by assuming a 15 percent yield loss as a representative figure for areas with high oxidant levels. This loss factor was then applied to the actual value of crops raised in these areas in 1973. Total damages were estimated at $2.9 billion for 1973 with a high–low range of $9.6 to 1.0 billion.

National Academy of Sciences (1975) is noteworthy for the inclusion of a section on the effects of acid precipitation on forestry and agriculture. (See chapter 5 of the report.) However they note that investigation of this set of issues is only beginning, and estimates of ag-

---

[1] These figures were "best estimates." Waddell expressed a range of uncertainty by stating high and low estimates as well. For materials, the high–low range was $3.1 to 1.3 billion. For vegetation it was $0.3 to 0.1 billion.

gregate physical or economic effects are not yet possible. This report also includes a critical review of the assumptions underlying Waddell's estimates of various components of materials damages, and the suggestion that actual damages may be four or five times higher than Waddell's figure. The principal criticisms focus on the assumptions about the inventories of exposed materials and the allocation of observed deterioration to different causitive agents—including acid precipitation and sulfate particles.

Heintz, Hershaft, and Horak (1976) present estimates of production damages due to water pollution in six categories: municipal water supply treatment costs, industrial water supply treatment costs, sedimentation damages to irrigation systems in agriculture, losses to commercial fisheries, damages to domestic plumbing and appliances, and damages to navigation systems due to sedimentation and corrosion. The total from these categories comes to $1.7 billion in 1973. The high–low range is $2.3 to 1.1 billion.

Bell and Canterbery (1976) is a comprehensive effort to estimate the benefits of improved commercial and recreational marine fisheries associated with achieving the goals of the Federal Water Pollution Control Act Amendments of 1972. They use expert judgments to derive functions relating changes in biological productivity and catch to changes in water quality indexes. They use a demand model to predict price changes due to additional supplies of fish and compute changes in consumer surplus. They estimate consumer benefits will be $354 million in 1985 (in 1967 dollars).

REFERENCES

Bell, Frederick W., and E. Ray Canterbery. 1976. *Benefits from Water Pollution Abatement: Coastal Waters.* 2 vols. Report to the National Commission on Water Quality (April) (NTIS PB 252-172-01, 252-172-02).
Council on Environmental Quality. 1975. *Environmental Quality—1975* (December) (Washington, D.C. CEQ).
Crocker, Thomas D. 1971. "Externalities, Property Rights, and Transactions Costs: An Empirical Study," *Journal of Law and Economics* vol. 14, no. 2 (October) pp. 451–464.
Grad, Frank P., A. J. Rosenthal, L. R. Rockett, J. A. Fay, J. Heywood, J. F. Kain, G. K. Ingram, D. Harrison, Jr., and T. Tietenberg. 1975.

The Automobile and the Regulation of Its Impact on the Environment (Norman, Okla., University of Oklahoma Press).

Heintz, H. T., Jr., A. Hershaft, and G. C. Horak. 1976. *National Damages of Air and Water Pollution*. A report to the U.S. Environmental Protection Agency (Rockville, Md., Enviro Control, Inc.).

Lind, Robert C. 1973. "Spatial Equilibrium, the Theory of Rents, and the Measurement of Benefits from Public Programs," *Quarterly Journal of Economics* vol. 89, no. 3 (May) pp. 188–207.

Mäler, Karl-Göran, and Ronald E. Wyzga. 1976. *Economic Measurement of Environmental Damage* (Paris, Organisation for Economic Co-operation and Development).

National Academy of Sciences, Commission on Natural Resources. 1975. *Air Quality and Stationary Source Emission Control*. Committee Print, Senate Committee on Public Works, 94 Cong. 1 sess. (March).

———, Coordinating Committee on Air Quality Studies. 1974. *The Costs and Benefits of Automobile Emission Control*, volume 4 of *Air Quality and Automobile Emission Control*.

U.S. Department of Health, Education and Welfare. 1970. *Air Quality Criteria for Carbon Monoxide* (March) (Washington, D.C.).

———. 1969. *Air Quality Criteria for Particulate Matter* (January) (Washington, D.C.).

———. 1970. *Air Quality Criteria for Photochemical Oxidants* (March) (Washington, D.C.).

———. 1969. *Air Quality Criteria for Sulfur Oxides* (January) (Washington, D.C.).

U.S. Environmental Protection Agency. 1971. *Air Quality Criteria for Nitrogen Oxides* (January) (Washington, D.C.).

Waddell, Thomas E. 1974. *The Economic Damages of Air Pollution* (Washington, D.C., U.S. Environmental Protection Agency).

Watson, William, and John Jaksch. 1978. "Household Cleaning Costs and Air Pollution" (mimeo.).

CHAPTER 10

Conclusions

The book has been about the economic theory underlying the measurement of welfare changes and its application to nonmarketed goods such as environmental quality. I have reviewed the conceptual basis for the measurement of welfare changes and discussed those methodologies and empirical techniques that can be derived from the theoretical framework. The number of empirical techniques discussed and the variety of references offered in the preceding chapters suggest that a far from empty tool box is available for the economist who must seek an answer to the question: what is the value of an environmental improvement?

Suppose the administrator of EPA wished to know the magnitude of the benefits accruing from a given pollution control policy. If asked, I believe an economist could specify the economic theory and models he would use, the data he would like to have, and the empirical techniques he would apply to the data to obtain measures of benefits. This is a fairly optimistic statement about the state of the art. One must be careful not to read too much into it. The appropriate models and techniques can be identified; and the data requirements can be established. But this does not mean that gathering the data and implementing the techniques would be easy. Moreover, the statement refers only to the economic aspects of the problem. Where the economic technique requires noneconomic data—for example, dose-response functions—economic analysis must be postponed until we gain a better understanding of the noneconomic aspects of the problem.

In all, there are five important qualifications which must be appended to this statement. First, most of the economic models and techniques discussed in this book rely on the analysis of interactions and interdependencies between public goods demands and private goods demands. They suggest ways in which market data can be analyzed to draw inferences about public goods demands. Where public and private good interactions are absent because of the nature of preferences, I have shown that it is not possible to infer public goods demands from observations of private market data. For nonuser benefits such as option value, preservation value, and so forth, there may be no techniques for inferring public good demands and benefits from market data. In these "hopeless" cases we must rely on alternatives such as surveys and bidding games. But we have seen that there may be serious questions concerning the accuracy of responses of individuals in the necessarily hypothetical situations they pose.

A second qualification involves the valuation of longevity benefits. Not all people agree that it is possible or appropriate to assign dollar values to the prolongation of life brought about by public policies such as pollution control. Economists have developed models of rational individual choice in the face of uncertainty regarding date of death. And these models seem to be able to explain some aspects of individual behavior, at least over short time horizons.[1] There is even some evidence that people do act in the ways described by the models. But even within the economics community, there does not appear to be broad acceptance of the notion that in this realm individuals' actions and the values they reveal should be the basis for policy evaluation.

Of course one argument for not accepting existing revealed preferences is that they may reflect choices made in the face of inadequate information about the consequences of alternative actions. If lack of information lies behind some people's reluctance to accept the consequences of individual choice as a basis for making policy, the solution to the problem is to provide more information to individuals and to make it easier for them to make informed choices. But the major thrust of public policy in the areas of environmental health, occupational health and safety, and consumer safety has been to restrict the range of choice through regulations and prohibitions on certain actions rather than to improve the basis for choice by providing better information. Thus even if economic research were to be successful in substantially narrowing the range of estimates of the values individuals assign to their own life expectancy, the acceptability of this information to politically responsible decisionmakers remains in doubt.

The third qualification arises from the distinction between equity and efficiency in the allocation of resources. The pattern of market prices in an economic system, and therefore observed willingnesses to pay for both private and public goods, depends in part on the pattern

---

[1] But as was shown in chapter 7, the possibility of inconsistent or myopic behavior cannot be ruled out over longer time horizons.

of distribution of income and wealth. Estimates of benefits derived from market data or from surveys or bidding games must be qualified by a statement such as the following: "Use with caution. This benefit measure is conditional upon the existing distribution of income. If you believe that the existing distribution of income is inequitable, that belief impairs the normative significance you can attach to this measure of benefits."

The fourth major qualification is that economic measures of benefits must be built upon noneconomic data such as dose-response functions, physical damage functions, and the like. And for some types of physical effects, these data are not available or at least are not reliable.

The last qualification concerns the availability of the appropriate economic data. It may be very difficult and costly to gather the detailed data required for empirical implementation of some of the models discussed in this book. This is particularly true where there are significant economic responses and adjustments to existing pollution levels. Some of the possible types of adjustments have been described during the discussion of averting behavior, water-based recreation demand, and materials and productivity benefits. In each case, accurate measurement of benefits requires detailed modeling of adjustments to pollution at the microeconomic level. The theoretical basis for modeling these adjustments is quite straightforward. But the empirical requirements for measurement are quite demanding.

I have argued here that benefit estimation is possible in principle, at least for some important classes of benefits; but that the task of benefit estimation is likely to be quite difficult in terms of obtaining data and building models. In the next section I review the state of the art of benefit measurement as reflected in existing estimates of benefits in several categories of air and water pollution effects. I shall then turn to a discussion of gaps and overlaps among aggregate benefit measures derived from different types of techniques and then briefly discuss the measurement of the distribution of benefits across categories of individuals. I conclude with some broad recommendations.

THE STATE OF THE ART

In chapter 2, I introduced a classification of the effects of pollutants according to whether they affected biological mechanisms in humans and other living organisms or operated through nonliving systems. This classification is repeated for convenience.

The Channels Through Which Environmental Changes Affect Man

Through living systems—biological mechanisms
    Human Health—morbidity, mortality
    Economic productivity of ecological systems
        Agricultural productivity
        Forestry
        Fisheries
    Other ecosystem impacts
        Recreational uses of ecosystems—fishing, hunting
        Ecological diversity, stability
Through nonliving systems
    Materials damages, soiling, production costs
    Weather, climate
    Other—odor, visibility, visual aesthetics

In this section, for each category of effect we consider what could be done to estimate benefits given existing economic theory and analytical techniques, what has been done and reported in the literature, and what should be done to improve our state of knowledge about benefits in that category.[2] The focus is primarily on techniques for assigning values that rely on market data.

Living Systems

Human health effects. The approach to measuring health benefits that is likely to be most fruitful involves three steps. The first is determining the relationship between exposure to or ambient concentrations of pollutants and mortality or morbidity rates. The second is to use this

---

[2] Unfortunately there are a substantial number of studies which purport to measure benefits but which are not adequately based on existing theory and do not utilize appropriate analytical techniques. Although something might be gained by reviewing the mistakes of others, that task might be better left to another time and place.

relationship to predict changes in mortality or morbidity associated with changes in ambient concentrations or exposure. The third step is to use monetary measures of willingness to pay to assign values to the predicted changes in mortality or morbidity.

This class of benefits is an example of one for which the measurement of economic benefits must be built upon a foundation of knowledge from outside the realm of economics. The most comprehensive effort to develop this information is that carried out by Lave and Seskin (1977) over an eight-year period. Through the use of multiple regression techniques they have investigated the relationships between a variety of air pollution variables and mortality rates. They have estimated cross-sectional, time series, and combination cross-sectional-time series models. The air pollution variables they used were intended to represent long-term or chronic exposures for typical residents of urban areas (standard metropolitan statistical areas—SMSAs). Pollution measures for each SMSA were used along with other possible causal variables in regressions to explain mortality rates by SMSA. In general their evidence supports the hypothesis that higher exposures to air pollutants lead to higher mortality rates. Lave and Seskin also investigated the relationship between short-term exposure (daily average and short-term moving averages) and daily mortality rates. They found some limited evidence that air pollution episodes increase mortality.

The Environmental Protection Agency has also been conducting a major epidemiological study of the effects of air pollution on human health.[3] Unlike the Lave and Seskin study, EPA has given a good deal of attention to the effects of air pollution on morbidity. The Community Health Environmental Surveillance System (CHESS) surveys have been criticized on the grounds that they have not included sufficient controls for other factors that might influence reported morbidity, and because the study design did not allow for direct measurement of the actual exposure of study subjects to air pollution.[4] There has also been some epidemiological work on the relationships between some forms of water pollution and morbidity and mortality. Most of the studies have focused on bacterial and viral disease.[5] Harris, Page, and Reiches

[3] See the various reports of EPA's Community Health and Environmental Surveillance System, for example U.S. Environmental Protection Agency (1974).

[4] See also Heintz, Hershaft, and Horak (1976), and Waddell (1974) for surveys and references to more narrowly focused studies of dose-effect relationships for air pollution.

[5] See Heintz, Hershaft, and Horak (1976) for a survey and references.

(1977) have now found some evidence linking chemical contaminants of drinking water from surface sources with cancer mortality.

Most of the studies referred to above have had the limited objective of increasing information on dose-response functions. They did not attempt to make predictions of changes in mortality or morbidity or to assign values. Lave and Seskin represent the major exception to the statement. They used EPA estimates of the percentage reduction in emissions of sulfur oxides and total suspended particulates to predict the percentage reduction in ambient concentrations of these pollutants. They assumed that the given percentage reduction in nationwide emissions would result in an equal percentage reduction in pollution concentrations across the nation. They then used the elasticity of their air pollution–mortality relationship computed at the mean to predict a percentage reduction in mortality. Finally they used a medical cost–human capital model to assign an economic value to the reduced mortality.

Given the aggregate nature of their data on air pollution exposure and mortality, that is, with no disaggregation within SMSAs, it might be argued that more refined computations of predicted mortality changes were not justified by the quality of the data. But different SMSAs experience different percentage reductions in pollution given the postulated federal control policy. It might be more accurate to compute changes in mortality for each SMSA separately (and for different groups, for example, by age, separately) based on that SMSA's particular circumstances and aggregate these changes across all SMSAs.

For health effects, there are two types of pressing research needs. The health effects of air pollution appear to be significant both in physical and economic terms. For water pollution, bacterial and viral health effects appear to be relatively minor at least compared to the other types of damages caused by water pollution. But as more evidence is gathered on the health effects of chemical contaminants of surface and ground waters, they may be found to comprise a significant fraction of total water pollution damages. For these reasons, additional information on dose-response relationships for both air and water pollution would be of great value. More effort should be devoted to large sample, carefully controlled epidemiological studies for the purpose of examining both chronic and acute effects of air and water pollutants on both morbidity and mortality. The objectives of such research should be the development of predictive models that could provide estimates of changes in mortality and morbidity for defined populations at risk as a result of specified changes in exposures of those populations to specified pollutants.

Research efforts to determine these health effects should be designed to implement and support efforts to determine economic values of reduced morbidity and mortality. For example, sample surveys to determine morbidity effects caused by air pollution should include questions that will obtain socioeconomic data. Socioeconomic variables are associated with health status and must be controlled for in estimating health effects. These data could then also be important in models designed to provide estimates of willingness to pay.

Economic productivity of ecological systems. Ecological systems are of direct economic significance because they are the source of agricultural, forestry, and fishery products which are allocated through markets. There are basically two types of approaches to estimating the value of pollution-induced changes in the productivities of these ecological systems. The first approach is to derive dose-response functions for particular components of the systems, and to use market-derived prices to assign values to the responses. For example, changes in the yields of spinach could be related to changes in ozone levels. Market data could be used to derive unit values for the spinach product. This is the most common approach to estimating productivity damages or benefits.[6] The problem with this approach is that it fails to take into account the possible adjustments on the part of producers. Some of these adjustments and their consequences for benefit estimation were discussed in chapters 6 and 9. Unfortunately, even the direction of error in estimates of benefits derived from this approach cannot be determined. If the dose-damage approach is applied to a situation where producers have already made their adjustment to existing pollution levels, the technique will underestimate true pollution damages since it does not take into account the costly adjustments that producers have already made. For example, if producers have shifted from spinach to an ozone-resistant crop of lower value, ozone damages might appear to be zero. But this ignores the loss of economic productivity caused by changing crop patterns. On the other hand, estimates of damages to spinach that ignore the possibility of producer adjustment will tend to be biased upward.

---

[6] See for example the relevant sections of Heintz, Hershaft, and Horak (1976) and Waddell (1974).

The second approach is to model the production processes and the markets in which products are sold so that one can infer benefits of pollution reduction from changes in product and factor prices and costs. To develop such models properly is, of course, a major empirical undertaking. The best example of such a study to date is the impact of water pollution on salt water fisheries undertaken by Bell and Canterbery (1976). They developed a set of biological production functions to capture the effects of water pollutants on harvestable stocks of various fishery species. Then they attempted to model the supply and demand side of fish markets in order to predict changes in harvest levels as well as prices to consumers. Increased harvests due to reduced pollution lowered fish prices, leading to increases in consumer surplus to households. These were counted as a major component of benefits.

The Bell effort was acknowledged to be preliminary and at best a first approximation. There were many instances where data gaps had to be filled by informed guesses and expert judgment. I am not aware of any comparable effort to model any part of the agricultural or forestry industries. More comprehensive research and modeling efforts might improve our understanding of adjustment processes as well as provide more soundly based estimates of expected benefits from various types of pollution control policies.

Outdoor recreation. Natural environments are used by people directly in utility-yielding activities such as recreation as well as indirectly as inputs in production processes. The value of these activities can be adversely affected by the presence of pollutants. The principal direct use of natural environments is for water-based outdoor recreation.

There is a substantial body of theoretical and empirical literature on estimating the demand for outdoor recreation activities and the value of specific recreation sites. But very little of this literature deals explicitly with the effects of water quality on demand and value. Gaining a better understanding of how changes in water quality affect recreation participation and willingness to pay is the major hurdle which must be overcome in developing sound estimates of the benefits of water pollution control.

In principle the Clawson-Knetsch technique could be applied to a body of data in which some measure of water quality was one of the variables included to explain variations in recreation participation rates. As was discussed in chapter 8, the two major barriers to the implementation of the Clawson-Knetsch technique are the development of adequate data sets to meet the requirements of appropriate model specification and identifying those measures of water quality which have the most impact on recreation behavior. The two most comprehensive efforts at integrating water quality to the Clawson-Knetsch framework are by Stevens (1966) and Reiling, Gibbs, and Stoevener (1973).[7] But neither of these studies was entirely satisfactory in the way in which water quality was defined and related to visitation rates. I think that a major research effort should be made to select an appropriate area and water bodies for study, to develop a properly specified model, and to gather the necessary data. Until such an effort is made, the practicality of the Clawson-Knetsch technique for estimating recreation benefits will remain an open question.

Another approach to relating recreation behavior to water quality is to utilize the results of surveys such as those conducted periodically by the Bureau of Outdoor Recreation. An effort could be made to relate participation rates and water-based activity to measures of the quality of water bodies readily accessible to respondants. In order to carry out this approach, a survey instrument would have to be designed to elicit adequate information on the supply of recreation opportunities to each respondent. One major difficulty in implementing the survey approach is in distinguishing between the quantitative and qualitative dimensions of supply as determinants of recreational behavior.[8]

---

[7] See chapter 8 for further discussion of these two studies.

[8] Heintz, Hershaft, and Horak (1976) have prepared for EPA an estimate of nationwide damages to outdoor recreation due to water pollution. They estimate these damages to be $6.3 billion at 1973 prices. But this estimate did not use either the Clawson-Knetsch or recreation participation approaches. The empirical basis of this estimate is a survey of recreationists in Green Bay, Wisconsin. They were asked, "What would you do if water conditions deteriorated at the place you do most of your boating, fishing, and swimming?" Recreationists were asked to choose from among responses such as "Would not bother me," "Stop recreating entirely," "Stay in same location but participate less frequently," and "Move to a different location." Values were imputed to these responses in terms of changes in willingness to pay or in the travel expenditures. These values were then aggregated for the Green Bay area and extrapolated to the nation as a whole on the basis of national recreational participation data. This approach can be criticized on several grounds:

1. The question is hypothetical, and it is not clear that survey responses would yield accurate predictions of actual behavior. See chapter 5 of the present book.

2. The nature and degree of pollution are not specified. Thus, these results could not be used to make predictions about the effects of specified changes in water quality or water pollution.

3. The basis for some of the value imputations is not well documented.

Other ecological system impacts. Pollutants can cause changes in ecological systems which have no obvious or direct impact on the production or consumption activities of humans. In such cases there is no obvious way of attaching monetary values to these effects within the conceptual framework outlined in this book. Westman (1977) has suggested that impacts that result in decreases in ecological functions be valued at the cost of replacing those functions. For example, if a pollutant reduces nitrogen fixation in soils, the damage should be calculated from the costs of manufacturing and applying an equivalent amount of chemical nitrogen fertilizer. This could be an appropriate basis for valuation if the replacement activities were actually undertaken. But the ecological functions lost may have little or no value at the margin, that is, for small perturbations from existing levels. In other words those lost functions would not actually be replaced because replacement costs exceeded the benefits.

I would prefer to acknowledge that these ecological impacts lie outside the economic rubric. This would emphasize our lack of knowledge concerning the significance of these effects for human welfare, and highlight the necessity for making explicit judgments about value and significance when weighing policy choices. Finally, if replacement cost measures of benefits were provided, people would be encouraged to add them up with benefit measures in other categories. This would reduce the usefulness of the overall figures because they would no longer be based on a common analytical framework and set of economic concepts and definitions.

Nonliving Systems

Impacts on production. As in the case with the economic productivity of living systems, there are two approaches to estimating benefits. The first is to apply market or shadow prices to impacts derived from dose-response functions, and the second is to model the production processes and related markets in an attempt to capture behavioral responses to potential or actual physical damages and related effects on prices and outputs. The first approach has predominated in the empirical

---

4. The extrapolation of a regional study to a national estimate does not adequately account for possible differences among regions in recreation behavior.

literature on benefit estimation.[9] Because of the variety of materials and production activities potentially affected by pollution, comprehensive application of the second technique may not be practical. Thus the dose-response approach is likely to continue to dominate the empirical literature. Users of estimates derived from this approach should be aware of its limitations and the potential for bias either up or down.

Impacts on households. Air pollution can affect households directly through increased soiling and reduced life of paints, curtains, and other materials. Several studies have estimated the increase in cleaning costs as a measure of pollution damages.[10] This approach may overestimate or underestimate damages depending on how the increased frequency of cleaning is estimated. If the increase in frequency is based on actual observations, it is likely to underestimate true damages because it omits any possible utility loss associated with the increased soiling rate. On the other hand if the increase in cleaning frequency is imputed from some estimate of the soiling rate, this may overstate benefits to the extent that individuals respond by accepting a higher average dirt level.

There is an alternative approach to estimating these benefits which relies on an explicit model of household behavior. Increased cleaning costs and disutility of higher dirt level both reduce the value of the stream of services flowing from the housing unit. If housing markets function well, this in turn should be reflected in housing prices. However the same argument applies to other types of effects which are location-specific, for example aesthetics (see below) and health effects associated with exposure to air pollution at home. The hedonic price approach can measure the aggregate value of all effects impinging on the house site. But it cannot indicate the distribution of these damages by category of effect.

Aesthetics. People may experience disutility when exposed to perceptible forms of air pollution even though there are no significant effects on health, materials and soiling, and so forth. Since these "aesthetic" effects are not typically linked to specific economic activities or tangible physical effects, they are particularly difficult to measure. How-

---

[9] See the appendix to chapter 9.
[10] See Waddell (1974) and Heintz, Hershaft, and Horak (1976) for reviews and summaries of these studies.

ever those aesthetic effects which are specific to housing locations may be reflected in housing price differentials. To the extent that this is so, aesthetic effects (along with others) can be captured by the hedonic price technique.

Climate and weather. Estimation of possible damages (or benefits) caused by man's having modified the climate poses serious theoretical as well as empirical problems. Not the least of these is understanding and modeling the physical processes so that reasonable predictions of climatic change can be achieved. Any degree of climatic change is likely to have effects on individuals directly, and also indirectly through production. Furthermore these changes are likely to vary significantly across space. Finally, with changes of this scope, it may not be possible to rely on the partial equilibrium modeling that underlies most of the benefit estimation techniques discussed in this book. For interesting discussion of some of these problems and approaches to solving them, see Ferrar (1976).

OVERLAPS AND GAPS

One major problem in estimating benefits is the possibility of overlap among or gaps between categories of benefits as estimated by presently used techniques. This type of problem can arise when two types of effects associated with the same pollutant are estimated separately. For example, do estimates of health effects and property value changes associated with particulates involve some double counting of particulate damages, or are there additional effects not captured by either measure? Although definitive answers to this question cannot be given here, the discussion will show that it should be possible to determine when such gaps and overlaps exist. It should also be possible to make some judgment as to the significance and likely direction of any biases in the estimated total benefit figures. And this should be useful in deriving confidence limits or high and low bounds surrounding best estimates of total benefits.

Consider the case of air pollution where health benefits are measured by mortality rate studies and aesthetic, soiling, and materials benefits are measured through property value differentials. The justification for measuring two classes of benefits separately and adding them to obtain aggregate benefits is that only those effects of air pollution which are perceived by individuals can influence property values, and that people have for the most part been ignorant of the effects of air pollution on their health and life expectancy.

But one can feel somewhat uneasy about this simple resolution of the problem. Some kinds of short-term health problems (eye irritation, shortness of breath) may be directly perceived as being caused by air pollution. Also, there has been a substantial increase in the information available to the general public about long-term health effects and relative air pollution levels around urban areas. Thus, perceptions of health effects may be influencing property value differentials and leading to the possibility of double counting. To gain a better understanding of the problem, it is necessary to consider in more detail exactly what is captured by each of the two approaches to measurement.

It will be helpful to develop a system of classification for different types of effects. Aesthetic effects such as odor and taste, reduced visibility, soiling, damage to external paints, and the like, are perceived by individuals. Impacts on health constitute the other broad class of effects. For purposes of this discussion, we need not distinguish between morbidity and mortality effects. But we can, at the conceptual level, distinguish between those health effects which are perceived by individuals and those of which they are ignorant. The former are likely to be primarily clinical manifestations of short-term exposures at relatively high levels. Finally, it is necessary to distinguish between those effects that are caused by pollution exposure at home and those that are caused by the person's exposure as he travels around the urban airshed, to work, for shopping, for recreation, and so forth. These "away-from-home" effects are independent of the individual's place of residence.

This classification scheme is displayed schematically in figure 21. There are six subsets of effects classified by aesthetics, "health perceived," "health unperceived," and in all cases further divided between home and away. Property value studies can only capture those effects associated with the home that are perceived. Health benefits derived from mortality and morbidity studies capture both home and away effects and both perceived and unperceived health effects.

Figure 21 illustrates both an overlap and a gap. Perceived health effects at home are captured by both the property value and health effects approaches. But aesthetics associated with away-from-home exposures are not captured by either measure. Whether the addition of property value and health effect benefits results in an overestimate or

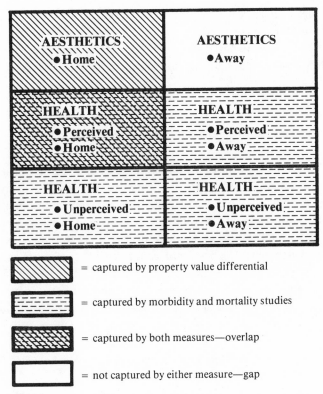

AESTHETICS • Home	**AESTHETICS** • Away	
HEALTH • Perceived • Home	**HEALTH** • Perceived • Away	
HEALTH • Unperceived • Home	**HEALTH** • Unperceived • Away	

= captured by property value differential

= captured by morbidity and mortality studies

= captured by both measures—overlap

= not captured by either measure—gap

Figure 21. Overlaps and gaps in property value and health benefit estimates

an underestimate depends on the relative size of the double counted and omitted categories. Nothing can be said about this question on a priori grounds.

There is a similar kind of problem in the case of water pollution when recreation benefits and property value benefits are both being estimated. Property value measures capture both the value of easy access to the improved water-based recreation opportunities and other nonrecreation aesthetic benefits (for example, wildlife appreciation, elimination of odor and unsightly flotsam). In estimating recreation benefits, the double counting problem can be avoided by identifying recreation participants as being either "from abutting property" or "from away" and counting for benefit purposes only participation by those from away. This can easily be accomplished if benefits are being estimated for a particular site, for example, by the Clawson-Knetsch method. However, if benefits are being estimated at the national level from a national recreation participation survey, it may not be possible to identify that part of participation attributable to property owners using abutting water bodies. Thus, adding property value benefits to those estimated from a national participation model would involve some degree of double counting.

THE DISTRIBUTION OF BENEFITS

The primary purpose in estimating benefits of environmental improvement programs is to provide data for benefit–cost analyses of alternative policies. Benefit–cost analysis is an application of the efficiency criterion. As such, it totals up benefits and costs to whomever they accrue without regard to their distribution. But there is ample evidence that policymakers are not concerned solely or even primarily with efficiency in resource allocation. It is clear that they are concerned with the equity or redistributive aspects of policies. This is as true in environmental policy questions as elsewhere.[11] Thus, in addition to providing information on aggregate benefits, economists could serve public policymakers by providing more information on who is being hurt now by environmental degradation and who will benefit from environmental improvements.

In what follows I will assume that policymakers' principal concern is with the distribution of benefits (and costs) by income levels. Other categorizations of individuals, for example, by age, race, or region, may also be of interest to policymakers. But it is more difficult to fit them into a comprehensive notion of social welfare. In any event, the analysis of the incidence of damages or benefits by other categories is a question primarily of data rather than of basic methodology.

A question to consider is whether the analysis of distribution effects requires a different methodological approach than the estimation of aggregate benefits. Basically the answer is no. At the conceptual level benefit measures are derived separately for each individual, and then aggregated to obtain total benefits. Distributional concerns can be reflected simply by aggregating individual measures over relevant subsets, for example, by income class. In practice, however, not

---

[11] See Freeman (1972) and Baumol and Oates (1975), especially pages 209–212, for discussions of the possible role of distributional information in environmental policymaking.

all benefit estimates are built from microeconomic foundations in this manner.[12] Where that is the case, analysis of the distribution of benefits may not be possible. The problem here is the inadequacy of the data base for benefit estimation, not the methodology.

In reviewing what is known about distributional aspects of environmental pollution, it is important to distinguish between the incidence of physical measures of effects and the incidence of monetary values. Different people may place different monetary values on equivalent physical effects because of differences in income, range of substitution possibilities, demographic characteristics, or tastes. Differences in these factors could result in differences in the demand functions for environmental quality. In addition, people with the same demand functions may have different willingnesses to pay at the margin because of differences in exposure to the physical effects. For example, it seems likely that high income households would have higher demand functions for environmental quality attributes such as air quality.[13] But to the extent that air quality can be purchased in the housing market, households will tend to sort themselves out by income class with higher income households settling in neighborhoods with high air quality.[14] Thus, high income households could have low marginal willingnesses to pay for improvements in air quality and low benefits from nonmarginal changes.[15]

RECOMMENDATIONS

It seems appropriate to close this book on techniques for estimating benefits with some suggestions for applications of these techniques and recommendations for further research to enhance our capa-

[12] See for example, Lave and Seskin's (1977) estimate of health benefits from air pollution control.

[13] See Freeman (1972) and Baumol and Oates (1975).

[14] See Freeman (1972). In contrast, Gianessi, Peskin, and Wolff (1977) found that higher income households experienced higher exposure to air pollution. The results follow from the quite different models used to distribute exposure by household. I used exposure at the residence as calculated from air pollution monitoring data within an urban area. Gianessi, Peskin, and Wolff assumed that exposures within each SMSA were uniform and examined differences in income and average exposures among SMSAs and between urban and rural areas.

[15] A recent study by Harrison and Rubinfeld (1977) tends to support this hypothesis, at least for all but the highest income class.

bilities. These recommendations fall into two categories: (1) those dealing with improvements in the basic data and analytical techniques, and (2) one proposing the initiation of ex post measurements of realized benefits.

Basic Data and Analytical Techniques

Earlier I distinguished between measuring effects and assigning values, both necessary steps in the determination of benefit estimates. In the key areas of mortality and morbidity from air pollution, and in the lesser areas of vegetation and materials damages from air pollution, as well as in sports and commercial fisheries and production benefits from water pollution control, the measurement of these effects lies largely outside the realm of economics. Economists' efforts to assign values and estimate benefits in these areas must await better information on physical effects.

The apparent importance of health effects of air pollutants suggests a high payoff for more information on dose-response relationships. Also, some attention should be given to epidemiological studies of water pollution health effects. In particular, attention should be given to the problems of persistent organic chemicals and viral pathogens in drinking water.

Research on the value of human life should be extended in two directions. First, the willingness-to-pay model in which one element of choice is a small change in the probability of death should be further developed. One important extension is to examine the implications of changes in the shape of the probability distribution of expected life. Second, government decisions and other collective decisions involving safety, health, medical research, and the like, should be carefully analyzed to determine the implied or explicit values placed on human life or changes in probability of death. This effort may give some insight into collective attitudes toward life valuations, and it may also stimulate efforts to achieve greater consistency among those making decisions in this area of public policy.

EPA should commission a series of microeconomic studies specifically designed for given regions in order to estimate the demand curves for specific recreation sites using the Clawson-Knetsch travel cost approach and to relate shifts in the demand curve to changes in various water quality parameters. This series of studies should be designed and coordinated so as to control for socioeconomic variables, the availability of substitutes and alternative sites, and other regional differences in recreation behavior. The objective of these studies would be to identify the underlying functional relationship between quality and willingness to pay for recreation experiences. If this effort is successful, it should be possible to generalize the results to additional sites and regions. This series of studies would emphasize the determination of the demand curve and valuation.

Another study should address changes in the quantity of use on the basis of a large, carefully constructed survey of recreation participation. Earlier surveys have not adequately dealt with the quantity and quality of the available water-based recreation sites and the availability and quality of alternative forms of recreation opportunity as determinants of water-based recreation participation rates. If such a data base were established, and participation rates could be successfully related to the quantity and quality of recreation opportunity, then the prediction of changes in participation rates associated with specific water pollution control programs would be relatively straightforward. Of course, this approach would not reveal values or shadow prices; nor would it capture the change in utility of existing recreationists.

There should be carefully constructed experiments with the survey techniques for estimating willingness to pay for reduction in pollution. These experiments should be coordinated with studies based on other analytical techniques in an effort to provide a cross-check or validation of benefit estimates obtained by different approaches.

Ex Post Evaluation

A careful and comprehensive program of ex post analysis of pollution control benefits should be developed and implemented. The period of the 1970s will have been characterized by a major commitment of resources to air and water pollution control. It would be penny-wise and pound-foolish not to plan to allocate 1 or 2 percent of the total funds to be spent on pollution control toward measuring and evaluating what we will have bought with that massive expenditure. In one sense, the nation has embarked on a large-scale socioeconomic experiment in altering environmental conditions. We should take advantage of this experiment with a carefully thought out and comprehensive program of data gathering and analysis.

REFERENCES

Baumol, William J., and Wallace E. Oates. 1975. *The Theory of Environmental Policy* (Englewood Cliffs, N.J., Prentice-Hall).

Bell, Frederick W., and E. Ray Canterbery. 1976. *Benefits from Water Pollution Abatement: Coastal Waters.* 2 vols. Report to the National Commission on Water Quality (April) (NTIS PB 252-172-01, 252-172-02).

Ferrar, Terry A., ed. 1976. *The Urban Cost of Climate Modifications* (New York, Wiley).

Freeman, A. Myrick III. 1972. "Distribution of Environmental Quality," in Allen V. Kneese and Blair T. Bower, eds., *Environmental Quality Analysis* (Baltimore, Johns Hopkins University Press for Resources for the Future).

Gianessi, Leonard P., Henry M. Peskin, and Edward Wolff. 1977. "The Distributional Implications of National Air Pollution Damage Estimates," in F. Thomas Juster, ed., *The Distribution of Economic Well-Being* (Cambridge, Mass., Ballinger).

Harris, Robert H., Talbot Page, and Nancy Reiches. 1977. "Carcinogenic Hazards of Organic Chemicals in Drinking Water" in *Origins of Human Cancer* (Cold Spring Harbor, N.Y., Cold Spring Harbor Laboratory) (Resources for the Future Reprint 148).

Harrison, David, and Daniel L. Rubinfeld. 1977. "The Distribution of Benefits from Improvements in Urban Air Quality." Discussion Paper D77-15 (Cambridge, Mass., Department of City and Regional Planning, Harvard University).

Heintz, H. T., Jr., A. Hershaft, and G. C. Horak. 1976. *National Damages of Air and Water Pollution,* a report to the U.S. Environmental Protection Agency (Rockville, Md., Enviro Control, Inc.).

Lave, Lester B., and Eugene P. Seskin. 1977. *Air Pollution and Human Health* (Baltimore, Johns Hopkins University Press for Resources for the Future).

Reiling, S. D., K. C. Gibbs, and H. H. Stoevener. 1973. *Economic Benefits from an Improvement in Water Quality* (Washington, D.C., U.S. Environmental Protection Agency).

Stevens, Joe B. 1966. "Recreation Benefits from Water Pollution Control," *Water Resources Research,* vol. 2, no. 2, pp. 167–182.

U.S. Environmental Protection Agency. 1974. *Health Consequences of Sulfur Oxides: A Report from CHESS, 1970–1971* (Research Triangle Park, N.C., Community Health Environmental Surveillance System).

Waddell, Thomas E. 1974. *The Economic Damages of Air Pollution* (Washington, D.C., U.S. Environmental Protection Agency).

Westman, Walter E. 1977. "How Much Are Nature's Services Worth?" *Science,* vol. 197 (September 2) pp. 960–964.

INDEX